THE CAMBRIDGE COMPANION TO
TONI MORRISON

Nobel laureate Toni Morrison is one of the most widely studied of contemporary American authors. Her novels, particularly *Beloved*, have had a dramatic impact on the American canon and attracted considerable critical commentary. This *Companion* introduces and examines her oeuvre as a whole, the first evaluation to include not only her famous novels, but also her other literary works (short story, drama, musical, and opera), her social and literary criticism, and her career as an editor and teacher. Innovative contributions from internationally recognized critics and academics discuss Morrison's themes, narrative techniques, language, and political philosophy, and explain the importance of her work to American studies and world literature. This comprehensive and accessible approach, together with a chronology and guide to further reading, makes this an essential book for students and scholars of African American literature.

D0221555

THE CAMBRIDGE
COMPANION TO
TONI MORRISON

THE CAMBRIDGE
COMPANION TO
TONI MORRISON

EDITED BY
JUSTINE TALLY
UNIVERSITY OF LA LAGUNA

CAMBRIDGE
UNIVERSITY PRESS

CAMBRIDGE UNIVERSITY PRESS
Cambridge, New York, Melbourne, Madrid, Cape Town, Singapore, São Paulo

Cambridge University Press
The Edinburgh Building, Cambridge CB2 8RU, UK

Published in the United States of America by Cambridge University Press, New York

www.cambridge.org
Information on this title: www.cambridge.org/9780521678322

© Cambridge University Press 2007

First published 2007

Printed in the United Kingdom at the University Press, Cambridge

A catalogue record for this publication is available from the British Library

Library of Congress Cataloguing in Publication data

The Cambridge Companion to Toni Morrison / edited by Justine Tally.
p.   cm. – (Cambridge companions to literature)
Includes bibliographical references and index.
ISBN 978-0-521-86111-3 (hardback) – ISBN 978-0-521-67832-2 (pbk.)
1. Morrison, Toni – Criticism and interpretation.   2. African Americans in literature.
I. Tally, Justine.   II. Title.   III. Series.
PS3563.O8749Z58   2007
813'.54 – dc22   2007003520

ISBN 978-0-521-86111-3 hardback
ISBN 978-0-521-67832-2 paperback

813.54
CAM

CONTENTS

CONTENTS

NOTES ON CONTRIBUTORS

ABENA P. A. BUSIA, Associate Professor in the Departments of English, and Women's and Gender Studies, at Rutgers University, lectures and publishes extensively on black literature and curriculum transformation for race and gender. Her edited works include *Theorizing Black Feminisms* (1994) with Stanlie James, and *Beyond Survival: African Literature and the Search for New Life* (1998) with Kofi Anyidoho and Anne Adams. She also co-directs, with Tuzyline Jita Allan, and Florence Howe of the Feminist Press, *Women Writing Africa*, a multi-volume, continent-wide publishing project of cultural reconstruction. Her poems have been anthologized on three continents and her collection *Testimonies of Exile* (1990) was published by Africa World Press.

JOHNNELLA E. BUTLER is the Provost and Vice President for Academic Affairs at Spelman College in Atlanta, Georgia. As a scholar, Professor Butler specializes in African American literature, American ethnic literature, and multicultural studies. She has taught numerous courses in American ethnic studies and American ethnic literature and has written many articles and books on American ethnic literature and the theory and pedagogy associated with multicultural studies. She is the editor of and lead contributor to *Color Line to Borderlands: Ethnic Studies and the Matrix of Higher Education* (2001) and co-editor of the *Encyclopedia of American Studies*.

MAR GALLEGO is Associate Professor at the University of Huelva, Spain, where she specializes in African American studies and the African diaspora, with a special focus on women writers and gender issues. She has authored *Passing Novels in the Harlem Renaissance* (2003) and has co-edited several essay collections: *Myth and Ritual in African American and Native American Literatures* (2001), *Contemporary Views on American Culture and Literature in the Great 60's* (2002), *Razón de mujer: Género y discurso en el ensayo femenino* (2003), *El legado plural de las mujeres* (2005), and *Espacios de género* (2005). She is presently working on a monograph on women writers of the African diaspora.

SÄMI LUDWIG was educated at the Universities of Bern and Geneva and did post-graduate research at the Kennedy Institut in Berlin, the University of California, Riverside, the University of California, Berkeley, and at Harvard. He wrote his master's thesis on Ishmael Reed's Neo-Hoodoo Aesthetic and his doctorate on intercultural communication in Ishmael Reed and Maxine Hong Kingston (*Concrete Language*, 1996). His second book is on the cognitive dimension in American realism (*Pragmatist Realism*, 2002). He lives in Switzerland and teaches at the Université de Haute Alsace, Mulhouse, France, which is part of the European Confederation of Upper Rhine Universities (EUCOR).

DWIGHT A. MCBRIDE is the Chair and Leon Forrest Professor of African American Studies and Professor of English and Communication Studies at Northwestern University. Author of *Impossible Witnesses: Truth, Abolitionism, and Slave Testimony* (2002) and, most recently, of *Why I Hate Abercrombie and Fitch: Essays on Race and Sexuality* (2007), McBride also edited *James Baldwin Now* (1999) and co-edited both the 2003 Lambda Literary Award winning anthology *Black Like Us: A Century of Lesbian, Gay, and Bi-Sexual African American Fiction* (2002) and *A Melvin Dixon Critical Reader* (2006). He lives in Chicago, Illinois, and Saugatuck, Michigan.

CLAUDINE RAYNAUD is Professor of English and American Literature at the University François-Rabelais, Tours, France; she now heads the nationwide African American Studies Research Group created in 2004. She is the author of *Toni Morrison: L'Esthétique de la survie* (1997) and has co-edited with Geneviève Fabre *Beloved, She is Mine, Essais sur "Beloved" de Toni Morrison* (1993). Two of her most current publications are "Coming of Age in the African American Novel," chapter 6 in *The Cambridge Companion to the African American Novel* (2004), and an anthology of articles on Gaines's *The Autobiography of Miss Jane Pitman* (2005).

DEIRDRE RAYNOR is Associate Professor at the University of Washington, Tacoma, where she teaches American ethnic literature and is the Faculty Co-ordinator of the Ethnic, Gender, and Labor Studies Concentration in the Interdisciplinary Arts and Sciences Program. Her primary scholarly interests include African American literature, Native American literature, multicultural pedagogy, and diversity in higher education. She has written and published scholarly articles on the work of Ann Petry, Edward Christopher Williams, and Julia Collins, and the Harlem Renaissance. She is currently editing a book on race in the humanities.

JUDYLYN RYAN is an Assistant Professor of English at Ohio Wesleyan University, where she teaches courses on African American and other diaspora literatures and cinema. Her scholarly work has been published in *Modern Fiction Studies, Toni Morrison: Theoretical and Critical Approaches* (1997), *Approaches to Teaching the Novels of Toni Morrison* (1998), *Women Preachers and Prophets through*

Two Millennia of Christianity (1998), *Studies in the Literary Imagination, Critical Voicings of Black Liberation: Resistance and Representations in the Americas* (2003), and *SIGNS: Journal of Women in Culture and Society.* She is the author of *Spirituality as Ideology in Black Women's Film and Literature* (2005), and is currently at work on a second book, *Teaching Black Women's Cinema.*

JOYCE HOPE SCOTT is Associate Professor of American Studies at Wheelock College in Boston where she teaches African American literature, African literature and theatre, literature and history of the Caribbean, and American popular culture. Her writings and research interests include representations of African spirituality in African American women's literature, the carnivalesque in African American fiction, African theatre for social intervention, and iconographic representations of the American national narrative. Professor Hope Scott is a former Fulbright Professor and Regional Scholar to West Africa. Her publications include *Camel Tracks: Critical Perspectives on Literatures of the Sahel* (ed. Boyd-Buggs and Hope Scott, 2003); "Official Language and Unofficial Reality," in *The Real Ebonics Debate* (1998).

SHIRLEY A. (HOLLY) STAVE is Associate Professor of English at the Louisiana Scholars' College in Natchitoches, Louisiana. She is the author of *The Decline of the Goddess: Nature, Culture, and Women in Thomas Hardy's Fiction* (1995), the co-author of *Living Witchcraft: A Contemporary American Coven* (1994), and the editor of *Gloria Naylor: Strategy and Technique, Magic and Myth* (2001) and of *Toni Morrison and the Bible: Contested Intertextualities* (2006). She has also published articles on film and on authors as diverse as Wilkie Collins and Toni Morrison.

ÁGNES SURÁNYI is Assistant Professor in the Department of English at the University of Pécs, Hungary, where she teaches contemporary British and American literature and translation theory and practice. Her publications in English include articles on Toni Morrison, Angela Carter, and Virginia Woolf. She has research interests in writing by African American women, in magic realism, literary influences and exchanges, and has centered her doctoral work on "Reading between Virginia Woolf and Toni Morrison."

JUSTINE TALLY is Professor of American Literature at the University of La Laguna, Tenerife, Spain, where she specializes in African American literature. She is the author of *Paradise Reconsidered: Toni Morrison's (Hi)stories and Truths* (1999) and *The Story of "Jazz": Toni Morrison's Dialogic Imagination* (2001). Her current work is on myth and regeneration in Morrison's *Beloved*, forthcoming from Routledge (2008). Having organized the first international conference for the Collegium for African American Research in 1995, she then went on to serve on the CAAR Board as treasurer for eight years and as a general editor of the FORE-CAAST series (*Forum for European Contributions in African American Studies*).

CHERYL A. WALL, Distinguished Professor of English at Rutgers University, is author of *Women of the Harlem Renaissance* (1995) and *Worrying the Line: Black Women Writers, Lineage, and Literary Tradition* (2005). She edited two volumes of writing by Zora Neale Hurston for the Library of America, as well as critical casebooks on *Their Eyes Were Watching God* and "Sweat." Along with Linda Holmes, Wall has edited *Savoring the Salt: Celebrating the Life and Legacy of Toni Cade Bambara* (forthcoming, 2007). Her current project is a study of Toni Morrison's career as editor.

HANNA WALLINGER is Associate Professor of American Studies at Salzburg University in Austria. She is author of *Pauline E. Hopkins: A Literary Biography* (2005) and has published essays on Hopkins, Alice Walker, Gloria Naylor, Sutton E. Griggs, W. E. B. Du Bois, Alice Moore Dunbar-Nelson, and others. She is secretary of the Collegium for African American Research.

1850	Fugitive Slave Act: "Compromise of 1850" after which run-away slaves could be legally recaptured in the North and returned to slavery.
1855	In *Beloved*, Sethe escapes, Denver is born. Celia, a slave, hanged for murdering her master in Missouri.
1856	Actual escape of Margaret Garner and other slaves (January 27).
1857	Dred Scot case.
1863	Emancipation Proclamation, which frees enslaved black people *only* in rebel states.
1865	End of Civil War (April 9). Lincoln assassinated (April 15). Thirteenth Amendment to the Constitution – which ends slavery. Ku Klux Klan created in Tennessee.
1865–1920	During this time, more than 50 identifiable all-black towns and settlements are established in Oklahoma. While all-black towns also appear in other states, no other state has as many of these towns as Oklahoma.
1865–1877	Reconstruction Period in the American post-Civil War South.
1867	Birth of Madame C. J. Walker: an illiterate poor woman turned into businesswoman in the beauty-cult industry (development of the hot comb and methods for treating black hair); accused of imitation of white Europeans; dies in 1919.

1872	Freedmen's Bureau is abolished.
1882 ff.	Lynching, massacres, and race riots resulting from reaction to Reconstruction; lynching peaked in 1892; the last lynching takes place in Alabama in 1981.
1882 ff.	Great Migration – mass movement of African Americans from the American South to the North to seek employment in the far more industrially developed region of the US; numbers peak in 1919 but continue through and after World War II.
1894–1937	Bessie Smith, the "Empress of the Blues." Enormously successful, travels widely in a custom-designed railroad car, allegedly trained by Ma Rainey.
1896	*Plessy vs. Ferguson* establishes "Separate but Equal," ruled constitutional by the Supreme Court; "one-drop" theory becomes law of the land.
1902–1974	Charles August Lindbergh is famous for the first solo flight (New York to Paris) across the Atlantic. He admires the Nazis and propagates the superiority of the white (Aryan) race.
1908	Madame C. J. Walker (Sarah Breedlove Walker) opens a college in Pittsburgh to teach her revolutionary hair-care procedure using products she herself developed. Her daughter, A'lelia Walker, inherits her mother's fortune, and establishes a gathering place for the artists and writers of the Harlem Renaissance.
1911	James Van Der Zee sets up a portrait studio; over the next several decades he was to record the lives of people in the Harlem area. In the 1940s, he puts together a series of photographs of African American funeral ceremonies, which is officially published in 1978 as *The Harlem Book of the Dead*; Toni Morrison is asked to write the introduction.
1914–1918	World War I.
1915	The "second wave" of the Great Migration of southern blacks to the North begins.
1917–1918	American involvement in World War I; around 400,000 African Americans serve in the US armed forces, but only 10 percent are assigned to combat duty.

1917   St. Louis race riots (July 1–3) – one of the worst race riots in American history; inaccurate statistics but somewhere between 40 and 200 people are killed and hundreds injured; 6,000 people are driven from their homes.

(July 28) Silent Protest Parade (NAACP Protest March) held in Manhattan in reaction to escalating violence against African Americans.

1918   Okeh Records, an independent record studio, is formed; in 1920, it becomes a subsidiary of Columbia Records. It quickly realizes money is to be made recording what are then called "race records" and launches many major African American musicians, including Louis Armstrong and King Oliver.

1919   The 369th Infantry Regiment, an all-black military unit that fought in World War I, makes a triumphant return to Harlem (February). But the summer of 1919 is called Red Summer because of the extreme number and severity of the race riots.

1920s   Harlem Renaissance (though critics differ as to specific dates).

1930s   The Great Depression; the rise of Hollywood as fabricator of dreams, and the launching of Shirley Temple, child prodigy.

1931   Birth date of Chloe Ardelia Wofford (February 18th). Though most sources cite "Anthony" as Morrison's second given name, John Duvall has published a copy of her birth certificate showing "Ardelia." Morrison is the name she takes when she marries.

1941   Pearl Harbor is bombed (December 10); the United States enters World War II, sending troops to Europe and the Pacific fronts until the war is over in 1945.

1954   The Supreme Court decision in the case of *Brown vs. Board of Education of Topeka, Kansas*, makes segregation of public schools unconstitutional, beginning the end of "Separate but Equal" mandate (May 17).

1955   Emmett Till is murdered in Mississippi (August 28). Beginning of the Montgomery Bus Boycott (December 5). This year is often cited as the beginning of the Civil Rights era.

1960s	The Black Aesthetic (Arts) movement, which closely parallels the Civil Rights and Black Power movements. Characteristics: art as political, anti-white, anti-American, and anti-middle-class; advocates the need for works of art that would be meaningful to black masses and promote racial pride. Outcome: emergence of black studies departments at various universities in the US in the mid-seventies.
1961–1975	US military involvement in the Vietnam War; disproportionately high number of black casualties.
1963	Assassination of civil rights activist Medgar Evers (June 12).
	Assassination of US President John F. Kennedy (November 22).
1964	Signing into law of the Civil Rights Act of 1964 (July 2); creation of Equal Opportunity Commission, beginning of affirmative action programs.
1965	Assassination of Malcolm X (February 21).
	Race riots in the Watts district of Los Angeles (August).
	Morrison becomes senior editor at Random House in New York City.
1968	Assassination of civil rights leader Rev. Martin Luther King in Memphis, Tennessee (April 4).
	Assassination of Robert F. Kennedy (June 5).
1970	Toni Morrison's *The Bluest Eye* published.
1971	Morrison becomes Associate Professor, English, at the State University of New York (SUNY), Purchase, New York (1971–1972)
1973	*Sula*
	Official end of US involvement in the Vietnam War.
1974	*The Black Book*
1975	Fall of Saigon to the North Vietnamese.
1975	*Sula* nominated for the National Book Award.
1977	*Song of Solomon*; receives National Book Critics Circle Award.
1981	*Tar Baby*

1982	*District Storyville*; directed and choreographed by Donald McKayle.
1983	"Recitatif"
1986	*Dreaming Emmett*, produced by the Albany Repertory Theater.
1987	*Beloved*; Morrison takes the Robert F. Goheen Chair at Princeton University, the first black woman to hold a named chair at an Ivy League university.
1988	Pulitzer Prize for Fiction for *Beloved*.
	Robert F. Kennedy Award for *Beloved*.
1989	"Unspeakable Things Unspoken: the Afro-American Presence in American Literature" (Hector Tanner Lecture on Human Values at the University of Michigan).
1991	Clarence Thomas Senate Hearings for confirmation as Justice of the Supreme Court. Anita Hill presents allegations of sexual harassment by Thomas during the time she worked as his assistant at the US Department of Education.
1992	*Playing in the Dark: Whiteness and the Literary Imagination* (the published version of the William E. Massey Sr. Lectures in the History of American Civilization at Harvard University).
	Race-ing Justice, En-Gendering Power: Essays on Anita Hill, Clarence Thomas, and the Construction of Social Reality, edited.
	Jazz
1993	Morrison awarded the Nobel Prize for Literature.
1995	O. J. Simpson tried for the murder of his ex-wife, Nicole Brown Simpson, and her friend, Ronald Goldman.
1996	National Book Foundation Medal for Distinguished Contribution to American Letters.
1997	*Birth of a Nation'hood: Gaze, Script, and Spectacle in the O. J. Simpson Case*, edited with Claudia Brodsky Lacour.
1998	*Paradise*
2003	*Love*

2005   Libretto for the opera, *Margaret Garner*, music by Richard Danielpour, performed in May in Detroit and in July in Cincinnati; and in Philadelphia in February of 2006.

2006   Morrison retires from Princeton.

JUSTINE TALLY

Introduction:
"All necks are on the line"

In her seminal essay, "Unspeakable Things Unspoken: the Afro-American Presence in American Literature," Toni Morrison throws down the gauntlet. What we do as writers and critics is not just important, it is crucial; it is not just informative, it is formative; it is not just interesting, it profoundly shapes the perception of the world as we, and others, come to "know" it. It is a responsibility that we as critics must take extremely seriously because what we do makes a difference, whether it is fawning over a popular writer whose subtext is actually pernicious to human relationships, or unfairly criticizing a more complex writer struggling to speak from a different world. The choices we make are not gratuitous; they are most often political, emerging from an ideology that we are not even, not necessarily anyway, aware of. If there is one thing that Toni Morrison – author, playwright, librettist, lyricist, Nobel Prize winner, social and literary critic – has taught us, it is that we are all responsible for those choices, and ignorance is not a lawful excuse for committing an infraction: For Morrison ". . . as far as the future is concerned, when one writes, as critic or as author, all necks are on the line."[1]

But as Morrison herself (following Bakhtin) has noted, "responsibility" is also "response-ability," the capacity for a dialogue between writer and reading public, often mediated by the critic, which demands that (1) we take the author and her work seriously and meet her on her own terms, and (2) we prepare ourselves, yes, academically, but equally important, psychically to free our minds from the strictures and constraints of the inherited, the given, the unquestioned, the "unspeakable," in order to meet "marginal" authors on their own terms. These days, however, it is more than inappropriate to define Morrison as "marginal," not because she has moved to the center of the canon, but because she has managed to move the center; or perhaps it would be more appropriate to say that because of her multi-faceted and untiring work, she has helped change a restricted, predominantly white, and male-centered literary world into a multicultural mosaic.

Not that it did not take enormous effort on her part to attain the canonization seldom granted to women writers, almost never to blacks. And yet Morrison was hardly the first non-white, non-male author to challenge the hegemony of the white-male center: that effort has also been both political and collective in nature as, for example, in the open letter to the *New York Times* by forty-eight black writers, decrying the non-recognition of *Beloved*, inexplicably passed over in 1987 for both the American Book Award and the Pulitzer. (She later indicated that that support and recognition by her own writerly community was one of the most meaningful "awards" she has ever received.) It is fascinating that in an informal survey among writers and other literati by the same news institution in May 2006, the very same book was voted the best piece of fiction written in the US in the last twenty-five years; in fact it was *a priori* considered to be the "front runner," no matter that one letter to the editor protested that not even 30 percent of those surveyed were women. It is fascinating as well to remember that the winner for the previous twenty-five years was Ralph Ellison's *Invisible Man*, an important reference for Morrison's first novel. Two hundred years after the proscription of literacy for slaves in the United States, black writes back: the exquisite taste of revenge, the profound dismay over the enforced silencing. Faulkner's two-word description of Dilsey and her family in his Appendix to *The Sound and the Fury*[2] – "they endured" – also succinctly epitomizes Morrison's abiding respect for her own black legacy.

The essays included in this volume are testimony precisely to Morrison's resonance on an international, intergenerational, and intercultural scale; the contributors include both men and women, "black" and "white," Americans and Europeans, younger scholars and more established critics. Some contributors have chosen to capitalize the "B" in "Black" as a political statement; others think it more political to use the lower case. As editor, I believe that Morrison's work demands that respect for difference, so I am simply explaining, not "apologizing" for, these choices. Because if there is one crucial link to be found in all of this author's multifarious work, and indeed among the distinctly varied approaches to be found in this volume, it is the concept that language is politically loaded and that in our critical writing, even in our everyday conversations, we must heighten our sensitivity to the use we make of it.

"[W]here your hands are. Now," to quote Morrison, is holding a vibrant addition to the copious scholarship already available on the author. What makes it all new is not only its cross-fertilization of international minds and critiques, but also the focus on the "entirety" of her work: not just new essays on her eight novels, but innovative discussions of her less well-known "shorter pieces," her influential career as editor and teacher, her ground-breaking literary criticism, and her perceptive social criticism. No volume before this *Companion to Toni Morrison* has attempted to look at her oeuvre as an entity – though she herself has stated: "It's one job" – yet doing so illuminates her life's project as a consistent attempt to make a difference.

It has been suggested that because of Morrison's investment in the recovery of black history, her novels might well be read in the chronological order of their respective time frames: the rural slave-holding South; the Great Migration to the North; post-World War I and the Harlem Renaissance; the Great Depression; World War II and pre-Civil Rights; the Civil Rights era and the Vietnam War; and the "Age of Greed" with its political, social, and personal backsliding, which also has witnessed an insidious return to scientific racism (as if it had ever really gone away). The Chronology included at the beginning of the volume is an attempt to reference many of the historical events mentioned (or at least tacitly understood) in these particular essays and relevant for the historical background, which is ever present in a Morrison novel and crucial for understanding other aspects of her work. It does not pretend to be exhaustive either for the historical data, or for Morrison's biography, simply helpful.

For the purposes of organizing this volume, however, the novels discussed in the essays in Part I appear in order of publication, with the exception of Abena Busia's discussion of Morrison's "shorter pieces." Rather than covering the historical bent of the novels (which is exceedingly difficult anyway, given the fusion of past and present so often at the core of her work), this "straightforward" setting out of her fiction facilitates an analysis of Morrison's development as a writer, both as to her narrative strategies and techniques as well as to the political concerns of contemporary society. As with most great authors, Morrison may be talking about the past, but she is speaking to the present.

Ágnes Surányi looks at both *The Bluest Eye* and *Sula* within the problematic of growing up black and female, on the one hand, and the crucial support systems offered by female relationships, on the other. Both novels speak to their respective moments: Morrison's reaction to "Black is Beautiful" in the first, and to the early women's movement in the second. For Surányi, the narrative technique of both novels, each in its own way, is highly innovative, emphasizing both the metaphors and the language itself as central to the author's vision, and mapping out early concerns that will continue to surface in her later work.

Joyce Hope Scott also emphasizes Morrison's language in *Song of Solomon* and *Tar Baby*, specifically from the point of view of Bakhtin's carnivalesque as a tool for subversion and survival in a hostile world. Milkman Dead and Jadine Childs may both be involved in quests for the meaning of their "blackness," but their decisions differ vastly even as they grow in humanity. In addition to extending the author's signature technique of "circularity," these texts are "open-ended," a characteristic that will also become a hallmark of Morrison's novels.

Because of the monumental impact of *Beloved*, and the extraordinary outpouring of critical work on this novel, Claudine Raynaud devotes her entire essay both to the critical work it has generated and the centrality of memory to the poetics of the text. Through the language of memory, metaphor, and dream, Morrison at once examines what was suppressed, determines what is useful for survival, and discards what is too painful to carry forward. Though history is central, it is a "history of consciousness," a "ghost story," which, simply because it lacks "materiality," is no less real. "Absence of evidence is not evidence of absence," as Carl Sagan has said.

Shirely A. (Holly) Stave also takes on "Historical Revisionism" in *Jazz* and *Paradise*, the "zero-moment" of the Harlem Renaissance, and the backdrop of the Civil Rights era and the Vietnam War, respectively. Though the present is serendipitous in *Jazz*, and the music of the 1920s resonant in both the text and the narrative technique, the past continues to haunt the migrants to the City. The playful yet ultimately unreliable narrator foregrounds the language of the story recounted again and again in multiple voices, "tracks" echoing the records, the hunt, the City itself. In *Paradise*, however, history becomes monolithic and lethal, and women its victims. Symbolic language is confronted with the *semiotique*.

I have always found the reluctance to examine Morrison's self-proclaimed "trilogy" (*Beloved, Jazz*, and *Paradise*) *as* a trilogy rather perplexing. My own contribution to this volume, then, is an attempt to open up the discussion, using various approaches, and suggesting ways in which we can understand the trilogy as one complete project, independently of the fact that each of its components brilliantly stands on its own. Again, the network of language, memory, and history supports and sustains the texts, but I also want to raise issues of Morrison's investment in the theoretical debates of the last three decades of the twentieth century. It is my hope that this essay will serve as a springboard for more investigation into the textual and extra-textual aspects that, I believe, securely link these three novels to each other.

Mar Gallego also looks at *Love*, Morrison's latest novel, through the lens of historical recovery, here the pre-Civil Rights movement of the "past" and the "present" of the 1990s, focusing on the loss that went hand-in-hand with the gains of the 1960s. Gallego, however, also emphasizes the heartbreak and breakdown in female friendships caused by the loss of traditional black communal values, and celebrates the value of a loving female relationship, free of patriarchal interventions and class distinctions. A valiant and valuable first approximation to a new text.

Except for Morrison's only published short story, "Recitatif," no critical work has to date been available on the author's incursions into other genres. Abena Busia's "field work" has itself been a diligent job of "historical recovery," given the fact that three of the four pieces discussed here have not even been published. Busia has relied on personal interviews, two with Morrison herself, and the fortuitous recovery of a manuscript of *Dreaming Emmett*, which the author kindly lent her for work on this piece. From a copy of the libretto and her attendance at two performances of *Margaret Garner*, and with personal input from the producers of the musical *Storyville*, Busia has creatively traced Morrison's "artistic impulse" for the benefit of everyone interested in the writer's complete works. Through this work Busia demonstrates Morrison's restless curiosity, willingness to experiment creatively, and her interest in close collaboration with others in different artistic fields.

Part II of this *Companion* deals with other, less well-known, but highly influential aspects of Toni Morrison's writing. Hanna Wallinger navigates the complexities of the author's literary criticism as set out in her two major contributions to the field, specifically her examination of "American Africanisms." Students of American literature will find Wallinger's explanations both clarifying and exceedingly useful as she follows the intricacies of Morrison's arguments, providing the historical background from which these arguments derive, and highlights the influence this new focus in criticism has had, and continues to have, on studies of American literature.

Given the avowedly political nature of Morrison's writing, it is somewhat surprising that more attention has not been given to her "social criticism." Sämi Ludwig uses cognitive theory to identify two different thrusts in the author's social criticism: first, the direct critique of the type of narration used to define and confine black participants in the national discourse (and the usefulness of such stereotyping in important national debates), and second, the more intricate examination of how language carries heavy ideological weight and the author's own struggle to achieve a language that is race-based but not racist. Ludwig's contribution also highlights Morrison's indebtedness to some of the great philosophers, and how she adapts certain of their premises to her own uses.

Again, to date no one has examined Morrison's influential work undertaken while she was a senior editor at Random House. Cheryl Wall has uncovered a wealth of information, both on the encouragement offered to young African Americans knocking at the doors of publishing houses, and the crucial role Morrison has played in shaping the American literary scene by getting their work into print. Wall's examination of the writers whose work was ushered into the light with Morrison as midwife lays bare the foundations of the world of publishing and what impact Morrison's personal politics have had on what we now read. Those politics are on display particularly here in Wall's in-depth discussion of the creation and compilation of *The Black Book*.

Part III is devoted to essays that take a comprehensive look at Morrison's oeuvre considered as a whole. Judylyn Ryan brings to her analysis of Morrison's language a background in the narrative techniques not only of writing but also of cinema. The resulting, innovative readings sustain Ryan's arguments that the author's "social vision" and "democratic narrative" are part and parcel of her "teacherly role . . . of the artist in a democratic society," designed to reclaim and strengthen reader competence. This essay once again supports the contention that Morrison's personal politics are indeed political.

It is more than just interesting that at a historical moment in which civil liberties in the US seem to be under threat, Ryan emphasizes the "democratic," while Dwight McBride, in examining Morrison as an intellectual, focuses on her "pursuits of freedom." History can produce such irony: it is seemingly the black community, too long shackled by slavery and discrimination, which may be shouldering the responsibility for the true meaning of the "American Dream." In McBride's essay, language again is the central force furthering the vision of the author. Even as he draws on textual examples that appear elsewhere in this volume, the reading he offers of these same words evidence the "heteroglossia" of Morrison's writing.

The last essay, written by Deidre Raynor and Johnnella Butler, is a diligent overview of the major critical approaches to Morrison's work to date, presented in succinct, easily accessible form. Here students, teachers, and researchers can get an idea of the breadth of Morrison scholarship and at the same time quickly locate specific sources for their own research. It is certainly a gigantic task to try to be "exhaustive," but Raynor and Butler's work is admirable in its comprehensiveness and certainly offers some much-needed "shorthand" for those daunted by the sheer range and volume of Morrison criticism.

The Further Reading section at the end of the volume includes only book entries and is intended for use as quick reference, on the one hand, and on the other, to inspire others to "keep on keeping on" with their reading and study of Morrison.

As editor I am deeply appreciative of the time, energy, and thoughtfulness that the contributors to this *Companion* have invested in their essays. If the work and vision of Toni Morrison is furthered in any meaningful way by the addition of these analyses to the scholarship, maybe somewhere down the line our necks will still be in tact.

NOTES

1. Toni Morrison, "Unspeakable Things Unspoken: the Afro-American Presence in America Literature," *Michigan Quarterly Review* 28.1 (Winter 1989): 5.
2. William Faulkner, *The Sound and the Fury: The Corrected Text with Faulkner's Appendix* (New York: Modern Library; Rpt. 1992). Though the novel itself was first published in 1929, Faulkner wrote his Appendix in 1946.

PART ONE

Toni Morrison's fiction

I

ÁGNES SURÁNYI

The Bluest Eye and *Sula*: black female experience from childhood to womanhood

The Bluest Eye

The publication of *The Bluest Eye* (1970) heralded the arrival of a brilliant young novelist – but it took almost five years for many to sit up and take notice. Though Sarah Blackburn remarks that Toni Morrison's first novel was published "at an auspicious time when a growing, middle-class women's movement was just beginning to acknowledge the reality of its black and poor sisters,"[1] an overview of the critical discourse of the time shows that from the readership the book received little, if any, understanding. It is noteworthy that after its first publication the novel was out of print for quite a long time. A tragic story of child abuse, with race, gender and class mixed in, *The Bluest Eye* is concerned with racial self-loathing, the loss of identity, and shame. Even though the setting for the story is 1940–41 – the beginning of World War II for the United States – it is also "presentist" in concept, ideologically grounded in the 1960s when "Black is Beautiful" entered into the popular, if more militant, discourse. Setting out to write a story that she herself wanted to read, Morrison worried that this slogan of racial pride would be unable to dispel the long-term psychic effects of prejudices rooted in racialism and sexism.

The locale of this imaginative narrative is Lorrain, Ohio, the protagonist Pecola Breedlove, a little black girl at the most vulnerable phase of her life. The title *The Bluest Eye* calls attention to itself immediately: the superlative degree of color as well as the singular form of the noun in the title is rather unusual, resulting in a pun. The singular noun may refer to the damaging white gaze; the omitted plural to the object of desire, an epitome of beauty according to mainstream society; or alternatively, to the saddest story of the demise of a child's identity (the "eye" as "I"), integral to the blues sung by Claudia's mother. The multivocality of the I/eye serves also to reinforce the text's emphasis on the visual, evident in everything from the white men's gaze as Cholly engages in his first sexual exploit, to the imposition of Hollywood icons in the cinema, and to Claudia's mutilation of the doll, punching out its startled blue plastic eyes in an attempt to find out what made it beautiful in the eyes of grown-ups. Pecola, desperately trying to escape the squalor of her life, finds that she can will her body to disappear, limb by limb, piece by piece, but never manages to free herself of her eyes, her invisibility never quite complete. Yet in her encounter with Mr. Yacobowski, the store-keeper who will sell her nine lovely orgasmic Mary Janes[2] without ever touching her dirty little hand, his refusal to even look at her confirms for her the insignificance and invisibility of a little black girl for the white gaze. Like Ralph Ellison's *Invisible Man* her "ugly" black skin impedes any acknowledgment of the child within. Told in the present tense, which suggests timelessness as well as repetitiveness, the incident confirms for Pecola her lack of self-worth. The dandelions she had formerly thought to be quite beautiful are now simply the weeds everyone has said they are.

Morrison's denunciation of the fetishism involved in the fixation on physical beauty is augmented by the time frame of her story, the moment the US is entering a war precisely to fight such racist ideology in the imposition of an Aryan "ideal." World War II is also present in Morrison's penchant for giving her characters poignant names, her "subtle delight in nominalism."[3] This grand narrative of history is represented in her designation of the three whores as Maginot Line, China, and Poland, significant places during the war. By merely giving hints of the distant world events Morrison emphasizes that it is the individual life-stories in the black community that are of interest to her. Yet, in Jennifer Gillan's insightful reading, *The Bluest Eye* is an indirect "commentary on the artificial boundaries of citizenship, gender, race, and history."[4] She points out the importance of Morrison's setting her story during 1940–1941, because in that year the United States was posing as the champion of democracy abroad, while ignoring its own long-standing history of obsession with racial purity and preference for blue-eyed and blonde-haired Aryans. "The names China and Poland signify the European and Asian fronts, Maginot Line refers both literally and metaphorically to the tendency to focus on the wrong front,"[5] i.e., projecting one's guilt onto another.

On the home front, distraction from the socio-economic collapse and the calamity of war in Europe of the 1930s was provided by Hollywood, a rising industry dedicated to creating illusions of wealth and happiness while simultaneously and insidiously reinforcing white notions of beauty. The oft-mentioned film stars in the text – Shirley Temple, Jean Harlow, Ginger Rogers, etc. – serve to emphasize the omnipresence of the white gaze and its pernicious influence on the identity formation of the psychologically weakest characters in the book. Only Claudia as a young girl has the security of knowing who she is, and the family and community support to reject an ideology that defines her as inferior.

Morrison's well-known predilection for using the narrative technique of inversion makes it clear that the text itself is "specifying" on a film adaptation of Fannie Hurst's novel *Imitation of Life* (1933). In Jean Caputi's interpretation, Morrison provides her heroine Pecola with the role of an "unimpeachable witness against the very system that caused *peola* [a very white black girl] to become a household word."[6] Pauline may have named her daughter after Peola, for "Pecola's name is an inversion of Peola, the mulatta who hates her black mother in the movie *Imitation of Life*."[7] In *The Bluest Eye*, the black mother hates her own child as a reminder of her hopeless situation and adores the young child of the white family she works for. Morrison clearly condemns a racist culture for its worship of white standards of beauty and reacts "against the damaging internalization of assumptions of immutable inferiority originating in the outside gaze"[8] projected onto popular images.

Inversion or "reversal" is again apparent in Morrison's division of the book into four larger units: fall, spring, winter, and summer. The implication of the cyclical seasonal structure is that the events in the story are likely to be repeated, but as Mark Ledbetter comments, in this novel "[a]utumn is not a season with leaves of beautiful colours, as one might expect, but rather a season of a child's sickness, coughed up on her bed, and the colours of autumn are used to describe her [Claudia's] vomit."[9] Furthermore, he argues that "the child's winter should be playful, and the primary emotion should be anticipation. There is no anticipation in the life of the victim . . . Spring echoes autumn and winter with references to death."[10] Ledbetter regards similar occurrences of unexpected disruptions in the text as a violation of the text by itself. To the contrary, I am contending that it is primarily a deliberate violation of the generic traditions by the author. Intertextual references to the genre of the *memoire*[11] are also undermined by reference to a children's fairy-tale, "The Ugly Duckling," though this duckling will never turn into a beautiful swan.

Since the earliest critical responses, various commentators have pointed out the relevance of the opening *Dick and Jane* excerpt to both the structure and ideology of the novel. Michael Awkward claims that by taking the primer as an intertext (or pre-text), the author revives and at once subverts "the convention of the authenticating document, usually written by whites to confirm a genuine black authorship of the subsequent text."[12] Morrison "signifies"[13] on the white hegemonic discourse that has nothing to do with the realities of black life and refuses to accept the definition of the African American experience according to white standards. Ironically, the textbook is designed to force the reader to see the world through rose-colored (or rather white) glasses, but the introduction into literacy is based on a text that is meaningless from the perspective of African American children. The inculcation of blackness as a "negative signifier" in the minds of the black community causes the destruction and madness of Pecola. The seven central elements of Jane's world – house, family, cat, mother, father, dog, and friend – are used to organize the chapters and become, in turn, "plot elements, but only after they are inverted to fit the realities of Pecola's world."[14] As a result, *The Bluest Eye* is centered upon the home and the danger of "being put outdoors" (17). The three-fold repetition of the pre-text, a descent into chaos, shows the lack of meaning of the text for poor black children; the text without spaces challenges the reader to make sense of a senseless world and calls for compassion.

Immediately thereafter the childlike voice cedes to the bittersweet memories of an adult Claudia, looking back upon the past that we are about to encounter. As a child, she and her sister Frieda naïvely felt guilty about the sad events of the fall of 1941. The baby and Pecola's father, Cholly, are dead at the time of Claudia's present. There is a metaphorical parallel drawn between the seeds of marigolds that she and her sister failed to plant deep enough to take root and the seeds of Pecola's father that he scattered in the wrong ground. The metaphor extends to Pecola herself, who was born in a hostile world, in the wrong place at the wrong time. Claudia's storytelling is oral, introduced by a phrase often overheard in women's intimate gossip: "Quiet as it's kept" (5), which suggests that it is a story to be told and withheld at the same time, a story of incest, of blame, of loss.

Claudine Raynaud describes *The Bluest Eye* as an "anti-Bildungsroman," for it is about "the gradual descent into schizophrenia of the young black protagonist."[15] Jacqueline de Weever, a scholar of myth criticism, has searched for analogies and contrasts between the Greek Demeter myth and the novel. She claims that Morrison's version is based (again) on the narrative tactic of reversal.[16] As Trudier Harris notes, the effect of this folkloristic technique is that "the outcomes consistently fall short of [readerly] expectations."[17] In the myth, Persephone plays with her friends in a field of irises, violets, hyacinths; the landscape Pecola sees every day on her way to school is the urban desert of weeds, dandelions, and tires. Persephone has a loving mother in Demeter; Pecola is slapped by Pauline Breedlove when she accidentally upsets the blueberry cobbler. Demeter does not allow the earth to bloom until her daughter is restored to her; Pauline remains "dry-eyed," when her daughter goes mad. While Persephone is returned to Demeter, a devastated Pecola is lingering "between Coke bottle and milkweed, among all the waste and beauty of the world – which is what she herself was" (205).

The myth of Philomela and Procne – favored by contemporary feminist writers – is also inverted in the book: Pecola has no loving sister like Philomela, and her brother may already have run away from home. While in the original myth Procne takes a horrible revenge on Tereus for the rape of her sister, Pauline is helpless against Cholly and refuses to believe Pecola when she tries to tell her about her father's abuse. Rather unexpectedly, Pecola's rape is related through the eyes of the abuser. Without turning away from the pain and the consequences for the victimized child, Morrison challenges us to understand the attacker: Cholly despises Pecola for loving him in spite of his painful failure, and in drunken stupor, in an attempt to give the love to his "ugly" daughter that she has never experienced, he "tenderly" rapes her.

Such dysfunctionality takes an inevitable toll on the life of eleven-year-old Pecola. Save for the MacTeers, everyone she meets, including the members of her family, is convinced of her worthlessness. Her lack of self-esteem is generated by her alleged ugliness and also by the neglect, abuse, and contempt heaped upon her. She is abused by her own mother and father, denied or made invisible by other adults, but is also the target of ridicule from other children who constantly pick on her. Ironically, the only semblance of love she experiences comes from the three prostitutes. As a result she believes that all this would change if only she acquired blue eyes. At the novel's end she has been raped by her father, lost the baby she was carrying, been driven into madness, but continues her quest for "the bluest eyes," conversing with her imaginary friend, her double. Ironically, having been denied a sense of self and a voice to articulate her pain, in the end an insane Pecola has found not one, but two voices.

Against this pervasive plague of self-hatred, also apparent in Geraldine, Soaphead Church, and even the family of the "high-yellow" Maureen Peel, Morrison sets Claudia, the young but self-confident narrator who voices an alternative to the dominant materialistic discourse. The complexity of narration is provided by the switch of the narrative point of view from first to third person and the presence of multiple perspectives: while much of the storytelling comes from Claudia as a nine-year-old child, she also reflects on the events as an adult. At the same time Pecola's mother is given voice and Morrison herself intervenes as an all-knowing narrator. Cholly remains mute though his story is related by the third-person narrator, whereas Pecola is silenced until the end of the novel because of Morrison's decision to show her as a victim of trauma who would be unable or unwilling to tell the story of her rape. According to Awkward, Pecola's ultimate finding of not one but two voices corresponds to the two-voiced narration of *The Bluest Eye*. As he demonstrates, Claudia narrates the first chapter in each section of the novel and relates matters about her own childhood experiences. The omniscient narrator controls the chapters that Claudia does not narrate, providing information about the histories of older characters as well as about incidents in Pecola's life of which Claudia could not have knowledge. But "after the onset of Pecola's schizophrenic double-voicedness, the distinctive narrative voices of *The Bluest Eye* merge into a single voice."[18] The adult Claudia possesses information of which earlier she was ignorant. In a revelatory moment she realizes that the whole community was guilty of the internalization of self-hatred and the related scapegoating of Pecola. There is a shift from "I" to "we" and an oscillation between "our" and "my" in the final part of Claudia's narrative, which generates ambiguity. "All of us . . . felt so wholesome after we cleaned ourselves on her. We were so beautiful when we stood astride her ugliness . . . Her inarticulateness made us believe we were eloquent. Her poverty kept us generous" (205). We learn that the formerly rebellious Claudia, as she herself admits, has "adjusted without improvement" (23). She has submitted to white middle-class norms, demonstrated by the fact that, with an undertone of egoism and possessiveness, she speaks about leaving a helpless Pecola behind in "my town" (206).

Morrison's constant fascination with language is revealed by her presentation of the vernacular of black people in her novels. Black style is not – she warns us – as some writers think, "dropping g's."[19] It is rather the oral quality and the restoration of the language to its original power. She likes to polish clichés and recover their original meanings. In *The Bluest Eye* even the most distressing experience is handled with delicate humor; much of the comic relief derives from the way the little girls mimic adult black women's talk, for example mispronouncing "incorrigible" as "incorrigival" and saying "ministratin'" instead of "menstruating." Yet Toni Cade Bambara found that her students could not appreciate the significance of the depiction of Pecola's first menses by Morrison because "the onset of menstruation is not something that is valued in our [mainstream] culture," observing that "the initiation or rites of passage of the young girl is not one of the darlings of American literature."[20] The taboo topic of menstruation, so bravely dealt with in *The Bluest Eye*, is certainly unlike anything I have read so far. Claudia's taking the lyrics of the blues her mother sings literally and Pecola's innocent nagging of the "three merry gargoyles" (55) with questions is at once funny and heart-wrenching. The language used by children is definitely different from the speech of the adults in the book; in both cases the author takes care to make the language "rich but not ornate."[21] Morrison's insistence on preserving the African American traditions can be seen, or rather heard, in the "specifying" between Maginot Line and the other women. The borderline between decent women and man-hating prostitutes is erased; only the latter are capable of giving love to Pecola, whose quest for it elsewhere is futile. They notice her bare-legged poverty, yet tell her about Prince Dewey instead of exposing her to the bleak reality of their lives. A comparison of Claudia's and the omniscient narrator's storytelling shows Morrison's deft manipulation of language, her awareness that for a child the language needed to describe the traumatic effect of violence and abuse is not available.

Sula

In her next novel Morrison continues to deal with black female experience, but the emphasis shifts from childhood experience to lasting bonding between girls-becoming-women. *Sula* (1973) spans the period from 1919 to 1965. The title of the novel is at first disorienting (until the end of the Prologue it is not specified whether it is the name of a character demanding the reader's attention, an African goddess,[22] or a place). The epigraph of the novel chosen from Tennessee Williams's *The Rose Tattoo* provides the reader "with a pithy statement of the novel's underlying theme, the ravages of time and misbegotten love."[23]

In the novel Sula's appearance is indefinitely postponed. After the horrible experience of the two world wars and the trauma of the holocaust contemporary writers can rarely afford to begin a novel by introducing the protagonist in a safe or idyllic environment. Morrison projects the history of the obliteration of a black community, and then reconstructs its history chronologically in retrospection. The Prologue of the novel focuses on specificity and difference, the history of the community, nostalgia for its past, the violence done to it, and the consequences of that violence, predicting the future that brings about total annihilation. The next chapter focuses on Shadrack, to be continued with the story of Sula's grandmother, Sula's girlhood, her maturation into a young woman, her absence, her death, Nel's epiphany, and the anticipated disappearance of the Bottom. The chronological mode of storytelling returns to its starting-point, resulting in a cyclical structure.

In her explanation of the writing process Morrison says that she knew she "[w]as writing a second novel, and that it would be about people in a black community *not just foregrounded but totally dominant*," but she has problematized her own prologue in *Sula* as a surrender to "a worn-out technique of novel writing: the covert announcement to the reader whom to pay attention to."[24] The technique she is not satisfied with, however, is innovative in my opinion, since she writes about the black community from the point of view of an outsider, a "valley man." White people may well remain peripheral in Morrison's novels, but with regard to her readership she had to face the dilemma of writing for mainstream white culture. Had she not begun with the Prologue, the reader would have come "into immediate confrontation with Shadrack's wound and scar and paid more attention to the traumatic displacement this most wasteful capitalist war had on black people in particular, highlighting their creative . . . determination to survive whole."[25] Even though the Prologue cushions the reader's entry into Shadrack's world, the chapters preceding and delaying the appearance of the novel's protagonist disorient the (conventional) reader.

The encounter first with Shadrack, the World War I veteran, is utterly unexpected. At this point, what I want to argue is that the appearance of the World War I veteran immediately after the Prologue of the novel – whose heroine is Sula – is a scar on the body of the text, which cannot be ignored in our interpretation. The chapter in which the war veteran's story is told is titled "1919," reflecting Morrison's concern with the neglect and humiliation that met the black soldiers who returned shocked and paralyzed from the European front. War is not a heroic hide-and-seek in the novel. Over 400,000 black men, including Shadrack, were drafted at the time. "The black 369th Infantry were under continuous fire for a record of 191 days, for which they won the Croix de Guerre and the honor of leading the victorious Allied armies to the Rhine in 1918."[26] The returning black soldiers that Helene Wright sees on the train still have to travel on Jim Crow cars.[27] Without questioning the great sacrifice of the black soldiers, Morrison records the flight of the American troops from the enemy instead of a dignified march. The way a comrade's head is blown off is naturalistically depicted, his anonymity underlining the futility and waste of this war. Morrison deals with both the physical and psychological damage done to the black soldiers. Importantly, there are two African American war veterans in the novel: Plum and Shadrack. As a result of their war experience, Plum becomes a heroin addict and Shadrack's mental instability deteriorates into permanent madness. The novel has a woman's experience at the center as well as that of a shell-shocked veteran suffering from the post-traumatic effect of World War I. The motif of the double (Doppelgänger) is an element of significance both at the formal and the thematic levels, which deserves scrutiny. Sula has not one, but two doubles, Shadrack and Nel. Relevant events are also doubled: there are two murders (one accidental, the other intentional); two deaths by fire (Hannah's and Plum's); and two self-mutilations (Eva's and Sula's). Delayed reactions as well as the threat of castration occur twice in the novel as well. Doubling, reversal, and indirection recur insistently. Whereas Sula and Shadrack share the painful experience of blackness and outlawry and are linked by their lack of the ability to feel, the bonding between Sula and Nel is based on their awareness of being "neither white nor male."[28] Shadrack is a probable witness of the accidental murder of Chicken Little and he is the last to see Sula laid out on the table dead. Morrison uses metonymy to symbolize Sula's and Shadrack's belonging together: in her fear Sula leaves her belt behind in Shadrack's hut (figuratively fastening Shadrack to herself). It is also mentioned that, according to rumor, there is intimacy between "the two devils" (117). Shadrack's enigmatic word "always" also strengthens their relationship. In my understanding, the word implies the promise that there is permanence in the face of change and death. Driven by the desire for immunity from change, Shadrack institutionalizes the National Suicide Day on January 3 (14), announcing that this was the only day to focus on death, to get it out of the way.

Shadrack's name alludes to the biblical Shadrach in the Book of Daniel. Readers of the Bible will know that Shadrach was "one of the three friends who were thrown into the fiery furnace by command of Nebuchadnezzar"[29] for refusing to worship the king's god and his idol of gold. For this refusal Shadrach and his two compatriots are thrown into this metaphorical hell, yet the flames have no power to destroy them. Unlike his biblical namesake, Shadrack does not come out of the fiery furnace of war safe and unsinged; on the contrary, he is "blasted" and "permanently astonished" (7). His main achievement is mere survival, as he manages to survive the war as well as the accident (mass suicide) in the tunnel. Shadrack is punished for refusing to worship the idol of war and to regard fighting as a male virtue after his war experience. In Medallion "even the most fastidious people . . . sometimes caught themselves dreaming what he must have been like a few years back before he went off to war" (7). In the chapter dedicated to Shadrack, his perspective is given priority, and the readers are invited to see the world through his lens. After the terrible trauma of war, against all his expectations "to be terrified or exhilarated" he "*could not feel* something very strong [either]. Ironically, *he felt only the bite of a nail in his boot*, which pierced the ball of his foot whenever he came down on it" (7–8, emphasis added). The contrast between the literal and figurative meanings of "feeling" in this passage is an example of defamiliarization based on inversion, just like Shadrack's embarrassment at hearing the word "private," which he deliberately understands as some "secret," being unwilling to heed the word that reminds him of his army rank and participation in the war.

The description of Shadrack's hands is a metaphoric allusion, on the one hand, to his inability to reach out and communicate, and, on the other, to the impact of the war on those who took part in it and do not know how and what to use their hands for after the terrible experience of learning and witnessing the art of killing. In hospital, "Shadrack noticed two lumps beneath the beige blanket on either side of his hips. With extreme care he lifted one arm and was relieved to find his hand attached to his wrist. He tried the other and found it also" (9). But then all of a sudden his hands began "to grow in higgledy-piggledy fashion" (9). After his dismissal from the hospital "[t]hrough his tears he saw the fingers joining the laces, tentatively at first, then rapidly. The four fingers[30] of each hand fused into the fabric, knotted themselves and zigzagged in and out of the tiny eyeholes" (13). His hands can no longer be controlled; even everyday activities like tying his shoelaces require an extraordinary effort.

Sula came out "at a time when the Black Aesthetic movement called for positive representations and role models."[31] As a consequence, Sula, a young black woman without any attachments or feelings of responsibility could hardly be expected to receive a favorable reception. But Morrison was determined to undermine the stereotyping as well as the false idealization of black characters. She admitted that though she didn't know anyone like Sula, still she took care "not to make her freakish or repulsive or unattractive."[32]

Sula is introduced within the family in parallel to her friend Nel. While Sula lives in "a household of throbbing disorder" (52), the Wrights' home is neat and tidy, a kind of prison. The relationship of Sula and Nel is complementary; many parallels and points of comparison connect them: while Sula is a rebel, Nel is her conventional counterpart, a "dutiful friend, respectful daughter, loyal wife and nurturing mother."[33] In contrast, when Eva asks her about the possibility of marriage and having children, Sula retorts: "I don't want to make somebody else. I want to make myself" (92). That is, Sula "extracts choice from choicelessness." [34] She rebels against the role she is assigned to take within the black community. Consequently, she becomes a transgressor and an outlaw, just like Shadrack. By focusing on the young women's bonding Morrison undermines the ethical binarities of the conventional (Euro-American) notion of the self and challenges the tradition of creating positive black characters, always consistent with themselves. Accordingly, the Bottom community offers various interpretations of Sula's eccentric behavior and her birthmark and peculiarities. Sula's birthmark is alternately seen by the various characters as a rose, a rattlesnake over the eye, a copperhead, a tadpole, or her mother's ashes.

Sula needs Nel because she "had no center, no speck around which to grow. She had no ego. For that reason she felt no compulsion to verify herself – be consistent with herself" (119). Robert Grant remarks that the lack of center in Sula's character is one of the reasons why "thematically and politically the novel is an unpredictable text," and that Sula is an enigmatic character whose "behavioral motivations" are morally and psychologically unclear.[35] He has also observed the "quasipalindromic"[36] structure of the novel (95) and the significance of the central lacuna in the body of the text, which intentionally calls attention to Sula's absence.

There is no doubt that Sula's and Nel's meeting "was fortunate, for it let them use each other to grow on" (152). Nel's mother, however, resented her daughter's choice of Sula as a friend. She expressed her dislike in an ambiguous manner, saying that "Sula's mother was sooty" (29). "Sooty" may be understood in two ways: it may suggest that Sula's mother is not clean or morally pure, but it may also refer to the fact that she is too black-skinned for the mulatto Helene's taste. Nel envies her friend's behavior, even though the latter is more uncertain and instinctive than she is. In reproaching her friend, she points out to Sula that she cannot be walking around "all independent-like," doing whatever she likes (142). In putting up a rebellion against racism and sexism, Sula cuts off the tip of her own finger in defense of Nel when they are confronted by a gang of Irish hoodlums. In this episode Morrison shows the damaging effect of ethnic resentment: the newly arrived Catholic immigrants – themselves victims of contemptuous treatment by the white Protestants of the town – turn into aggressors in order to regain confidence and feel superior. Sula's reaction is ambiguous. It seems likely that her act echoes Eva's (intentional) loss of her leg; this is her response to a situation of sexist and racist assault. Alternatively, it may be also read as Morrison's comment on Freud's theory of penis envy.

Sula and Nel do have a special (homoerotic) relationship. The game in which they engage at the time of their sexual awakening is crucial for understanding the relationship of the two young women. Even though Nel is the initiator, she disrupts Sula's joy by starting to compete with her, and finally destroying the hole they have made together. The game symbolizes the future burial of their friendship. This particular episode shows that Nel has little self-knowledge, and she fears "funky" experimentation. All she wants is a clean house and a good husband. No wonder that later she fails to understand Sula's act of seducing her husband Jude, or that Sula values their friendship much more than the casual sex she may have with men. Nel acts as the wronged wife and mother, yet "she refuses to look at the unacceptable aspects of herself. Nel and Sula appear to be different but they are also similar."[37] Love that is accompanied by possessiveness and inhibits the development of the subject is the Western kind of love that Morrison condemns. Nel realizes the true nature of her feelings towards Sula too late.

Although in accord with other critics Grant regards *Sula* as a radically feminist text, he has reservations. He asserts that "feminist appropriations of *Sula* as solely a novel about 'black female friendship' or as a 'black lesbian novel' is too monistic."[38] I agree with Grant's claim that Sula cannot be interpreted in a monolithic way, but it remains a fact that black-female bonding (with lesbian connotations) is the central concern of the novel. As Morrison herself has stated, "*Friendship between women* is special, different, and *has never been depicted as the major focus of a novel before* Sula. Nobody ever talked about friendship between women *unless it was homosexual*, and there is no homosexuality in *Sula.* "[39]

Despite Morrison's denial of having written this story with the intention of depicting homosexuality, Barbara Smith assumes that *Sula* works as a lesbian novel mainly because of the author's consistent criticism of heterosexual institutions. She underpins her claim by analyzing the dreams of the girls before their first meeting, their shared fantasies as well as their description as two halves of the same equation.[40] In contrast with Smith, Barbara Johnson acknowledges that the texts she has selected for analysis – including *Sula* – are not necessarily lesbian, but in her (lesbian) reading they "could . . . be said to have a crypto-lesbian plot."[41] Her conclusion is that ultimately *Sula* does not work as a lesbian novel because even though compulsory heterosexuality blinds Nel and Sula to the possibility of not looking upon each other as sexual rivals, "protracted and intense eye-contact and involuntary re-encounters ungrounded in conscious positive feelings"[42] are missing in it.

Nevertheless, one cannot question the intensity of the relationship between the two women, which is disrupted by Jude's appearance. Nel realizes the real loss only after Sula's death. The term Johnson uses to designate this belated reaction is *"the dissociation of affect and event,"* which she regards as "one of Morrison's most striking literary techniques in this novel, both in her narrative voice . . . and in the emotional lives of her characters."[43] The dissociation noted above is present on the microlevel of the novel as well: when the mother of Chicken Little sees her son's clothes lying on the table in the basement of the mortuary, "her mouth snapped shut, and when she saw his [dead] body her mouth flew wide open again and it was seven hours before she was able to close it and make the first sound" (64). Eva Peace has to postpone her anger and hatred for her womanizing ex-husband until his visit two years later. Hearing his new lover's "high-pitched big-city laugh," which "hit her like a sledge-hammer . . . it was then that she knew what to feel" (36).

Johnson has also drawn attention to two prominent words, "aesthetic" and "rapport," in the text. (In the novel the italicization of these words signals their significance.) After witnessing the love-making scene between her husband and Sula, Nel is ruminating: "I waited for Sula to look up at me any minute and say one of those lovely college words like *aesthetic* or *rapport*, which I never understood but which I loved because they sounded so comfortable and firm" (105). It is out of place for Nel to be thinking about the meanings of these words in the given situation. Johnson's argument that the arbitrariness of these words provides a key to the novel is supported by the ambiguity of the episode when an "interested" Sula is watching her mother fall victim to the flames. It is impossible to say whether she was in shock, or, as Eva was convinced, she had watched the spectacle of her mother burning "not because she was paralyzed, but because she was interested" (78).

The first term signals that the dilemma Morrison faces is not unlike that of Sula, who is an artist without an art form: in a sense the artist should contemplate life aesthetically, keeping her distance from her subject at the same time. The second word implies that she should have a sympathetic relation to the pain of the characters in her fictional world. I agree with Johnson's claim, these two words are of key significance for the reader, indeed, but I need to add that they are equally important for the author. By means of giving prominence to "aesthetic" and "rapport" Morrison merges and highlights the central issues of the novel with her own writerly dilemmas.

The Bluest Eye and *Sula* are experimental texts, radically innovative in terms of theme and form. Both books contrast the alternative responses of resistance and subjugation to sexist or racist oppression. Several commentators have remarked that apart from the stunning imagery, the alternately lyrical and dramatic depiction of violent acts, the hallmark of Morrison's fiction is death-watch: the characters – as willing or enforced spectators – often witness violent (natural or unnatural) deaths. The fact that "invisibility" serves as the grounds for racism against blacks accounts for Morrison's preoccupation with violence in terms of the spectacle, the inexorable white gaze. In consequence, Johnson is perhaps right: sometimes Morrison "runs – indeed courts – the risk of transforming horror into pleasure, violence into beauty, mourning into nostalgia."[44] Such is the haunting loveliness of these texts.

NOTES

1. Sarah Blackburn, "Review of *Sula*," *Toni Morrison: Critical Perspectives Past and Present*, ed. Henry Louis Gates, Jr. and K. A. Appiah (New York: Amistad Press, 1993), p. 6.
2. Toni Morrison, *The Bluest Eye* (New York: Alfred Knopf, 1970, rpt. 1997), p. 50. All subsequent references will be included in the text.
3. Houston A. Baker Jr., "When Lindbergh Sleeps with Bessie Smith: the Writing of Place in Toni Morrison's *Sula*," *The Difference Within: Feminism and Critical Theory*, ed. Elizabeth Meese and Alice Parker (Amsterdam: John Benjamins, 1989), p. 90.
4. Jennifer Gillan, "Focusing on the Wrong Front: Historical Displacement, the Maginot Line, and *The Bluest Eye*," *African American Review* 36.2 (2002): 283.
5. The name of a powerful defensive line built by France to stop a German invasion. The line was a complete failure: in 1940, Nazi armies invaded northern France by going through neutral Holland and Belgium, bypassing the Maginot Line. (See detailed explanation in Gillan, "Focusing on the Wrong Font," p. 285).

6. Jean Caputi, "'Specifying' Fannie Hurst: Langston Hughes's 'Limitations of Life,' Zora Neale Hurston's *Their Eyes Were Watching God*, and Toni Morrison's *The Bluest Eye* as 'Answers' to Hurst's *Imitation of Life*," *Black American Literature Forum* 24.4 (Winter 1990): 710.

7. Quoted in Caputi, "'Specifying' Fanny Hurst," p. 711.

8. Toni Morrison, "Afterword," *The Bluest Eye*, p. 210.

9. Mark Ledbetter, *Victims and the Postmodern Narrative or Doing Violence to the Body: An Ethic of Reading and Writing* (London: Macmillan, 1996), p. 27.

10. *Ibid.*

11. Justine Tally, *The Story of "Jazz": Toni Morrison's Dialogic Imagination*. FORE-CAAST 3 (Hamburg: Lit, 2001), p. 31.

12. Michael Awkward, *Inspiriting Influences: Tradition, Revision, and Afro-American Women's Novels* (New York: Columbia University Press, 1983), p. 62.

13. See Henry Louis Gates, Jr., "The Blackness of Blackness: a Critique of the Sign and the Signifying Monkey," *Black Literature and Literary Theory* (New York: Methuen, 1984), pp. 4–19.

14. Raymond Hedin, quoted in Michael Awkward, "Roadblocks and Relatives: Critical Revision in Toni Morrison's *The Bluest Eye*," *Critical Essays on Toni Morrison*, ed. Nellie McKay (Boston: G. K. Hall, 1988), p. 58.

15. Claudine Raynaud, "Coming of Age in the African American Novel," *The Cambridge Companion to the African American Novel*, ed. Maryemma Graham (Cambridge University Press, 2004), p. 114. In contrast with the developmental novel the "anti-Bildungsroman" deals with the protagonist's regression.

16. Jacqueline de Weever, *Mythmaking and Metaphor in Black Women's Fiction* (London: Macmillan, 1991), p. 107.

17. Trudier Harris, "Escaping Slavery but Not Its Images," in *Toni Morrison: Critical Perspective*, ed. Gates and Appiah, p. 12.

18. Awkard, *Inspiriting*, p. 93.

19. Judith Wilson, "A Conversation with Toni Morrison," *Conversations with Toni Morrison*, ed. Danille Taylor-Guthrie (Jackson: University Press of Mississippi, 1994), p. 136.

20. Quoted in Ruth Rosenberg, "Seeds in Hard Ground: Black Girlhood in *The Bluest Eye*," *Black American Literature Forum* 21.4 (Winter 1987): 436.

21. Thomas LeClair, "The Language Must Not Sweat," in *Conversations*, ed. Taylor-Guthrie, p. 121.

22. Michele Pessoni, "'She Was Laughing at Their God': Discovering the Goddess within Sula," *African American Review* 29.3 (1995): 443.

23. Lynn C. Munro, "The Tattooed Heart and the Serpentine Eye: Morrison's Choice of an Epigraph for *Sula*," *Black Literature Forum* 18.4 (1984): 150.

24. Toni Morrison, "Unspeakable Things Unspoken: the Afro-American Presence in American Literature," *Michigan Quarterly Review* 28.1 (Winter 1989): 23–24.

25. *Ibid.*, p. 26.

26. Patricia Hunt, "War and Peace: Transfigured Categories and the Politics of Sula," *African American Review* 27.3 (1993): 448.

27. Jill Matus, *Toni Morrison* (Manchester University Press, 1998), p. 57.

28. Toni Morrison, *Sula* (1973. London: Picador, 1993), p. 152. All subsequent references will be included in the text.

29. Peter Calvocoressi, *Who's Who in the Bible* (London: Penguin Books, 1988), p. 217.
30. The "four fingers" will establish another link with Sula, who cuts off the tip of one of her fingers in the book.
31. Matus, *Toni Morrison*, p. 38.
32. Morrison, "Unspeakable Things Unspoken," p. 23.
33. Rita A. Bergenholtz, "Toni Morrison's *Sula*: a Satire on Binary Thinking," *African American Review* 30.1 (1996): 92.
34. Morrison, "Unspeakable Things Unspoken," p. 25.
35. Robert Grant, "Absence into Presence: the Thematics of Memory and 'Missing' in Toni Morrison's *Sula*," in *Critical Essays*, ed. McKay, pp. 91–92.
36. That is, *Sula* is divided into two parts of nearly the same length: characters introduced and developed in Part One are brought back in Part Two in reverse order.
37. Bergenholtz, "Toni Morrison's *Sula*," p. 92.
38. Grant, "Absence," p. 93.
39. Quoted in Claudia Tate, "Toni Morrison," *Black Women at Work* (New York: Continuum, 1983), p. 118; emphasis added.
40. Quoted in Barbara Johnson, *The Feminist Difference: Literature, Psychoanalysis, Race, and Gender* (London and Cambridge, MA: Harvard University Press, 1998), p. 158.
41. *Ibid.*, 159–160.
42. *Ibid.*, p. 80.
43. *Ibid.*, pp. 82–84.
44. *Ibid.*, p. 86.

2

JOYCE HOPE SCOTT

Song of Solomon and *Tar Baby*: the subversive role of language and the carnivalesque

In *Song of Solomon* (1977) and *Tar Baby* (1981) Toni Morrison artfully employs African American vernacular language and folklore to foreground her concern with subversion both in the language itself and in narrative structure. Indeed these two novels effectively exemplify M. M. Bakhtin's theory of the carnivalesque through the enactment of ritual spectacles, comic verbal exchanges, and various examples of "abusive" language. In both *Song of Solomon* and *Tar Baby* the carnivalesque is at once "heteroglossic" – simultaneously producing multiple meanings – and "disruptive" – challenging hegemonic structures on two levels. First, it establishes an interracial dialogue that challenges white America's view and ordering of the world; and second, it give voice to an intra-racial dialogue, which confronts a privileged black middle-class materialism with the vernacular discourse of the black folk community.

Song of Solomon

For Milkman Dead, Morrison's protagonist in *Song of Solomon* (*SOS*),[1] history, identity, and spiritual healing are linked to the power of naming and the verbal facility to impress his experience on the language. This he ultimately achieves through initiation into the discursive formulas of the African American vernacular. Milkman must acquire the vernacular speech and culture of black urban males in order to be spiritually reborn and "discursively" reinserted into a history from which he and his family have been estranged. The narrative structure of Milkman Dead's quest depicts a series of initiatory phases of reappropriation of folk knowledge through encounters with black culture-bearers who actively engage in the production of their own meaning.

Morrison affirms the authoritative role of African American language and culture to her literary art:

I wanted to write literature that was irrevocably, indisputably Black, not because its characters were, or because I was, but because it took as its creative task and sought as its credentials those recognized and verifiable principles of Black art.[2]

She defines "the characteristics of [Black] art forms: . . . the group nature of art, its functionality, its improvisational nature, its relationship to audience performance, the critical voice which upholds tradition and communal values and which also provides occasion for an individual to transcend and/or defy group restrictions."[3] It is into this "art" that Milkman is initiated in his quest for historical knowledge and identity, and it is only through increased facility with subversive black discourse that he gains personal power and ultimate spiritual healing.

Linda Krumholz's study, "Dead Teachers," foregrounds the functions of African American vernacular language and culture in Morrison's text, noting that Morrison invokes the practice of *signification*, to establish a discursive world-order that runs counter to the dominant white culture. "Signifyin'" in black language is simply a form of parody that undermines the original intent of words or phrases, giving rise to new meanings, which in this novel affirm the black self and enable resistance to an insidiously prescribed "inferiority":

> In *Song of Solomon*, Morrison provides . . . an African American cultural literacy composed of folk stories, . . . biblical stories, [myth], individual and collective history, and a spiritual openness and perception, all of which comprise the "subversive memory" . . . which generate a sense of agency . . . self-valuation . . . and resistance . . .[4]

For example, the myth/legend of the Flying Africans, a "canonical tale" which forms a part of the racial memory of people of African descent, is used in this novel as the *narrative* structure on which the story of Milkman Dead and his quest for wholeness turns. As a subversive *linguistic* technique, Morrison employs language which contains a riveting critique of socio-political conditions of African Americans, though laced with humor and biting satire:

> "Doctor Street" was never used in any official capacity. And since they knew that only Southside residents kept it up, they had notices posted in the stores, barbershops, and restaurants in that part of the city saying that the avenue running northerly and southerly from Shore Road fronting the lake to the junction of routes 6 and 2 leading to Pennsylvania, and also running parallel to and between Rutherford Avenue and Broadway, had always been and would always be known as Mains Avenue and not Doctor Street. It was a genuinely clarifying public notice because it gave Southside residents a way to keep their

memories alive and please the city legislators as well. They called it Not Doctor Street, and were inclined to call the charity hospital at its northern end No Mercy Hospital. (4)

At this early juncture of the novel, Morrison invokes the practice of signification, establishing a discursive universe based on "folk humor and a rebellious deployment of language," as Krumholz notes.[5] Full of parody and blasphemy, it offers an example of specifyin' in the African American vernacular. This subversive discourse marks the revisionary aspect of black male speech acts, and it is what Milkman learns to appropriate and negotiate as he engages in a search for his true history and identity. It is through increased facility with the black vernacular, its language and rituals, that he gains personal power and transformation. The subversive use of language throughout *SOS* creates and sustains the carnivalesque in the text. Through acts of naming and un-naming, characters foreground the dialogic struggle between official and unofficial histories and the spiritual vacuity of materialistic middle-class values.

The narrator, modeled on the traditional African figure of the griot (official storyteller and oral historian of the community), comments on the politics of names and naming as it has occurred in the community. He serves as both a praise singer and counselor to the reader, as well as a chorus commenting on the action. Morrison underscores the quality of black art, its functionality and improvisational nature, its performative dimension and its communal value as a way for the individual to "transcend and/or defy group restrictions."[6] "It seems to me that the best art is political," she argues, "and you ought to be able to make it unquestionably political and irrevocably beautiful at the same time."[7]

This reimmersion into the revisionary aspect of black male discourse begins for Milkman in chapter 3 in Feather's pool hall and Railroad Tommy's barbershop. The pool hall and barbershop are traditional sites of black masculine wisdom for young men growing up in the urban environments of American cities. Milkman is thirteen years old, the traditional age of initiation for men in a number of cultures. His lesson begins with Hospital Tommy's deconstruction of Milkman's and Guitar's desire for a beer with a litany of wisdom about "other stuff [they] are not going to have . . ." (59). In the barbershop the disruptive, "political voices," comical inversions, namings and un-namings become, as Mae Gwendolyn Henderson argues, "an expressive site for a dialectics/dialogics of identity . . .,"[8] in essence, the carnivalesque.

The discussion of Emmett Till's murder in the barbershop reflects, again, Bakhtin's notion of comic verbal composition, which sets up a linguistic sparring between those men who articulate the beliefs and values from both middle-class Afro-America and the mainstream media and others who counter that discourse through various forms of African American vernacular speech acts. Freddie offers a black folk perspective by suggesting that Till was detached from the collective memory of the race relative to proper protocols of engagement for black men in the American South (Till was from the North). He asks: "What'd he do it for? He knew he was in Mississippi. What he think that was? Tom Sawyer Land?"(89).

Here a clear distinction is drawn between the mythical South of white American literature and the brutal lynching-South of African American reality. "Thought he was a man, that's what," Railroad Tommy rejoins, but Freddie replies, "Well, he thought wrong . . . Ain't no black men in Bilbo country" (81). The verbal sparing continues with Walters's calm observation, "'Oh, they'll catch them' . . . 'Catch 'em? Catch 'em?' Porter was astounded. '. . . They'll catch 'em, all right, and give 'em a big party and a medal'" (82). The narrator informs the reader that "[t]he men began to trade tales of atrocities . . . A litany of personal humiliation, outrage, and anger turned sicklelike back to themselves as humor" (83). What Milkman witnesses approximates a musical composition, a finely toned and deeply textured exposé of signifyin', jonin', rappin', and woofin', all forming the linguistic patterns of urban black male discourse, a textual landscape for young black boys to learn "life rules" (83). This signifying on the younger Milkman and Guitar by the older, wiser Tommy serves as a pedagogy of black manhood, as well, "an initiation into the world of adult black [male] discourse . . ."9

Another pedagogical occasion in black male discursive fluency is presented in Milkman's brawl with Saul in Shalimar. Milkman is the northern outsider, unaware of the rules of engagement in the black community and the proper protocols for behavior among southern black men. He has entered a "completely new order of things."10 The conflict arises because of Milkman's failure to assess the implications of his presence, a middle-class black man from the North, in a small Virginia town. When he comments that there are "pretty women" (267) in Shalimar, it leads to the rhetorical game of playing-the-dozens between him and the men assembled in Solomon's store: "Milkman sensed that he'd struck a wrong note. About the women, he guessed. What kind of place was this where a man couldn't even ask for a woman?" (268).

He follows the comment about the women of Shalimar with one about needing to throw away his old car and buy a new one. The signifying turns deadly when Saul and Milkman engage in a denigrating exchange about the sexual prowess of northern black men employing the discursive forms of woofin', signifyin', and ultimately playing-the-dozens: "You mean to tell me pussy different up North?" says one man. "Naw," says a second. "Pussy the same everywhere . . ." "Maybe the pricks is different . . ." "How different?" "Wee little. That's why they pants so tight. That true?" (270) he asks Milkman, who then joins in the game of signifying aimed at the sexual denigration of the speakers. The game ends in a knife fight in which both he and Saul are wounded but in which Milkman has won a certain amount of respect from the men.

The third example occurs during the hunt in Virginia where he experiences a spiritual transformation that puts him in contact with the natural world, as opposed to the artificial, materialistic world of northern capitalism. On the wildcat hunt (276–283) Milkman is surrounded by a physical darkness to parallel the spiritual darkness in which he has lived for more than thirty years of his life. In this instance, the darkness fosters illumination and psychic clarity, as Milkman learns another phase of the discourse of intuition:

> It was all language. An extension of the click people made in their cheeks back home when they wanted a dog to follow them. No, it was not language; it was what there was before language. Before things were written down. Language in the time when men and animals did talk to one another. (281)

The hunting scene is another vehicle for Milkman's reintegration into southern black male folk vernacular and African/African American communal rites. It echoes Bakhtin's third form of carnivalesque, that of ritual spectacle. In the scene, Morrison invokes the memory of traditional hunter societies of West Africa continued in the African American southern tradition of hunting. It is a premier cultural ritual of black male initiation and bonding. Indeed, the hunt in Shalimar harkens back to the Djoliba Hunters of Mali who claim that: "les chasseurs *donso[dozo]* ont un statut à part. Leur confrérie se situe au-dessus des clivages d'ethnie, de caste, de religion. Elle est la plus vieille institution traditionnelle du Mali."[11] (The hunters/"donso" have a special status. Their brotherhood transcends ethnic, caste, or religious designations. It is the oldest traditional organization in Mali.) The *donso/dozo* are spiritually tuned to nature and can "speak" the ancient language between the land, the animals, and man. They are also traditional healers.[12]

While Milkman is not a member of the Shalimar "brotherhood" historically, he is taken on the hunt by the "initiatory priests/elders, Luther and Calvin,"[13] who invite him because of the way he handled himself with Saul in the knife fight. Morrison's griot discloses the events of the wildcat hunt and delineates the evolution and healing that Milkman undergoes as he sits under a sweet gum tree to rest from the chase (278–279). Her language is a retrieval of the structure and style of jazz music, which invokes the cultural, performative, and spiritual dimensions of the hunt. This reimmersion in the southern rural tradition of his ancestors before their migration to Michigan enables Milkman to gain an understanding of the language of nature from which the African and African American vernacular takes its base.

In this milieu the dead are omnipresent and animals, trees, spirits, and, indeed, the earth itself can enter into dialogue with man. After the hunt, Milkman resembles an African initiate of the Poro and Vodoun secret societies of West Africa. He has "enter[ed] the forest [a novice], symbolically dies through the act of circumcision [Guitar's near strangulation of him with a piece of wire] and returns to the village, having successfully completed his initiation."[14]

The hunt completes Milkman's literacy lessons; he is then prepared for an application-of-learning through an encounter with the Shalimar children and their ring game about Solomon, the Flying African. The song they sing is the same one sung at the time of his birth when the insurance man attempts to fly from the roof of Mercy Hospital. The verses of the song, which at first are perceived as "nonsense words," take on a liberatory and instructive power when Milkman begins to understand their meaning. As Dolan Hubbard suggests:

> So overwrought is he by his discovery that he becomes intoxicated not with happiness but with joy ... As he becomes more enmeshed in names and naming, Milkman undergoes ritual transformation as well. The history that Milkman discovers behind the buried names [of his ancestors] transforms his journey back into a mission fraught with [spiritual] overtones; hence his insatiable need to proclaim.[15]

We see this "transformation" when Milkman goes back to see his lover, Sweet. He sings snatches of the children's song and praises the exploits of his great grandfather in the language of the black male vernacular that he has now mastered:

> "He could fly! You hear me? My great-granddaddy could fly! Goddam!" ...
> "The son of a bitch could fly! You hear me, Sweet?"
> ... He just took off; got fed up ... My great-granddaddy could flyyyyyy and the whole damn town is named after him."   (331 and 332)

Later, as he reconstructs the subversive role of names and naming in African American communal history: "Their names. Names they got from yearnings, gestures, flaws, events, mistakes, weaknesses. Names that bore witness" (333).

Historical changes such as black migration to urban areas, assimilation into the middle class, and acculturation to Western values, have all impacted the traditional values and beliefs that provided the common stock of knowledge for captive African people in the Americas. Morrison's novel addresses these changes and their consequences. Thus, we can say that *SOS* bears witness to the power of lost and discredited traditions to heal and reconnect the psychically fragmented and spiritually detached individual to the communal whole. The African American folk tradition, Morrison suggests, is a "site of memory" with the power and mystery to inform and transform characters and the literary stage on which they act out their fictive roles.

Tar Baby

In *Rabelais and His World*, Bakhtin focuses on the monolithic worldview of the Middle Ages and the subversive acts of language and representation which parodied and ridiculed this view through the carnivalesque. In this view, the carnivalesque is a genre of parody and blasphemy that undermined official cultural authority. Like *SOS*, Toni Morrison's novel, *Tar Baby* (*TB*)[16] exemplifies Bakhtin's carnivalesque. In *TB* Morrison reappropriates the humorous African American folk fable of Br'er Rabbit and the Tar Baby to foreground the foibles and incongruities of human nature. The heteroglossic (and "glossalalic") nature of the narrative positions sentient nature, characters, and the griotic narrator in "contestatorial" dialogue with the white master narrative, represented by Valerian Street.

In opposition to Street is the trickster (Son Green), traditional figure of black humor, invoking disruptive, primal creativity and destructiveness in the neatly ordered world of the white capitalist/patriarch. Son, like the classic African trickster, is an outrageous figure of the margins yet somehow at the center of the tale. Henry Louis Gates, Jr. defines tricksters "as . . . mediators, and their mediations are tricks."[17] Yet, despite the multi-layered contentions of Morrison's text, it is this very dramatizing of oppositions that forms the principle of coherence for the disparate and contentious voices of the narrative. This contention is what represents the carnivalesque in the novel. The narrative dialogic is what enables a reenvisioning of definitions and a reshaping of them to construct a new and enlightening, but painful, reality for the characters in this fictive universe.

The story of Br'er Rabbit and the Tar Baby has a number of versions in African American folklore. In fact, the tale, like that of the Flying Africans in *SOS*, has its roots in West African lore. As in *SOS*, this very "act" of making a folktale from a marginalized discourse, the signifying and transformative device on which the novel turns, is in itself disruptive of the novelistic tradition, and thus, representative of the carnivalesque. In addition, the narrative structure replicates a jazz sequence. For as "[v]oices blend and change, then shift into viewpoints that switch and slide, then become voices again, [the reader has] to be alert at all times, the ear at the ready to pick up and put together the . . . echoes of sound and meaning that these connected voices release."[18]

Son Green, like Milkman Dead, embarks on a quest leading to his reinscription into the indigenous culture of the Africana people of the Caribbean. Set on a mythical island in the Caribbean, Isle des Chevaliers, *TB* is the only one of Morrison's novels to feature white characters in a central relationship to her black protagonist(s). On this privately owned island is a magnificent dwelling called L'Arbe de la Croix, the retirement home of Valerian Street and his wife Margaret. Now in the twilight of his life, he has gone into a type of self-imposed exile. He has also transported his faithful black retainers, Sydney and Ondine Childs. Jadine, Sydney and Ondine's niece, a successful model in Paris, has been educated at Valerian's expense and represents a peculiar kind of accomplishment for him.

Into this tranquil world comes Son Green, an interloper of the black underclass, a dreadlock-wearing, black sailor who has jumped ship and swum to Isle des Chevaliers where he hides, steals food, and watches the beautiful Jadine as she sleeps. Clearly an outsider, Son is a figure in the margins of history who, nevertheless, critiques the effects of history upon all of the characters. On the issue of the outsider, Bakhtin argues that only by being outside of a culture can one understand his own culture. This posture opens new possibilities for each culture, reveals hidden "potentials, . . . promotes renewal and enrichment"[19] and creates new potentials, new voices, that may become realizable in a future dialogic interaction. Thus "outside" groups, like African Americans, marginalized by a dominant ideology within "non-carnival" time, not only gain a voice during carnival, but also disrupt the ideology that seeks to silence them. Carnival – and its accompanying components – Bakhtin suggests, represents a theory of resistance: "Carnival is the place for working out a new mode of interrelationship between individuals.[20] The narrative structure of *TB* turns on the dialogic interaction of the marginalized and the dominant.

As in the various topoi in *SOS*, *TB*'s setting in the Caribbean is characterized by overtones of capitalist exploitation on the one hand and magic and myth on the other. While Bakhtin's theory of the carnivalesque was based on his reading of the European tradition of carnival, *TB* draws on the idea of carnival as it emerged in the Caribbean, as a manifestation of the spirit of African resistance seen in maroon communities of runaway slaves and freed Africans who revised and reformulated the European celebration brought by English, French, and other European slavers and colonists to the Islands. For Afro-Caribbean people carnival became a way to express the disruptive power of new forms to pervade and illuminate contrarieties within their society. Extended forms of carnival, like Calypso, "began in Kaiso, chanting songs sung by the Mandingo people of West Africa."[21] These songs either mocked or praised people or institutions, a performative style appropriated in kotèba theatre and the griotic traditions of West Africa.

That the reader is entering a world subject to magical transformation, located in carnival time, is evidenced by the narrative voice affirming nature's sentience with a series of Bakhtinian "comic verbal compositions": "clouds gathered together [and] stood . . . [and] looked at each other . . . as the river [scuttled] around the forest floor [and crashed] headlong into the haunches of hills . . . ill and grieving . . ." because "men had . . . folded the earth where there had been no fold and hollowed her where there had been no hollow" (7). As flowers, groves, and trees were cut down to make way for vacation homes for the wealthy, we are told that "those trees that had been spared dreamed of their comrades for years afterward [in nightmarish] mutterings" (8).

Morrison's narrator takes the reader further "into" the language of nature that Milkman begins to understand on the hunt in Shalimar. Nature is allowed the utterance that has been denied to the local West Indians who remain voiceless as they work the land and produce the sugar and chocolate used in Valerian's candy factory. Yet, among them, there is the liberating spiritual force of Vodoun, peopled by the Loa who are "fundamentally rooted in history" and who are "visible manifestations such as plants, animals . . . but chiefly ancestors."[22] Morrison invokes this alternative cosmos through the agency of speech given to the natural environment and to mythic/spiritual forces like the Swamp Women who hang upside down from the trees.

The novel's various intersecting narratives represent an example of the assault of African American vernacular language on the ideological hegemony of Euro-American capitalism and its trend of exploitation of the Caribbean landscape and indigenous peoples. Despite the imposition of a tyrannical and arbitrary order, with the development of palatial homes and manicured subdivisions, a kind of insurrection and chaos abounds in the landscape of Isle des Chevaliers. Nature has a "dialogic life" of its own. Its narrative is a prelude to the discursive tensions that will arise between the black trickster, Son Green, and the white business tycoon, Valerian Street. Morrison speaks of the narrative universe of TB as "an animated world in which trees can be outraged and hurt, and in which the presence or absence of birds is meaningful."[23] She continues with the observation: "[We] have to be very still to understand these so-called signs, in addition to which they inform [us] about [our] behavior."²⁴

Street's paradise of L'Arbe de la Croix is part of a carefully crafted community of expensive homes built by exploited local laborers; constructed above a swamp called Sein de Vieilles or witch's tit, it can be said that his world stands symbolically over the myths and metaphors of former African slaves. We are told that "[t]he world was altered" by wealthy white capitalists who "had gnawed through the daisy trees until, wild-eyed and yelling, they broke in two and hit the ground" and "[i]n the huge silence that followed their fall, orchids spiraled down to join them" (8). This language revises capitalistic discourse of "development" and "improvement" with alternative definitions of violation and destruction of the natural environment. Yet, the land recoils with the transgressive force of one hundred blind black horsemen, descendants of African captives: "They learned to ride through the rain forests avoiding all sorts of trees and things. They race each other, and for sport they sleep with the swamp women in Sein de Vieilles" (131). The comic parody of "blind horsemen" riding through forests echoes the same subversive pattern of language that we see operating in *SOS*.

Son Green's entry supposes another intrusive narrative, creating the heteroglossia of carnival. As a speaking subject, he is the black outlaw/bad nigger of Euro-American nightmare who sneaks in at night from the waters of the Euro-American unconscious self as Br'er Rabbit sneaks into the farmer's garden in the folktale. Like the trickster rabbit, Son is the manifestation of the pariah in Western culture, the terrorizing black male referred to in the novel as "swamp nigger" (85), a black beast with dreadlocks. As soon as he is discovered hiding in Margaret's bedroom after swimming ashore at Isle des Chevaliers, he is immediately cast as the undesirable transgressor intruding into the picturesque "garden" created by Valerian Street. Street and his "extended family" at L'Arbe de la Croix live in a world of illusions – Valerian Street hiding in his greenhouse in the middle of wild and contentious nature, his wife Margaret in her dreams of past glory, and Jadine, Sydney, and Ondine locked in a deracinated escape from their cultural heritage.

Son is an oppositional character to all of them. As a self-defined black male, his existence is framed by a discourse of idealized black culture. Racial and cultural difference is his signifying trait, and the narrative reinforces that difference. His entry is marked by a frightened Margaret Street who can utter only one word: "Black!" Son's social idiolect is reminiscent of the men at Hospital Tommy's barbershop and Solomon's store in Shalimar – monosyllabic and colloquial, in direct contrast to the largely stilted language of Margaret and Valerian. To Margaret, Jadine, and Ondine, Son is the perverse subhuman. In this sense, then, he typifies the trickster and the flying African of myth and folklore. Son, like Solomon, is one of Morrison's "dangerously free characters,"[25] in sharp contention with Valerian's rigid, authoritarian household:

> In those eight homeless years he had joined that great underclass of undocumented men.
> . . . They were an international legion of day laborers and musclemen, gamblers, sidewalk merchants, migrants, unlicensed crewmen on ships with volatile cargo, parttime mercenaries, fulltime gigolos, or curbside musicians. What distinguished them from others – was their refusal to equate work with life and an inability to stay anywhere for long.   (142)

The struggle between Son and middle-class Sidney Childs echoes the conflict between Pilate and Macon Dead in SOS. A "Negro" from Philadelphia, Sidney defines Son through the assimilationist discourse of his class and the language of his white employer:

> You the kind of man that does worry me. You had a job, you chucked it. You got in some trouble, you say, so you just ran off. You hide, you live in secret, underground, surface when you caught. I know you, but you don't know me. I am a Phil-a-delphia Negro mentioned in the book of the very same name. My people owned drugstores and taught school while yours were still cutting their faces open so as to be able to tell one of you from the other.   (140)

As Bakhtin's carnival opens up the world, breathes new life into it, and thrusts everything into new possibility for the future, Morrison's Son Green thrusts the Street household into a "contestatorial" dialogue with black vernacular culture and the anarchic jazz and blues rhetoric of the urban hipster. Son is a wanderer. His speeches are replete with flicks of irony and touches of humor, classic examples of the signifyin', specifyin' discursive patterns of urban black male speech found in SOS.

Morrison links the African American traditions of jazz music, black vernacular, and folklore to the cultural creations of carnival and syncretic religious forms of Africana people in the Caribbean in Son's transformation of his history into a magical jazz performance – a speech act staged for his L'Arbe de la Croix audience. We see this in his reaction to Jadine's question: "What do you want out of life?" (145). His response is replete with clipped, jazzy, disarming irony:

> "My original dime. That's all. My original dime . . . The one San Francisco gave me for cleaning a tub of sheephead . . . Nothing I ever earned since was like that dime . . . That was the best money in the world and the only real money I ever had . . . Something nice and simple and personal, you know? My original dime."   (145–146)

Bakhtin's carnivalesque spirit, which turns on reversals, leads also to a change in language. On this feature in Morrison's work, Rodrigues notes that:

The voice [Son's] is a written voice [that] hurtles along offering no explanations, dropping more bits of information that stubbornly refuse to come together and make sense . . . Here is a musical score that has to be made to spring into audial life, into sound and rhythm and beat. The inner ear listens to what one reads, and the words . . . take wing, leap into sound.[26]

When Son speaks, his words replicate the notes of jazz, "[creating] run-on sounds . . . rhyme [they] connect . . . but leave the connection a mystery . . ."[27] "My dime, girl. The dime . . . Really great . . . Nothing was ever like that sheephead dime. That original dime from Frisco" (145). This audible quality of the narrative exhibits a resistance aimed at those Euro-American definitions of success, power, and powerlessness. Son is a "participant" of Bakhtin's carnival claiming, rather than resisting, his designation as other. Thus, he challenges Jadine Childs about her education in Paris and its value to her as a black woman:

Truth is that whatever you learned in those colleges that didn't include me ain't shit . . . they tell you what was in my heart? If they didn't teach you that, they didn't teach you nothing about yourself. And you don't know anything, anything at all about your children and anything at all about your mamma and pappa. You find out about me, you educated nitwit!   (227–228)

Such a disruptive position relative to widely accepted notions of the superiority of European education transgresses boundaries of the acceptable to underscore Bakhtin's notion of new connections and new potentialities for transforming meaning through dialogic encounters. Son Green's presence/being invokes those decentralizing forces that mitigate the official order, power, and ideology of Valerian's and white America's neatly ordered ideological universe. It is a presence of mind that Milkman Dead searches for and ultimately finds at the end of his quest in SOS.

Valerian's established social order deteriorates into disorder during the Christmas dinner. Arguments and fights break out between blacks and whites, faithful servants and patronizing employers as Ondine and Margaret fight, scratching each other and pulling each other's hair. In the ensuing exchange, the narrative positions the two men at the crossroads of consciousness – domain of the god Legba/Eshu-Elegbara – where black and white men have been constructed in a contentious dialogue throughout the four-hundred-year history of slavery, colonization, and racial oppression in the Americas. At Isle des Chevaliers, this contest is represented by the myth of origins of the island of Dominique:

> Somewhere in the back of Son's mind one hundred black men on one hundred unshod horses rode blind and naked through the hills and had done so for hundreds of years. They knew the rain forest when it was a rain forest, they knew where the river began, where the roots twisted above the ground; they knew all there was to know about the island and had not even seen it. (177)

Ultimately, Son Green as trickster succeeds in outwitting his stronger more powerful foe, as the trickster often does in folktales, myths, and legends. Through his verbal facility, like that of his fabled brothers, Br'er Rabbit, the Signifying Monkey, and Anansi, the Spider, Son manipulates Valerian into a compromising position.

In a particularly insightful reading of *TB*, Terry Otten suggests that Morrison refigures the mythic "fall" from the Garden of Eden (perhaps for her the original template for the carnivalesque) as a parallel mythic structure to the African American animal fable of Br'er Rabbit and the Tar Baby. Morrison's own view is that evil, i.e., the fall, operates to redeem the "sinfully" innocent inhabitants of L'Arbe de la Croix. Thus, Son's "sin" of transgression in this reading articulates Morrison's existential theology in which "[t]hose who sin against the flawed order become agents of experience [and change, but] they also run the risk of freedom. Those who do not are doomed to moral entropy."[28]

It is Son, the transgressor, who can set free the spiritually bound Valerian. He intrudes into the false sense of security of Valerian's world and thus causes all to "fall" into enlightenment. Ironically, Valerian and Margaret wait for their son, Michael, to visit them. However, it is not the son they expect who comes, but rather the alienated black outlaw, America's own "native son" – sneaking out of the mental corridors of their self-deceit – who confronts them and forces them to face up to the beast in their own closet. This beast is the memory of Margaret's abuse of their son Michael when he was a child.

Son as a subterranean operative and transforming force is more evident through Morrison's signification on Milton's Satan as Son hides in Jadine's room, watching her sleep. In *Paradise Lost*, Satan – represented in the text as a disgruntled general rebelling against God – is seen "whispering insinuations into Eve's ear . . . Assaying by his Devilish art to reach / The Organs of her Fancy, and with them forge / Illusions as he list, Phantasms & Dreams . . ."[29] as she sleeps. Son, likewise, wants to transform Jadine and disrupt her neatly ordered existence by imposing his "insinuations" onto her psyche through spiritual intrusions into her dreams:

He could adjust his breath to hers and breathe into her open mouth his final dream of the men in magenta slacks who stood on corners under sky-blue skies and sang "If I Didn't Care" like the Ink Spots . . . but [his] animal smell got worse and her breathing was too light and shallow for his own lungs . . . the sun . . . strutted into the room like a gladiator so he barely had time to breathe into her the smell of tar and its shiny consistency before he crept away . . . hoping that . . . the animal smell would not alarm her or disturb the dream he had placed there. (102)

While Son cannot "[re]forge the organs of [Jadine's] fancy," his presence does create confusion and destabilization as her Euro-centric "hierarchical structure[s] and all the forms of terror, reverence, piety, and etiquette connected with it" are momentarily displaced.[30] Giving in to her sexual desire for him amounts to becoming like the "bitch in heat" she saw as a child – unjustly beaten for provoking the male dogs. Despite his success in seducing Jadine and confronting Valerian, however, Son does not escape the force of history. Morrison inverts the traditional ending of the tar baby tale as Son, unlike Uncle Remus's Br'er Rabbit, is unable to extricate himself from the tar baby's, i.e., Jadine's, entrapment; she is beautiful but completely assimilated and estranged from her history and culture, having, as Marie Thérèse says, "lost her true and ancient properties" (304). Thus, he remains emotionally attached to her even though she leaves him.

The blind horsemen are for Son what Solomon and other Flying Africans are for Milkman. Susan Willis points out that "The myth of blind horsemen [like other lore in Morrison's texts] has its roots in the many real Maroon societies [of the Caribbean] whose very existence depended on seclusion and invisibility. [Thus] this is the social reality for which blindness is a metaphoric reversal."[31] Gideon recounts that the horsemen had children who, as they got older, went blind too. "What they say, they saw with the eye of the mind" (152–153). Thérèse, he notes, "was one such" (152). Willis refers to this blindness in Morrison's text as a "basis for the group's cohesion" and as such it represents "an absolute alternality."[32] Blindness here is a communally shared way of being in the world; in its "alternality," it represents liberation. And because of its ideological "outsidedness," it is a trope of the carnivalesque, confronting and dismantling preconceived notions of the acceptable found in dominant discourses about normalcy and appropriate ways of being in the world.

Bakhtin points out in "Discourse in the Novel" that every apparently unified linguistic or social community is characterized by heteroglossia, whereby language becomes the space of confrontation. Such confrontation is found from the beginning to the end of this novel. Ironically, Marie Thérèse "saves"

Son by taking him to the mythic blind horsemen: "The men. The men are waiting for you . . . You can choose now. You can get free of her. They are waiting in the hills for you" (306). Afraid and temporarily "blinded" by the mist, Son moves cautiously through the brush. Then, "as the mist lifts from the trees," he runs, like the legendary rabbit, "Lickety-split. Lickety-split. Looking neither to the left nor to the right" (306). This action can be read as Son's achievement of his truest nature by becoming one, not with the storytellers, but with mythic tales themselves.

In his role as trickster, Son manages to turn the materialistic world of L'Arbe de la Croix upside down. But like the trickster, who sometimes loses in the tale, he has not gained the object of his desire, Jadine, the tar baby. The quest over, he disappears, like Milkman, into myth – into the freedom and spiritual regeneration of the symbolic briar patch of Br'er Rabbit, into the hills of the legendary African maroons of the Caribbean. Only the story-teller and the myths remain as it is ultimately they who have silenced white male authority and committed the final "comic assault" on traditionally held notions about idyllic retirement retreats in the Caribbean.

To conclude, Bakhtin's notions of the literary carnivalesque suggest that cultural processes are intimately related to social relations and that culture (specifically language) is the site of social struggle. Those in power struggle to make and control "the sign," language, and endow it with static per-manence. Those oppressed struggle for liberation through confrontational dialogue with this language. The liberatory, de-privileging power of black language and culture is a hallmark of both *Song of Solomon* and *Tar Baby*. Trudier Harris argues that Morrison "consistently succeeds in questioning our assumptions, challenging the ways in which we view characters and cultures, and reminding us of the inherent dangers in taking absolute posi-tions on anything in life."[33] In *Song of Solomon* and *Tar Baby* this challenge unfolds in Morrison's exposé on the ways in which language, conveying cul-tural forms and knowledge, can create alternatives as well as disrupt hege-monic order. Subversive language shapes the complex structure of meaning in Morrison's fiction and underscores her skill in taking the "stuff of life," the carnivalesque, and using it for the imaginative purposes of art, psychic healing, and spiritual regeneration.

NOTES

1. Toni Morrison, *Song of Solomon* (New York: Signet, 1977). All references to this novel will be cited in the text and will refer to this edition.
2. Toni Morrison, "Memory, Creation, and Writing," *Thought* 59.235 (December 1984): 389.

3. *Ibid.*
4. Linda Krumholz, "Dead Teachers: Rituals of Manhood and Rituals of Reading in *Song of Solomon,*" *Modern Fiction Studies* 39.3–4 (1993): 551.
5. *Ibid.*
6. Morrison, "Memory," p. 388.
7. Morrison, "Rootedness in the Ancestor," *Black Women Writers (1950–1980): A Critical Evaluation,* ed. Mari Evans (New York: Anchor Books, 1984), p. 345.
8. Mae Gwendolyn Henderson, "Speaking in Tongues: Dialogics and the Black Woman Writer's Literary Tradition," *Changing Our Own Words,* ed. Cheryl A. Wall (London: Routledge, 1990), p. 37.
9. Russell A. Potter, *Spectacular Vernaculars: Hip-Hop and the Politics of Postmodernism* (Albany: State University of New York Press, 1995), p. 83.
10. Mikhail M. Bakhtin, *Rabelais and His World,* trans. Helene Iswolsky (Cambridge, MA: MIT Press, 1968), p. 34.
11. "En cultivant la diversité – Afrique de l'Ouest," Association des chasseurs de Djoliba, S/C ONG Femmes et Ecologie, www.grain.org/gd/fr/case-studies/cases/wa-abstract-mali-fr.cfm. (Retrieved July 5, 2006.)
12. *Ibid.*
13. Wilfred D. Samuels and Clenora Hudson-Weems, *Toni Morrison: Twayne's United States Authors Series* (New York: Twayne, 1990), p. 66.
14. *Ibid.,* p. 67.
15. Dolan Hubbard, *The Sermon and the African American Literary Imagination* (Columbia: University of Missouri Press, 1994), p. 136.
16. Toni Morrison, *Tar Baby* (New York: Signet, 1981). All references to this novel will be cited in the text and will refer to this edition.
17. Henry Louis Gates, Jr., *The Signifying Monkey: A Theory of African American Literary Criticism* (New York: Oxford, 1988), p. 6.
18. Eusebio L. Rodrigues, "Experiencing *Jazz,*" *Toni Morrison: Critical and Theoretical Approaches,* ed. Nancy J. Peterson (Baltimore: Johns Hopkins University Press, 1997), p. 257.
19. M. M. Bakhtin, *The Dialogic Imagination,* ed. Michael Holquist, trans. Carl Emerson and Michael Holquist (Austin: University of Texas Press, 1981), p. 271.
20. *Ibid.,* p. 123.
21. Arthur Lewin, *Caribbean: West Indian African American or African?* (Milltown, NJ: Clarendon Publishing, 1979), p. 56.
22. Sämi Ludwig, "Dialogic Possession in Ishmael Reed's Mumbo Jumbo: Bakhtin, Voodoo, and the Materiality of Multicultural Discourse," *The Black Columbiad: Defining Moments in African American Literature and Culture,* ed. Werner Sollors and Maria Diedrich (Cambridge, MA: Harvard University Press, 1994), p. 328.
23. Charles Raus, "Interview with Toni Morrison," in *Conversations with Toni Morrison,* ed. Danille Taylor-Guthrie (Jackson: University Press of Mississippi, 1994), p. 100.
24. *Ibid.,* p. 100.
25. Phillip Page, *Dangerous Freedom: Fusion and Fragmentation in Toni Morrison's Novels* (Jackson: University Press of Mississippi, 1995), p. 48.
26. Rodrigues, "Experiencing *Jazz,*" pp. 245–246.

27. *Ibid.*, p. 246.
28. Terry Otten, *The Crime of Innocence in the Fiction of Toni Morrison* (Columbia: University of Missouri Press, 1989), p. 4.
29. John Milton, *Paradise Lost* (New York: Penguin, 2000), chapter 4, lines 801–809.
30. M. M. Bakhtin, *Problems of Dostoevsky's Poetics*, trans. Caryl Emerson (Minneapolis: University of Minnesota Press, 1985), pp. 122–123.
31. Susan Willis, *Specifying: Black Women Writing the American Experience* (Madison: University of Wisconsin Press, 1989), p. 103.
32. *Ibid.*
33. Trudier Harris, *Fiction and Folklore: The Novels of Toni Morrison* (Knoxville: University of Tennessee Press, 1991), p. 185.

3

CLAUDINE RAYNAUD

Beloved or the shifting shapes of memory

> I must trust my own recollections. I must also depend on the recollections of
> others. Thus memory weighs heavily in what I write.[1]

> There is a necessity for remembering the horror, but of course there's a
> necessity for remembering it in which . . . the memory is not destructive.[2]

Beloved (1987) occupies a singular place in Morrison's oeuvre. One of the
most important American novels of the post-war era, it went on to win the
Pulitzer Prize for fiction (1988) after a national controversy that mobilized
Black intellectuals and artists.[3] When first writing the book, Morrison was
obsessed with fragments of stories about two different incidents: a child-
murder by an ex-slave,[4] and the forgiveness of a young lover who helped
her murderer escape the police. Although she cannot explain the connection,
something seemed clear to her: "a woman loved something other than herself
so much. She had placed all the value of her life in something outside herself" (*CTM*, 207). The project later developed into the trilogy *Beloved*, *Jazz*
(1992), and *Paradise* (1998). The topic – remembrances of slavery around the
tragic core of infanticide – partly accounts for the novel's success. Situated
in 1873, after the abolition of the Peculiar Institution, *Beloved* deals with
the recollections – what people remember – and the memory of slavery – the
act of remembering. It probes its effects on the individual psyche of black
and white people, but also the repressed memory of slavery in the make-up
of the American nation.

What makes *Beloved* stand out is the centrality of memory in the poetics of
the text and as subject matter. As she acknowledges, Morrison set out to write
about the "interior lives" of the slaves to "fill in the blanks" that were left
out of the slave narratives when the narrators drew a veil over "proceedings
too terrible to relate" (*SM*, 193,191). "Ripping the veil" leads to exploring
the burden of grief and the possibility of mourning in a text animated by the
twin gestures of recovery (of what is lost) and of reconstruction (of the past
and of the self destroyed by violence). Memory work, like dream work, like
the work of mourning, shares the complexity of different temporal modes
together with a profound alteration of the psyche through the processing

of subconscious elements that come to consciousness. The porosity of the characters' consciousnesses, made possible by subtle transitions from one focalizer to another, the leveling out of different time frames enable the novel to mimic and reflect the process of memory: the actual act of remembering as well as the incorporation of told memories into the oral tradition.

The instability of the text can best be illustrated by a metaphor that exemplifies this process. Of the slaves who "danced the antelope" Sethe recalls: "They *shifted shapes* and *became something other*. Some unchained, demanding other whose feet knew her pulse better than she did" (31; italics mine). This transformation – taking on other shapes and consequently undergoing a profound alteration – must be taken literally. Sethe first calls the baby kicking in her womb by that name when she tells her daughter Denver the story of her birth: "When she stopped the little antelope rammed her with horns" (30). Yet, as she has never seen an antelope, she cannot know the referent for a word that harbors the secret of its original meaning. Its migratory character – in the text as metaphor and historically, as it is handed down diachronically – together with the trace that it bears of the lost reality of the native country, calls for a theoretical frame in which the origin is constantly mourned and reaffirmed. Performance (here dance) means to be transported elsewhere (Africa) in a different state (unchained, free). The metaphor of the antelope performs a healing. Whereas Sethe describes herself as beckoning death, the tenor of the metaphor is the baby's impendent birth. The text thus explores the burden of the past and, through performance and ritual, the possibility of being rid of the pain by accessing a moment before the trauma.

Reluctant to deal with the subject of "slavery" (*CTM*, 256), Morrison was kidnapped by it in the same way as the slaves were abducted from Africa. The metaphor also extends to the reader "[who] is snatched, yanked, thrown into an environment completely foreign, and [Morrison] want[s] it to be as the first stroke of the shared experience that might be possible between the reader and the novel's population. Snatched just as the slaves were from one place to another, from any place to another, without preparation and without defense."[5] Hence to read *Beloved* is to engage in a process of transformation as the reader is urged "into active participation in the non-narrative, non-literary experience of the text, which makes it difficult for [him] to confine himself to a cool and distant acceptance of the data."[6] In the same way as Sethe confronts the past by revisiting it thanks to Paul D, the reader faces the "unspeakable" and is altered in the process. The ending of the text, which explains how Beloved was forgotten, also threatens a reappearance of the ghost if the "footprints" fit (275). Revenants, by definition, can return.

Beloved is not a "realistic" novel but bears rather all the marks of post-modernism which, Morrison explains, stem from the coincidence between slavery and the modern period: "From a woman's point of view, in terms of confronting the problems of where the world is now, black women had to deal with 'post-modern' problems in the nineteenth century and earlier."[7] Even so, the trace of a story line can be recovered. The non-linear narrative follows a progression which leads from the manifestations of the ghost in the house to its first physical appearance (50), to its exchanges with the main characters (Sethe the mother, the surviving daughter Denver, and Paul D, a slave from the same plantation as Sethe) and finally to its exorcism (262). The beginnings of the three distinct chapters typed in capital letters indicate that shift: "124 was spiteful" (3)/ "loud" (169) / "quiet" (239). Yet the novel does not end with the closure of the love story between Sethe and Paul D and Sethe's anxious questioning about her own self: "Me? Me?" (273). The ending remains open, the meaning ambivalent: "It was / This is not a story to pass on" (274–275) – a sentence which is repeated three times with telling variations. The story had to be told and at the same time could not be passed on to younger generations. The rewording of this "burden" from past ("was") to present ("is") shows how the two are bound up. The change from "It" to "This" shifts the emphasis from the story retold, that of Margaret Garner, onto the novel *Beloved* that now encompasses the event, Sethe's murder of her child. The text calls attention to itself in a self-conscious self-reflexive manner. The last word "Beloved" beckons the reader back, in a circular motion, to the title, and to rereading. It is an echo of the name that Beloved wants Paul D to utter when she tempts him into making love to her: "[Y]ou have to call me my name" (117). The sounds – and the letters – recall the moment when Beloved spells her name, reminding Paul D of the illiterate (52). *Beloved* is a poetic burial stone – a *"tombeau"* for the *"Sixty Million and more"* of the epigraph, the dead of the Transatlantic Passage. The final "Beloved" is also addressed to the readers, thus brought into a communion around the grief of a mother, a family, a people, a nation.

Since its publication, and after the Nobel Prize for literature was awarded to Morrison, a plethora of critical interpretations have given the text different and increasingly intricate twists.[8] The elaboration of these readings often runs counter to the novel's purposeful strategy of textual echoes and correspondences set in never-ending motion. "The truth was simple," Sethe declares in one of the core monologues: "[She] knew that the circle she was making around the room, him, the subject, would remain one. That *she could never close in, pin it down* for anybody that had to ask" (163; italics mine). The core of the murder remains elusive because pinning down, "fixing," leads to death. Similarly, Beloved's "identity" is never "fixed" and the verb reverberates with its vernacular meanings: "Your woman she never fix up your hair?" Beloved asks Sethe (60), whereas Paul D warns Sethe that the ghost has "fixed" him (127), after he has been forced into making love to her.[9] "Identities" overlap because of the similarity and the persistence of traumas uttered in a common language: "The language of both experiences – death and the Middle Passage – is the same," Morrison affirms (CTM, 247). Indeed, the fact that rape occurs on the slave ship, during slavery, and in the aftermath of the Emancipation Proclamation is the point brought home by having one "character" (Beloved) represent these three traumatic circumstances irrespective of a realistic time frame. The repetition of the crime is a comment on historical "progress," on racism, on the travails of black womanhood, on the links between cultural experience and memory, on generational memory.

Making memory real

Both a historical novel and a ghost story, Beloved addresses and displaces historical categories, such as the period known as "Reconstruction," thus undoing official readings of the national text as it goes back, beyond slavery, to the Middle Passage, trying to redress what Morrison calls "national amnesia" (CTM, 257). Privileging "history as life lived" over "history as imagined," the novelist becomes "the truest of historians" because the novel tells of the ways in which "the master discourse" has repressed the history of the oppressed, those left voiceless by the history books and by accounts, such as slave narratives, that obeyed the fixed rules of a genre and erased the other's point of view.[10] As critics have remarked, the whole process of making history with the tools of the master (reading/writing) is reflected in the character of Schoolteacher who represents scientific racism. The white slavemaster, who divides up Sethe's animal and human characteristics, stands for the normative white male system, the creation of "knowledge" from a priori and racist hypotheses and its link to power. Schoolteacher writes books in which this knowledge becomes the "truth" that is then passed down to later generations. The nephews' milking Sethe like a cow, taking her baby's milk, is both an application of the lesson and an abrupt literalization of the fact that slaves used to nurse white children. In the same way in which Morrison uses paroxystic behavior (infanticide) – translated as excessive mother love – to probe the "horrors" of slavery, the rape of Sethe's milk is a narrativization of the historical position of slave women in a racist economy. The double transitivity of the verb "to nurse" – "the nephew, the one who had nursed her" (150) – underscores how power deprives the slaves of any agency.

Seen through slaves' eyes, official history is pushed to the margins. The Civil War, for instance, does not seem to make sense: "The War had been over four or five years then, but nobody white or black seemed to know it" (52). Slaves served in both camps and were used as manual labor by both armies (269). History is also redefined as the history of consciousness of those who took part in everyday tasks (the cobblers, the field hands, the cooks). In her numerous interviews, Morrison explains how she has used documents to ground the narrative in historical "reality." The bit, the shackles, the collar, the whip, the chain gang – all these elements derive from identifiable historical sources. Their fictionalization is an attempt to imagine the context, both material and psychological, in which these traces can be relocated. Unlike the sudden irrepressible emergence of memory, this act of creation is linked to remembering. Morrison asserts that "memory (the deliberate act of remembering) is a form of willed creation" ("MCW," 385). The bit, for instance, is worn by Paul D when Halle witnesses the rape of Sethe, a detail withheld from Sethe until Paul D owns up to it: "I had a bit in my mouth" (69). It is one of the reasons why he does not intervene. The bit is also brought into the metaphoric exploration of the "face." Sethe's mother had worn it to such an extent that she wore a permanent smile: "when she wasn't smiling, she smiled" (203). Likewise, the evocation of slave marriage – which was forbidden – yields the image of the making and the unmaking of the wedding dress as a metaphor for the resourcefulness of the slaves and self-reflexively explains the aesthetics of the novel. Sethe steals and sews different pieces of material, which she then returns to their former domestic use (pillows, a mosquito net, the netting used to strain jelly). The ritual is "stolen," like the bits of cloth, since Sethe was sewing "on the sly" (26). It did happen, although none of its traces are visible to the master. The history of slavery that Morrison chronicles is thus "real," although the master discourse could carry on without ever acknowledging it. Invisibility is borne to its conclusion at the end of the book when the text stresses how loss can only be the expression of subjectivity: "She [Beloved] cannot be lost because no one is looking for her" (274).

Morrison complicates the master–slave relationship on the plantation by portraying Garner as a benevolent slave-master who wants his slaves to be "men" (10). The inherent contradiction between his assertion and the impossibility of its accomplishment is clear in Paul D's realization that "definitions belonged to the definers" (190). Baby Suggs's freedom is bought by her son Halle, who is used as "labor" to pay for her, when she is too old for it to mean anything. Like her husband, the white mistress Lillian Garner is softhearted: she gives Sethe "earrings" for her wedding that the latter cannot wear but steals away, sewn in the seam of her dress. Her muteness and the growth on her neck at the end of her life translate the inner corruption of the system and echo Paul D's forced voicelessness through the wearing of the bit.

The unvoiced and disremembered historical–cultural memory of the Middle Passage is cultivated in *Beloved* along genealogical lines. It goes back three generations from Beloved to Sethe and to Sethe's mother, who is the link to African reality. While the "history" of the Middle Passage is handed down by Nan, Beloved as African daughter is recreated in the middle section where she is the girl-child on the slave ship. After Sethe's (200–204) and Denver's (205–209) monologues, the text graphically reproduces the gradual coming to language of the slave girl in the hull in increasingly more grammatical sentences. She moves from the timelessness of an eternal present ("All of it is now" [210]), to the loss of the mother ("she goes in the water" [212]), and to her final desire for fusion ("I am looking for the join" [213]). Concurrently, the novel self-reflexively points toward the construction of history from primary sources, such as newspapers, and effects a critique of historicism. However, Paul D refuses to look at the clipping representing Sethe since the picture cannot capture the experience: "That ain't her mouth" (154). The insistence on his non-recognition of her face implies dissociation from the murder. If we recall that Morrison went back to actual reports of Margaret Garner's story, Paul D's distance echoes her own recreation of Garner's experience: she did not want to remain "faithful" to that story, which only served as a foundation. Moved out of 124 by Beloved, Paul D eventually sleeps in the coldhouse on newspapers stored there. Newspapers are recycled as "material," they return to what they are, mere paper. Without primary material produced by slave labor, the history of the masters simply could not be, a fact Sethe stresses: "He liked the ink I made" (37).

On the individual level, the novel illustrates the contradictions inherent in remembering a traumatic experience. The characters move from a refusal to acknowledge the past to confrontation and to reconciliation with the pain made bearable through retelling. Sethe and Paul D illustrate that position. Remembering and making peace takes love. Denver is temporarily spared the trauma of the past although she will eventually have to face it, and it finally catches up with her in the shape of Beloved. The first memory of Sweet Home – "the picture of the men coming to nurse her" (6) – arises even when Sethe is not directly connected to her past by an olfactory stimulus, such as the "scent of ink": "She worked hard to remember as close to nothing as was safe. Unfortunately her brain was devious" (6). The plash of water and the sight of her shoes and stockings are enough to reactivate the past. The surge of memory cannot be blocked since it works through the unconscious. Both random and precise, its logic is not that of the rational mind or the will, but rather of the emotions. Beloved's presence initiates the same process in Paul D's mind: "She reminds [him] of something. Something, look like, [he's] supposed to remember" (234). The subject is temporarily barred access to the traumatic event and cannot willfully pass on to something else. In fact, Sethe's memory is "terrible" (6) since it brings back the beauty of the landscape along with the horror: "Boys hanging from the most beautiful sycamores in the world" (6). *Beloved* tells the troubled ambivalence of memory, its double-edgedness. Recalling the trees brings a certain aesthetic *jouissance* (shamelessness) but it also contains the horror of lynching (shamefulness) (5). As such, Sethe stands in for the writer confronted with the necessity for aesthetics and the unsayable of murder, torture, sexual atrocities.

The trope of memory is born by the character of the ghost who "embodies" memory as when Denver catches sight of the "dress" and her mother embracing: "[I]t was the tender embrace of the dress sleeve that made Denver remember the details of her birth – that and the thin, whipping snow she was standing in, like the fruit of common flowers. The dress and her mother looked like two friendly grown-up women – one (the dress) helping out the other" (29). "Beloved" in this case appears as Amy's ghost; later, she is identified as Beloved herself (119). Predictably, Denver wants to go back to the story of her birth for security: "[she] stepped into the told story" (29). Memory is kept alive by storytelling while, conversely, untold stories must be told for repressed memories to emerge. The novel also fuses the characters' memories, for instance, by juxtaposing Sethe's memory and Paul D's after they make love, shifting focalization as the characters physically "shift" and turn over. Sethe crosses and uncrosses her ankles. She remembers the first time she made love with Halle in the cornfield. Looking at Paul D's back, she recalls corn stalks breaking over Halle's back. The text moves from her consciousness to Paul D's through the mediation of Paul D's "thinking" of Halle making love to Sethe: "[N]ow Paul D couldn't remember how finally they'd cooked those ears too young to eat. What he did remember was parting the hair to get to the tip, the edge of his fingernail just under, so as not to craze a single kernel" (27). The unmediated "shift" from one focalizer to the other leads to a meshing of memories that culminates in the poetics and an erotics of corn shucking: "How loose the silk. How quick the jailed-up flavor run free" (27).

The novel also insists on memory loss, blanks, ruptures in oral transmission, oblivion, "disremembering." Baby Suggs contrasts the triviality of memory and the loss of her children as all she can remember is how the first born out of her eight children loved "the burned bottom of bread" (5). Sethe fears that, if she gets to her daughter too late, the child will have forgotten her (16). Memory, at its most profound and archaic, originates in the repetition of nursing; it founds the mother–child (here daughter) bond. Ironically, the very daughter Sethe wants to feed is the one she kills. The text plays up milk (nurture) and blood (murder), life and death – "Denver took her mother's milk right along with the blood of her sister" (152) – a repeated ambivalence: "I drank your blood / I brought your milk" (216). Yet the memory of slavery is not simply there to be recovered. It is reworked in the present, in keeping with the Freudian notion of the workings of memory. Sethe thus arrives at the conclusion that she can forget certain things now that Beloved is back (191), but she is eaten up by that past, consumed by her memory, a psychological state that translates into a refusal to let Beloved leave (272). The true work of mourning means letting go of the memory as loss, and the ghost thus illustrates Sethe's refusal of her daughter's death, a death she must acknowledge and forgive in order to move forward. The concepts of "belatedness" and retroactive logic are applicable to *Beloved* in the sense that different temporalities inhabit the same subject.[11] The present is inhabited by the past and the past can only be reoriginated as past from the vantage point of the present moment.

"Word-shapes" beyond the racial subject

Morrison deploys strategies for grounding her work in both "race-specific yet race-free prose. Prose free of racial hierarchy and triumphalism."[12] Such a double-edged and seemingly contradictory approach signifies that her narratives are embedded in African American culture and history. At the same time, she attempts to nullify "race" in the projection of a utopia where race does not matter. *Beloved* depicts the making of a black subjectivity by having the reader "identify" with the black subject through the rendering of the slave's consciousness and concurrently exposes the incidence of racism on the white psyche. Baby Suggs exclaims: "There is no bad luck in the world but whitefolks" (89). Stamp Paid's interrogation – "What *are* these people?" (180) – and his analysis of the racial subject explains the interdependence of racism and the projection of whites' own self-hatred:

> The more coloredpeople spent their strength trying to convince them how gentle they were, how clever and loving, how human, the more they used themselves up to persuade whites of something Negroes believed could not be questioned, the deeper and more entangled the jungle grew inside. But it wasn't the jungle blacks brought with them to this place from the other (livable) place. It was the jungle whitefolks planted in them. And it grew. It spread. In, through and after life, it spread, until it invaded the whites who had made it . . . Made them bloody, silly, worse than they ever wanted to be, so scared were they of the jungle they had made. The screaming baboon lived under their own white skin; the red gums were their own. (198–199)

"Black people" are an internalized projection of white people's fears. The reciprocity of the construction (the whites are what they fear) and its deadly and devastating effects are produced by the change from the literal to the metaphoric use of the word "jungle." The section that is handled from Schoolteacher's point of view presents the white psyche: the logic of animal behavior applied to the slaves has Schoolteacher scold his nephews for not having trained Sethe properly. Animal metaphors run through the text. Sethe becomes a snake in the grass when she flees, whereas Paul D envies the freedom of a rooster named Mister.

One of the threads of the novel is a reflection on the body that stems from the fact that subjectivity being denied, the black male and female body – in pain, suffering – becomes a synecdoche for the slave. *Beloved* indeed begins with the disruptive presence of a "haint": Baby Suggs's house is "haunted" by a ghost that disrupts inanimate objects. The notion of the uncanny, the familiar defamiliarized, is literalized with the presence of the ghost in 124 Bluestone Road. *Beloved* starts with a "spirit" and the letters that did not exorcize that spirit. The inscription "Beloved" – "the one word that *mattered*" (5; italics mine) – written on the gravestone is truncated. "Dearly" has been left out because Sethe, who exchanged sexual favors for the engraving, did not allow more time. The omission describes a process analogous to the text of the novel that can be seen as making up for the missing word. It does indeed explain how the child was loved, how "dear" she was to her mother. The work of "beating back the past" (73) that Sethe engages in every morning is defeated: the past comes back embodied in the young woman Sethe finds on a stump upon returning from the carnival with Paul D and Denver. Beloved is made flesh, reappears and is eventually pregnant with Paul D's child. At the same time, the novel displays the "uncapturability of the life that it mourns."[13] Moreover, by appropriating the preacher's interpellation of his congregation as the name of her dead daughter, the murderous mother takes it away as a communal address to the survivors.

In keeping with the biblical overtones of the text, the disjunction between body and flesh is the location of the trauma.[14] The body is exchanged in the economy of slavery, reduced as it is to its physical strength (labor force) and to its reproductive capacities (chattel slavery). Schoolteacher's appraisal of Sethe is clear. She is "the one he said made fine ink, damn good soup, pressed his collar the way he liked besides having at least ten breeding years left" (149). Loving one's body is what the slaves should do as Baby Suggs's sermon in the Clearing makes explicit (88), and indeed Paul D performs the gestures of love, the touching that heals Sethe. He holds her breasts (17), makes love to her, bathes her (272). For the slave body bears the traces of torture, the owner's mark: Sethe's mother has a circle and a cross branded in her flesh, and Sethe's scarred back, whipped by Schoolteacher's nephew when she was pregnant, becomes a metaphor for another kind of writing, body writing.[15] She cannot see the writing that is on her back: others read it for her. When Paul D touches it, it becomes a piece of artwork "too passionate for display" (17) while the whitegirl Amy told Sethe that she had a "chokecherry tree" growing on her back (79). The different interpretations of the scar point to the necessity of finding a metaphor for physical suffering. It is metonymic of the novel as a whole in so far as it rescues the slave body from commodification. It celebrates the beauty of these marked bodies and also constructs a history of the body as the site of historically inflicted oppression and violence. The cut throat of the little girl becomes a necklace; the collar Paul D wears turns into "neck jewelry – its three wands, like attentive baby rattlers, curving two feet into the air" (273).

To stress that the murder of the daughter is the ultimate referent of the assault inflicted on the slave body, the body is constantly on the verge of being dismembered. Physical dismemberment is the translation of the splitting up of families and of the precariousness of memory, "disremembering." Beloved pulls a tooth out of her mouth and fears disappearance: "[she] had two dreams: exploding, and being swallowed" (133). The last section at the end of the novel depicts an explosion: "In the place where long grass opens, the girl who waited to be loved and cry shame erupts into her separate parts, to make it easy for the chewing laughter to swallow her all away" (274). Baby Suggs remembers how she never saw her children who were sold off and how she learned that they were all gone or dead (139, 143–144). When she is free, she tries to find them and cannot as the leads turn out to be dead ends (147). Remembering is an act of gathering the pieces, as the body parts need to be held together, collected. When Sethe finally agrees to be bathed by Paul D, he remembers his friend Sixo's words about the woman he loved: "She is a friend of my mind. She gather me, man. The pieces I am" (272).

As object, the novel stands in direct relation to the headstone that Sethe places on the child's grave: the inscription on the title page reiterates that of the tombstone. The story told attempts to exorcise the pain just like the ghost is finally exorcised by the community of women (216). The loss of a child is insufferable. The red light into which Paul D steps at the beginning of the novel is described as "grief" (9). He is the man in whose presence women allow themselves to cry and both Sethe and Denver shed tears in his presence, relieving themselves of some of the sorrow. Paradoxically, Sethe mourns a child that she has herself put to death, but mourning shifts to the "undoing" at the core of slavery that made her do what she did. She also acts out in infanticide the ambivalence of giving birth – which is also giving death – that motherhood exemplifies. Sabotage, self-destruction is the fruit of a love that is excessive. Sethe wanted to "outhurt the hurter" (234) and

Paul D describes her love as "too thick" (164): "Unless carefree, motherlove was a killer" (132).[16]

Selfhood is impossible when one does not own oneself. The slaves are goods exchanged in an economy in which each one of them has a price. Thus the novel explores the impact of that equation on the character's consciousness: "Bit by bit, at 124 and in the Clearing . . . [Sethe] had claimed herself. Freeing yourself was one thing; claiming ownership of that freed self was another" (95). Indeed, the abolitionists wanted the real Margaret Garner tried as a murderer and not as someone who had destroyed somebody else's property. In such a context, subjectivity can only be spelt in the negative: "The sadness was at [Baby Suggs's] center, the desolated center where the self that was no self made its home" (140). The words bluntly explain the absence made of loss, the emptiness, because bondage negates all "bonds": she is nobody's wife, nobody's mother, nobody's sister. Only when she is free does she realize that her hands are hers. She laughs out loud (141) and questions in disbelief that she can be paid: "Money? Money?" (144). Ownership and possession are explored both figuratively and literally: love is possession. The three women at 124 Bluestone Road are caught up in a deadlock, as they appropriate Beloved: "She is mine," they all proclaim in turn. In the central monologue, the daughter refuses to be separated from the mother: "I saw her face coming to me and it was my face too. I wanted to join" (214). She is longing for a state of fusion with the mother that is akin to the oneness of mother and child before birth. Indeed Sethe, Denver, and Beloved are "one" when mentally uttering the words "You are mine" (216). The mother is the daughter. The live daughter is the dead daughter. The circulation of roles is made possible thanks to the fluidity of Beloved's "identity." A projection of Denver's desire to be loved as much as the dead daughter, Beloved is also the imaginary friend that she invents in order to fight back the reality of a murderous mother. At the same time, the swallowing mother is the literary version of the psychoanalytic devouring mother who does not allow separation, the all-powerful mother, the ogress. Denver as the other daughter fears that she may suffer the same fate as Beloved at the hands of Sethe. Her presence at the scene of the murder is brought home to Denver by Nelson Lord. Hence Denver leaves school and walls herself up in silence, a silence that can be seen as acting out Sethe's refusal to speak about the murder.

In the end, Beloved's voice – "I am Beloved and she is mine" – explains that possession and dispossession are the same. Sethe has lost herself in the exchange with Beloved and she indeed grows very thin while Beloved blooms. Realistic elements overlap with the fantastic since Beloved is pregnant with Paul D's baby. The ghost of Beloved has so totally overtaken Sethe that it might kill her. The resolution of that loss is a recovery of her own foundation, her own sense of self. Sethe believed that the baby "was [her] best thing" (272); Paul D insists: "You your best thing, Sethe. You are" (273). Feminist critics have been prompt to seize the text as exemplifying the ambivalence of the mother–daughter dyad. For *Beloved* is a reflection on motherhood: the love of the baby daughter that transcends reason. Morrison states that "[s]lavery represented an ideal situation to discuss the problem. That was the situation in which Black women were denied motherhood" (*CTM*, 254). The mother kills the daughter and the daughter comes back to avenge that excessive love. Vampire-like, she swallows the mother who becomes her daughter's baby. From the beginning, Sethe claims that she escaped from Sweet Home to bring milk to her baby. Nursing the daughter is forbidden under slavery where Sethe only sees her mother from afar, and mother and daughter always run the risk of being forever separated. Sethe's mother tells her that she can recognize her by the slave-owner's mark on her body, and slaps her when she naïvely demands the same mark. Denver is the daughter who was born in the middle of the river. On the border between slave and free territory, in a boat, Denver's birth is one of the stories repeated throughout the novel, as if that story of birthing could compete with the story of the child-murder. That moment on the river is a repetition of the Middle Passage with a signal difference: the whitewoman Amy helps Sethe deliver Denver. In the section on the slave ship, the mother abandons the daughter who sees her join the hill of dead people pushed into the sea by the crew members (212).

The importance given to the theme of motherhood has led critics to overlook the carefully balanced treatment of black manhood in the novel.[17] The rape of the slave woman is echoed by the sexual abuse of the black man in the hands of the overseers who force them to perform fellatio, and the passage on the slave ship also signals the death of the father: "the man on my face is dead" (210).[18] The whole question of back manhood under slavery is explored in the mention that Garner prided himself at having men and not slaves. Moreover, the sexual negation of the black man by such a system is made explicit by Paul D's remark: "[N]ow he discovers his worth, which is to say he learns his price. The dollar value of his weight, his strength, his heart, his brain, his penis and his future" (226). The ghost Beloved takes possession of Paul D and moves him out of 124 Bluestone Road because he had thrown her out in the first part of the novel. The symbolism of the tobacco tin, in which his heart is lodged and locked, serves as a counterpoint to Sethe's refusal to remember. Indeed, Sethe's sorrow is not singular but exemplary of the other sufferings that the text relates. The paroxystic quality of the murder reverberates with the conditions of slavery: Sethe's rape, her whipping at the hands of Schoolteacher's nephew, the horror of the Middle Passage, the other stories of rape (Ella's, her own mother's), domestic murder, such as Stamp Paid's murder of his wife. The abuse of Paul D, held prisoner on a chain gang and made to perform oral sex on the overseer, parallels Sethe's own rape. It constructs an obscene symmetry of sexual exploitation and humiliation, an abjection written in words that make it overlap with the nausea of the Middle Passage: "in the beginning we could vomit" (210). The men on the chain gang are held prisoners in underground boxes that turn out to be literal graves when the mud slides in and threatens to bury them. Their "bond" through the chain makes individual plight dependent on the plight of the group. The "chain" reproduces the line of Pauls on Garner's plantation and the escape attempt that links them all in a common tragic fate.

Rocking a roaming loneliness

Beloved is a both story and lullaby, threnody and soothing words. The characters are "forced to tell the story: they don't want to remember, they don't want to say it, because they are afraid of it – which is human" (*CTM*, 248). They make comments on the effects of narrative technique: "Sethe learned the profound satisfaction that Beloved got from storytelling" (58). Denver loves to hear the story of her birth from her mother because she is present in it, unlike the stories in which she is displaced by Beloved. Other stories include Sethe's escape, which she relates to Paul D, who in return recounts the horror of his own experience on the chain gang. From Sethe's own telling and retelling, her "strings" of narratives, Denver weaves the story of her birth, "a net to hold Beloved" (76). One of the other governing metaphors for storytelling is "feeding," between mother and daughter, and between daughters: "The monologue became, in fact, a duet as they lay down together, Denver nursing Beloved's interest like a lover whose pleasure was to overfeed the loved" (78). Fusing a concern for the mind (telling) and body (eating), the orality of the text is both language and instinct.

The aesthetic limits of such a work are that it should still be readable as a novel, hence the fragments of narrative. It is also a reflection on the character of storytelling, its reliance on a storyteller and an audience, on the material of experience. Fragmentation is justified through the use of different narrative viewpoints and the very character of memory. The poetics of the text are its other border. When narrative breaks into poetry in the middle sequence of the novel (210–217), it is the logical outcome of what it is trying to tell: "unspeakable thoughts, unspoken" (199). Central to the novel is thus a questioning of the capacity of language to convey the "story." "[H]ow can

I say things that are pictures," laments the voice of the slave girl on the ship (210). The novel as a whole hinges on the question of "images" that fall outside of the realm of articulated language. Images also fall outside the bounds of the singular subject's consciousness. In Sethe's account of memory, "rememory" detaches itself, stands outside the subject who bumps into it since it is a "rememory that belongs to somebody else" (36). The past does not pass on: "Places. Places are still there. If a house burns down, it's gone, but the place – the *picture* of it – stays, and not in my rememory, but out there, in the world" (36; italics mine).

As it fights effacement, writing means "complementing" (SM, 199) and enters the Derridian logic of the supplement, i.e., the undecidability created by adding something which completes the text of slavery, and which, because of the very nature of writing, further points to the precariousness of the record. The novelist's "filling in" finds resonance in the insistent thematics of censorship and silencing that crystallizes around the symbol of the bit. "The disremembered and the unaccounted for," the anonymous slaves, haunt the pages, Beloved being one of their manifestations. Stamp Paid hears the voices in 124 and cannot make out what they say. These are the voices of "the people of the broken necks, of fire-cooked blood, and black girls who had lost their ribbons" (181). The "unspeakable" and "unspoken" thoughts of the three women express the opposition between speech and the unuttered: "The section in which the women . . . close up and begin to fulfill their desires begins with each one's thoughts in her language and then moves into a kind of threnody in which they exchange thoughts like a dialogue, or a three-way conversation, but unspoken – I mean unuttered" (CTM, 249). The novelist writes thoughts that did not make it into language; she imagines the thinking subject of slavery.

If the novel is about disruption, unsettling, derangement, breaking points, it also projects the obverse of this splintering: mediating, metamorphoses, repetitions of motifs, passages, seamlessness, communing. The word "bridge" is crucial to Morrison's worldview: "The gap between Africa and Afro-America and the gap between the living and the dead and the gap between the present and the past does not exist. It's bridged for us by assuming responsibility for people no one's ever assumed responsibility for" (CTM, 247). Beloved remembers the bridge of the slave ship: "Other than that, the clearest memory she had, the one she repeated, was the bridge – standing on the bridge, looking down" (119). Ella and Stamp Paid's dialogue attempts to piece together information: "'All I ever heard her say was something about stealing her clothes and living on a bridge.' 'What kind of bridge?' 'Who you asking?' 'No bridges around here I don't know about. But don't nobody live on em, under em neither'" (235). Indeed words act as "bridges" through their recurrence in different contexts. Their connotations, their literal and poetic uses, are activated in a constellation of meanings as in Beloved's monologue: "Sethe is the face I found and lost in the water under the bridge" (214).

Ultimately, sound marks the limits of writing, the limits of articulated language: "In the beginning there was the sound" (259). When women in the Clearing find the sound that "[breaks] the back of words" (260), the metaphor of slave labor and submission is used to denounce the prescriptive, normative, tendencies of language. The poetics of the text moves beyond meaning and information, relying on what Jakobson calls the poetic function of language.[19] Figured as the song of the women in the Clearing, sound is also the African language of the mother, a lost tongue one understands but does not speak, and the voices behind the numerous songs quoted in the text. Paul D is a singing man who makes songs about Sethe (263); Amy also soothes Sethe with a lullaby (80–81), and surprisingly Beloved sings a song that Sethe had sung only to her children. The intimacy of a mother's song is a sign of recognition that links women across generations of nurturing and passing on knowledge, across race. The poetics of the blues and of the spirituals, the hybridity of the heritage from work songs to European lullabies, are thus inscribed in the fabric of the novel to remind the reader of the force of the singing voice as a tool for survival and as beauty. In this way, Morrison reworks African American folklore and history, weaving its varied threads to recreate the moving texture of memory.

NOTES

1. Toni Morrison, "The Site of Memory," *Inventing the Truth: The Art and Craft of Memoir*, ed. William Zinsser (Boston: Houghton Mifflin, 1987), pp. 191–192. Further references will be cited as "SM" within the text.

2. Danille Taylor-Guthrie, ed., *Conversations with Toni Morrison* (Jackson: University of Mississippi Press, 1994), pp. 247–248. Further references will be cited as *CTM* within the text.

3. Toni Morrison, *Beloved* (New York: Plume Fiction, 1988). Further citations will refer to this edition and be included in the text.

4. Morrison first encountered that story as a newspaper clipping which had appeared in the *American Baptist* (Feb. 12, 1856) when she edited *The Black Book* (1974).

5. Toni Morrison, "Unspeakable Things Unspoken: the Afro-American Presence in American Literature," *The Black Feminist Reader*, ed. J. James and T. Denean Sharpley-Whiting (Oxford: Blackwell, 2000), p. 54.

6. Toni Morrison, "Memory, Creation, and Writing," *Thought* 59.235 (December 1984): 387. Further references will be cited as "MCW" within the text.

7. Toni Morrison in P. Gilroy, "Living Memory: a Meeting with Toni Morrison," *Small Acts: Thoughts on the Politics of Black Cultures* (London: Serpent's Tail, 1993), p. 178.

8. Critical "readings" of the novel have become more elaborate as the tools of narratology, psychoanalysis, post-colonialism, post-modernism, Foucaultian discourse theory, Bakhtinian dialogism, Derridian de-construction, Althusserian interpellation have been used in turn in a display of critical fireworks. Two examples of psychoanalytic readings are J. FitzGerald's analysis of the mother–daughter link in view of Melanie Klein's object-relation theory: "Selfhood and Community: Psychoanalysis and Discourse," *Modern Fiction Studies* 39 (1993): 669–687; and Peter Nicholls's "The Belated Postmodern: History, Phantoms and Toni Morrison," *Psychoanalytic Criticism: A Reader*, ed. S. Vice (Oxford and Cambridge: Polity Press, 1996), pp. 50–67, which explores the concept of *Nachträglichkeit* (belatedness). Postmodernism (Baudrillard, Lyotard, Jameson, Fukuyama) is analyzed more specifically by K. Chabot David, "'Postmodern Blackness': Toni Morrison's *Beloved* and the End of History," *Twentieth Century Literature* 44 (Summer 1998): 242–260. Post-colonialism in relation to American novels is studied by M. J. Suero Elliott in "Postcolonial Experience in a Domestic Context: Commodified Subjectivity in Toni Morrison's *Beloved*," *MELUS* 25 (Autumn 2000): 181–202. A. Keizer, *Black Subjects: Identity Formation and the Contemporary Narrative of Slavery* (Ithaca and London: Cornell University Press, 2004), uses Althusser's theory of subject formation.

9. See B. Christian, "Fixing Methodologies: *Beloved*," *Cultural Critique* 24 (Spring, 1993): 5–15.

10. Toni Morrison, "Behind the Making of *The Black Book*," *Black World* (Feb. 1974): 88.

11. P. Nicholls, "The Belated Postmodern," explores how memory does not mean remembering a past event but bringing two moments, a present one and a past event, in relation, with the present moment acting as a reworking of the past event.

12. Toni Morrison, "Afterword," *The Bluest Eye* (New York: Plume, 1994), p. 211.

13. Toni Morrison, *The Nobel Lecture in Literature, 1993* (London: Chatto & Windus, 1994), p. 21.

14. H. Spillers, "Mama's Baby, Papa's Maybe: an American Grammar Book," in *The Black Feminist Reader*, ed. James and Sharpley-Whiting, pp. 57–88.

15. S. Bröck, "*Beloved*: a Trace of Body Writing," *Beloved. She is Mine. Essais sur "Beloved" de Toni Morrison*, ed. G. Fabre and C. Raynaud (Paris: Université de la Sorbonne Nouvelle, 1993), pp. 133–138.

16. See C. Raynaud, "Figures of Excess in Morrison's *Beloved*," in *Beloved, She is Mine*, ed. Fabre and Raynaud, pp. 139–150.

17. See D. Ayer Sitter, "The Making of a Man: Dialogic Meaning in *Beloved*," *African American Review* 26 (Spring 1992): 17–29.

18. See C. Raynaud, "The Poetics of Abjection in Morrison's *Beloved*," *Black Imagination and the Middle Passage*, ed. M. Diedrich, H. L. Gates, Jr., and C. Petersen (New York: Oxford University Press, 1996), pp. 70–85.

19. Some readers have seen in that moment an ode to the return to the preverbal, Kristeva's semiotic.

4

SHIRLEY ANN STAVE

Jazz and *Paradise*:
pivotal moments in black history

Jazz

Toni Morrison might be considered an "author's author" for her willingness to discuss the process through which her works develop. She shares with her readers the impetus behind each novel's origin, disclosing how the artistic mind transforms memories, folklore, and other works of literature into potent, compelling, and highly individualistic texts. As is the case with *Beloved*, which was prompted by her unearthing documentation regarding a slave woman who murdered her child to prevent it from being enslaved, both *Jazz* (1992) and *Paradise* (1998) were set into motion by similar literary finds. A photograph of a young Black girl in her coffin, taken by James Van Der Zee and reprinted in a collection of his funereal photography entitled *The Harlem Book of the Dead*, for which Morrison wrote the foreword, provided the impetus for a novel set in 1926, precisely the year in which the photograph was taken. In an interview with Gloria Naylor, Morrison explained how the girl, at a party, refused to tell anyone why she was suddenly very weak and bleeding, saying only, "I'll tell you tomorrow," thereby enabling her lover, who had shot her, to escape safely. The incident haunted Morrison because, in her words, "a woman loved something other than herself so much. She had placed all of the value of her life in something outside herself."[1] In this novel, then, Morrison again interrogates the devastation caused by love. As she wrote earlier, in *The Bluest Eye*, "Love is never any better than the lover. Wicked people love wickedly, violent people love violently, weak people love weakly, stupid people love stupidly."[2] Her major characters in *Jazz*, Joe and Violet Trace and Dorcas Manfred, are neither wicked, nor violent, nor weak, nor stupid, but they do carry the trauma of orphaned childhood made more devastating by the racial terror to which they have borne witness.

Joe and Violet, the middle-aged couple around whose lives the novel revolves, are born in the American South during the Reconstruction era, but escape via the Great Migration to Harlem during its Renaissance; neither is prepared for the return of the repressed which overwhelms them once their lives are more secure, both economically and physically. Violet, the child of a mostly absent father and a mother who commits suicide, is raised by her maternal grandmother, who fills her head with stories of Golden Gray, the beautiful mixed-race child she has helped raise, initiating the "bootblack" young girl into a pattern of insecurity and despair that haunts her even after she marries Joe and convinces him to abandon the violence-ridden, racist South. Joe is similarly orphaned, raised from birth by foster parents; however, he is led to believe he is likely the child of Wild, a feral woman who lives in a cave, and an anonymous father. Obsessed by the idea that his mother is "[t]oo brain-blasted to do what the meanest sow managed: nurse what she birthed,"[3] Joe is both desperate to be acknowledged as Wild's child even as he is mortified that others in the community identify him as her offspring. Loving and marrying Violet allows him to forego his fixation with his birth to some degree, which results in his arriving in middle age still filled with mother-longing. Joe and Violet endure the post-Reconstruction carnage as well as they can, but after they are first burned out and then driven off the land they have bought, they join the mass migration of African Americans to the North. Dorcas, Joe's teen-aged lover, has lived only a portion of Joe's years, but her youth has been equally traumatic. The child of a father who is stomped to death by a mob and a mother who is burned to death the same day during the race riots in East St. Louis in 1917, Dorcas is taken in by her aunt, who means well but who is herself too terrified of the racial situation to rear her charge with love and affection. As a result, Dorcas reaches her teen years eager to throw off the restraints her aunt muddles with morality, and acts out by taking a man twenty-some years older than her as a lover.

To argue, however, that, in treating love as the site where untamed demons from the past resurface to wreak havoc, Morrison is merely reworking early themes overlooks the historical and cultural specificity of the setting of *Jazz*. Choosing to use the Harlem Renaissance as the backdrop for the novel's diegesis, Morrison interrogates a cultural space that has heretofore been regarded as a cultural Mecca for Americans of African descent, focusing the text not on "the artistic, cultural, or political milestones that African Americans achieved in those years,"[4] but on the lives of very ordinary people who work hard at commonplace jobs to provide for themselves. As Anne-Marie Paquet-Deyris points out, "Just like the Middle Passage of slaves across the Atlantic, the City of the Harlem Renaissance in the 1920s is some sort of 'zero moment' in black history."[5] While the splendor of the city and the sophistication of the lives of many of the middle class are well known, what has remained unspoken have been the other lives, the less-than-splendid existence teeming with economic uncertainty, internal color-line issues, sexism, depression, and the violence people assumed they had left behind.

Denise Heinze discusses Morrison's acute limning of the predicament encountered by émigrés from the South: "Black people may experience a newfound sense of individuation and autonomy in the city, but they relinquish a sense of responsibility to community and the selfless love that communities require to survive."[6] The City as Morrison articulates it is bold and flamboyant, inviting and provocative, yet it resists the attempts of its residents to put down roots, to establish a secure life; in fact, it is the antithesis of security in its rashness, its daring, its invitation to walk on the wild side. Morrison's narrative states,

> everything you want is right where you are: the church, the store, the party, the women, the men, the postbox (but no high schools), the furniture store, street newspaper vendors, the bootleg houses (but no banks), the beauty parlors, the barbershops, the juke joints, the ice wagons, the rag collectors, the pool halls, the open food markets, [and] the number runner. (10)

In the plentitude of available resources, the brief parenthetical asides underline the unstable foundation on which the City is founded. The City lives in the moment, with no blueprint for the future, no contingency plan that indicates an understanding of the ongoing cycle of existence, in which people give birth, grow old, and die. Hence, it is rough terrain on which to battle those ghosts who refuse to remain buried in the past.

Each of the major characters in the novel experiences a crisis driven by horrifying memories of racially inflected trauma and maternal loss: "The unrelenting and destructive influence of racism and oppression on the black family is manifested in *Jazz* by the almost total absence of the Black family. Even Morrison's mothers, previously incomparable in their strength and endurance, succumb to the social/economic/political forces of history."[7] Violet's mother, Rose Dear, abandoned by her husband and forcibly removed from her home, commits suicide when she can no longer eke out a living for herself and her children. Violet's grandmother, True Belle, nurtures her grandchildren but fills Violet's head with stories of a much-adored, mixed-race child, thereby inculcating in her granddaughter racial self-hatred and an infatuation so severe that Golden Gray "tore up [Violet's] girlhood as surely as if [they'd] been the best of lovers" (97). Violet later recognizes that her middle-life hopelessness stems from those childhood longings. From her mother, she learned to shun motherhood so that "[w]hatever happened, no small dark foot would rest on another while a hungry mouth said, Mama?" (102). Too late, Violet's maternal desires overwhelm her, leading her to more or less kidnap an infant and, when that enterprise fails, to sleep with a doll in her arms. Perhaps even more alarming, Violet comes to realize that, from the beginning of her relationship with Joe, she wished he were Golden Gray, and understands that perhaps Joe also chose Violet in lieu of an unattainable dream, "[w]hich means from the very beginning I was a substitute and so was he" (97).

Reading Violet's comments from a Lacanian perspective, we understand that all adult love operates on the principle of substitution, that the beloved always functions as the *objet petit a*, the desire that masks the ultimate desire, the return to the body of the mother. Nevertheless, some adults do manage to achieve fulfilling, mutually sustaining love relationships, the kind of love Joe and Violet experience at the novel's end. Furthermore, reading all adult love as equally invested in recapitulating infantile abundance expunges the specificity of lived race experience. Significantly, Violet's process of healing begins when she seeks out the murdered girl's aunt, Alice, and the two women bond through their discussion of the lives of Black women, their own and others. Peterson maintains that "[t]ogether they figure out that 'sisterhoods' are necessary between black women if they are to avoid becoming wild, armed, and dangerous."[8] This insistence on women's essential connection with each other is not new to Morrison's fiction, but the extraordinary circumstances in which that bond is forged in this novel underscores the urgency the author attributes to such contact. In choosing to privilege her relationship to Joe and later to Acton rather than to Felice, Dorcas, by contrast, denies herself the strength that she requires to continue to live. Felice muses angrily on what she rightly perceives as Dorcas's betrayal of their friendship: "Her best friend, I thought, but not best enough for her to want to go to the emergency room and stay alive" (213). Furthermore, Felice recapitulates Violet's curious gesture – seeking out the aunt of the girl she mutilated – by seeking out Joe and Violet and making herself a part of their lives. That her fate will likely be far different from Dorcas's becomes evident when she relates, "My mother wants me to find some good man to marry. I want a good job first. Make my own money . . . Like Mrs. Trace" (204). Although Felice, the daughter of a woman she sees only forty-two days a year, also feels bereft of mother-love, in seeking out women as friends and role models she indicates that she already understands what she requires to survive the racist geography she must by necessity inhabit.

Joe also desires the mother, in his case presumably the feral woman known as Wild. Having been told by his foster parents that his parents "disappeared without a trace" (124), Joe, assuming he is that "trace" that was left behind, adopts the last name Trace, a fanciful gesture on Morrison's part, inviting Derridian speculation. For Derrida, the trace represents "the erasure of selfhood, of one's own presence, and is constituted by the threat or anguish of its irremediable disappearance."[9] Carolyn Jones alleges that Joe "is the fragment that he has to investigate, on which he has to base, and with which he must recreate his identity. [He] becomes the hunter, tracking himself back to his origins: his mother." When he meets Dorcas, her acne scars appear to him as "tracks that mark the way to what he has lost."[10] After Dorcas's betrayal, when Joe stalks her, tracks her as if she were an animal, he ignores the instruction given him by Hunter's Hunter during his earlier stalking of Wild: "Now, learn this: she ain't prey. You got to know the difference" (175). Jones argues that Joe is incapable of respecting difference "because his difference is not acknowledged by Wild."[11] Hence Joe regards Dorcas as an extension of his desire, the treasure he has won by his years of perseverance, and never acknowledges her autonomy, her agency.

Morrison's most stunning coup lies in her choosing to define the City in terms of jazz, which functions both as the pulse of life, the metronome determining human action, and the rhythm of the narration, which interfaces with the music in a shimmy of sound and vibration. In an interview, Morrison explained how self-consciously she modeled the novel's narrative on the performance of a piece of jazz. For this reason, she reveals the entire plot of the piece on the first page, comparing that bit of narration to the melody of the work; just as in a piece of jazz, where the melody is reworked and manipulated by the various players, so Morrison envisioned her readers "bumping up against that melody time and again, seeing it from another point of view, seeing it afresh each time, playing it back and forth."[12] At the same time, she talked about the discipline integral to a jazz performance, a reining in of excess even amid a plenitude of sound, which she modeled in her narration: "It's an exercise in restraint, a holding back – not because it's not there, or because one had exhausted it, but because of the riches, and because it can be done again."[13]

Paula Gallant Eckard goes so far as to argue that "[i]n effect, jazz is the mysterious narrator of the novel," calling attention to the "syncopated rhythms" and the "classic blues themes of love and loss"[14] evident in the work. Additionally, she points out how the narrative voice shifts registers when it narrates rural scenes; there, "the narrator's speech does not contain musical language or jazz imagery. More conventional, nonmusical forms are used."[15] More obviously, other writers have addressed the novel's narrative style in terms of improvisation, the jazz technique whereby each solo player can remake the melody to fit his/her needs, not obligated to cater to the musical score or to the initial performance of the melody. As Peterson elaborates, "jazz offers another example of a (narrative) line that resists predetermination; although a jazz composition has a set melody, the room for improvisation and the spontaneity of performance create a fluid and shifting text."[16] Improvisation becomes a way for players – and characters – to seize control of their own lives, to resist cultural determinism and thereby to disallow a racist script (or score) to play itself out. Hence, Joe and Violet's story does not end as the narrator had anticipated; they reclaim their lives and break the cycle of violence and despair that some would claim is inevitably their fate. The narrator states, "I was sure one would kill the other . . . I was so sure it would happen. That the past was an abused record with no choice but to repeat itself at the crack and no power on earth could lift the arm that held the needle . . . Busy, they were, busy being original, complicated, changeable – human, I guess you'd say while I was the predictable one" (220). This affirmation of the possibility of change, of salvation, of agency is predicated upon improvisation, upon another voice, another tune, running up against expectations in such a way as to alter the entire outcome of the composition.

Improvisation in the musical sense can also provide the key to understanding the narrator of the work. Astute readers have commented upon the complexity, as well as the outright contradictions, evident in the narrator's words; Peterson, for one, describes the narrator as possessing "the detachment and overarching knowledge typically associated with a reliable omniscient narrator, but also [with] the limited knowledge, biases, and involvement associated with an unreliable first-person narrator."[17] One might argue, then, that the omniscient voice lays down the melody, the theme, the statement that determines the novel's plot, while the unreliable voice questions that claim, replays it in a different cadence, bringing in more complicated instrumentation, until neither the original narrator nor the reader can hear the original strain apart from the mediation that rearranges and inverts it. Because the narrative voice is so stunning, both so very personal, almost as if communicating gossip to the reader, and so willing to admit oversight, many, including Peterson, argue that the narrator functions as "an individual voice, a quasi character, one who shapes the story as she tells it."[18] Peterson's "she" will not raise eyebrows or opposition from most readers; critics have generally treated the narrator as female. The novel's opening sentence, "Sth, I know that woman" (3), implies a sense of intimacy with the reader, an acquaintanceship based on many prior conversations. While perceiving the statement as communicating gossip should not immediately identify the speaker as female, readers familiar with Morrison's *Beloved* will recognize the "sth" as the sound a *woman* makes "when she misses the needle's eye."[19] The narrator begins her performance by laying out the story line of the novel. In under four pages, we learn about Joe's affair with and murder of Dorcas, Violet's despair and attempted mutilation of Dorcas's corpse, and Violet's developing friendship with Dorcas's aunt; the section ends with the narrator confidently announcing the arrival of another young girl in Joe and Violet's lives, claiming, with the assurance of foregone knowledge, "that's how that scandalizing threesome on Lenox Avenue began. What turned out different was who shot whom" (6).

However titillated the reader might be by the narrator's preliminary assertion, by the novel's end, no "scandalous threesome" is unearthed and no more murders are committed. As Peterson points out, the narrator "confesses to having serious inadequacies"[20] in her understanding of the complexities of these characters. As she begins to assess her limitations, the narrator herself appears to be yet another rural immigrant seduced by the City: "It was loving the City that distracted me and gave me ideas. Made me think I could speak its loud voice and make that sound sound human. I missed the people altogether" (220). She also indicates that she and the characters mutually constitute each other, even as they have an existence apart from her narration: "I thought I knew them and wasn't worried that they didn't really know about me. Now it's clear . . . they knew me all along . . . They knew how little I could be counted on . . . I was sure one would kill the other . . . I was so sure, and they danced and walked all over me" (220). The metaphor of the needle in the groove of a record, which is referenced repeatedly throughout the text, stands in contradiction to the concept of a jazz performance, in which the music will always vary from earlier iterations of it. The narrator's players are not obligated to repeat the score exactly as it has been written, but maintain the privilege of improvising on it.

Narration functions on yet another level within the text as well. Joe, Violet, and Felice all narrate their stories – to each other, to the metanarrator, to the reader, to themselves. Peterson claims, "Morrison's novel emphasizes the role of narration in achieving [their] bond. By talking about their individual lives and pasts, Felice, Joe, and Violet heal themselves through a collective and reciprocal effort to face, tell, and renegotiate what has happened to them."[21] Joe's beginning an affair with Dorcas sets into motion the drastic events which enable the characters to heal, but it is his sense of loss and despair that prompt his seeking out the young woman in the first place. Violet's post-mortem attack on the body of Dorcas by way of response to Joe's betrayal must be read in the context of her repeated pattern of slipping into fugue states, indicating a move toward complete psychic disintegration. Felice, though decades younger, has attempted to deal with parental rejection by playing at living dangerously and must face the reality that Dorcas's situation could conceivably have been her own. However, by novel's end, through the performance of speech, through the spaces allowed for the past to be revisited, through authentic communication with another person, all three characters are moving toward wholeness, an understanding of self, and a genuine acceptance of life. However, lest we too blithely celebrate the novel's affirmation of self and the potential of healing it tenders, Jill Matus reminds us of Dorcas's death, arguing, "Even if Dorcas does sabotage herself, the tendency to blame her for her death does not deal with the complexities of her marginalization in this narrative," adding that "Dorcas remains at the close of *Jazz* as the cost of the blues."[22]

The novel ends, however, with the narrator speaking of herself and identifying herself with the book itself. In an ironic inversion, the narrator, whom we would presume has, as a function of the author, created the characters whom she employs for her purposes in storytelling, reveals that not only have those characters eluded her completely but also that she envies them, longing for the love they are capable of experiencing, a love that is revealed through touch, through a caress. Hence, she confesses her desire to say

> *That I want you to love me back and show it to me. That I love the way you hold me, how close you let me be to you . . . But I can't say that aloud . . . If I were able I'd say it. Say make me, remake me. You are free to do it and I am free to let you because look, look. Look where your hands are. Now.*   (229)

Paradise

Morrison's next novel takes place during another significant historical period for African American people. Set primarily in Oklahoma during and immediately after the Civil Rights struggles of the 1960s, *Paradise*, as the title indicates, interrogates the concept of utopian societies, playing race and gender against each other in an exploration of the constitution of oppression. Morrison has once again discussed the impetus for the novel's conception. In this case, a tract inviting African Americans to come west to settle in all-Black communities proclaimed, "Come Prepared or Not At All," leading her to speculate on the rarely mentioned Black westward expansion that paralleled the much more well-known white migration.[23] Additionally, a story she had heard, which she later discovered was fictional, dealt with the massacre of a convent of Brazilian nuns who had begun practicing Candomblé, an Afro-Brazilian religion. The two sources, one documented and one ultimately not credible, led to the construction of the powerful novel whose opening sentence has become common knowledge: "They shoot the white girl first."[24]

In a dazzling narrative montage, Morrison chronicles the creation and development of the all-Black town of Ruby, Oklahoma, and the serendipitous assembling of a collection of lonely social misfits, all women, in a mansion seventeen miles away. The town, once a mecca of sanctuary and community, has become a festering sore, teeming with greed, rivalry, and patriarchy run rampant. By contrast, the Convent, as it is called, is initially a chaotic way-station for the forlorn and aimless women who arrive there mostly by happenstance, but who, through the guidance of Consolata, after a visitation by a spiritual presence, commence on a journey to enlightenment by way of taming the demons that terrorize them. The seventeen miles that divide the communities are frequently traversed by some residents of each community, with the Convent functioning on multiple occasions as a refuge for Ruby residents driven to distraction by the town's repressiveness. The town fathers, faced with a resentful, disobedient younger generation and intra-familial feuding, ignore their own culpability in the town's degeneration, choosing rather to scapegoat the Convent women, whom they decide to massacre. Their strategy backfires, however, when the entire town fractures as a result of their actions; to complicate matters, none of the bodies of the slain women are ever found, although all appear again to family members and on the shore of a mysterious ocean located "down here in paradise" (318).

One of the central issues engaged by the text is that of racial purity. As Missy Dehn Kubitschek asserts, the novel "confronts one of African American culture's most sacred cows, the myth of unity and perfection in black society relieved of white oppression."[25] However, for the citizens of Ruby, white skin is not the only marker of tyranny; light-skinned Blacks are equally antipathetic, a hostility stemming from the event that has frozen history for all time for these characters, an incident they refer to as the Disallowing. Confronted by the bloodlust fueled by Reconstruction, several clusters of families flee the American South for the West, intending to settle in one of the all-Black towns that invited ambitious and respectable former slaves to relocate there. However, once they arrive, they are informed that they are "too poor, too bedraggled-looking to enter, let alone reside in, the communities that were soliciting Negro homesteaders"(14). However, they comprehend that what prompts their rejection is not their poverty but their "racial purity," their 8-rock [the term used throughout the book to describe the purely black residents of Ruby] skin. Coming upon one such all-Black town, the wanderers are given food, blankets, and money, but they are permitted only one night's rest before they are forced to move on. The psychic trauma of this "Disallowing" haunts the descendants of the original pilgrims decades later. The annual Christmas pageant at the school depicts not the holy family en route to Bethlehem, but their own forebears on their journey to a new home, turned away, year after year in its reenactment, from the town they had hoped to claim as their own. Matus points out that while the narrative insists on the importance of remembering black history, it also "explores how too zealous a remembrance of the past can hold a community in its grip," and further claims that Ruby "has memorialized its history in a way that threatens its capacity to adapt and respond to the present."[26] Trapped in one moment of their collective past, the citizens of Ruby refuse to acknowledge the demands of their own children to participate in the lived experience of the community, precipitating the rebelliousness that sparks the massacre at the Convent.

Believing they are reacting against the "one drop" rule that determined Black identity in the post-Civil War South, the founding fathers of Haven, the first town founded by the original wilderness wanderers, as well as those of Ruby, impose a racial isolationist parameter on their citizens, rejecting not only whites but any Blacks whose skin color reveals mixed-race ancestry. Unaware that they are replicating the character of racist white America, "[t]hey think they have outfoxed the whiteman when in fact they imitate him" (305). Pat Best, virtually the only mixed-race citizen of Ruby, understands that her mother died because the Ruby patriarchs, harboring hostility toward "a wife of sunlight skin, a wife of racial tampering"(197), refused to find a physician to attend her during a complicated delivery. Pat's daughter, Billie Delia, is condemned in the town's eyes from the day when, as a three-year-old baby girl she pulled down her panties in the street to ride naked on a horse. Pat realizes that "had her daughter been an 8-rock, they would not have held it against her" (203). Deliberating on the town's practices, Pat comprehends the significance of gender in the overall design: "The generations had to be not only racially untampered with but free of adultery too . . . [E]verything that worries [the town fathers] must come from women" (217). While the women of Ruby were fairly easily controlled in the past, the women of the Convent merely by their presence provide an alternative paradigm of womanhood that confounds the Ruby patriarchs.

The irony of Ruby's isolationist politics lies in the novel's historical setting during the Civil Rights movement, when integration rather than further segregation was foregrounded. However, just as *Jazz* recounts the Harlem Renaissance from the perspective of those who were not artists, musicians, or writers, so this novel, as Richard L. Schur points out, "tells the story of the inner life of events that have become larger than life and have been subsumed under the names of heroes like Martin Luther King and Malcolm X."[27] Morrison does not allow us to forget that African Americans cannot be viewed monolithically or that the values of the vocal revolutionaries were not in all cases unanimously shared. Soane Morgan, confused by the gesture of some of the young, who have adopted names she considers "ugly names. Like not American. Like African," reflects, "She had the same level of interest in Africans as they had in her: none" (104). Pat Best concurs, telling the Reverend Misner, "I just don't believe some stupid devotion to a foreign country – and Africa is a foreign country . . . is a solution for these kids"

(210). And when Misner attempts to raise money for a legal defense fund for four teenage boys arrested on trumped-up charges during a Civil Rights demonstration, Steward Morgan responds, "Little illegal niggers with guns and no home training need to be in jail" (206). Hence, as Schur maintains, "The tensions in Ruby result from the changing meaning of race in the post-civil rights era," adding that for men like Steward Morgan, "undoing the racial rules of Ruby would unravel the meaning of gender and sexuality as well, turning the social order of Ruby upside down."[28] The Convent women become a menace precisely because of their project of challenging conventional meanings of gender in a way that liberates them from the patterns of abuse and self-hatred that have demonized them throughout their lives. Schur continues, "The Convent, the town's double, haunts the community precisely because the fears and psychic wounds that they [the town] brought with them get mapped onto . . . the women of the Convent."[29]

In founding Ruby, the town patriarchs envisioned a paradise free from the violence and depravity of the outside world, but also a world free of racial prejudice. However, unwittingly, the town fathers tyrannize members of their own community, treating Roger Best's wife and Menus Harper's "pretty redbone girl" (278) as pariahs. Morrison has stated that traditional ideas of paradise always portray "male enclaves, while the interloper is a woman, defenseless and threatening. When we get ourselves together and get powerful is when we are assaulted."[30] The Convent, never formally constituted as any kind of community, much less a paradise, nevertheless "[approaches] that state by offering its inhabitants what they need most."[31] However, the word "paradise" always carries with it theological overtones, and what becomes immediately evident with this novel is that, political and social agendas notwithstanding, the work is heavily inflected with religious imagery and exploration.

As many critics have pointed out, Morrison knows the Bible very well and uses it effectively for her own purposes. Here, the narratives of the Exodus from Egypt, the Ark of the Covenant, the Nativity of Jesus, among many others, are used, not merely by the novel's extradiegetic narrator, but by the residents of Haven and Ruby themselves as conceptualizations of their own lives. However, while the devotion of the original wilderness wanderers, such as the self-named Zechariah and his sons, may be unquestionable, it is equally obvious that many of the current generation of patriarchs, Steward and Deacon Morgan among them, use religion sanctimoniously to justify their intolerance and domination, even as they avoid any sense of obligation to be just or benevolent. As Anna Flood muses, they "behaved as if God were their silent business partner" (143) and they themselves, reflecting on the fervent conviction of their forebears that God provided for them, believe,

"He did, safe to say, until He stopped" (16). Not surprisingly, these men go so far as to use Christianity to rationalize their slaughter of the Convent women: "These here sluts out there by themselves never step foot in church and I bet you a dollar to a fat nickel they ain't thinking about one either. They don't need men and they don't need God" (276).

Undeniably, the Convent women have no desire for what passes for religion in Ruby. However, after an extended period of mourning the death of her beloved mother-figure, Mother Mary Magna, Consolata undergoes a spiritual epiphany heralded by an encounter with a mysterious man who appears to be her male twin, pulls herself out of the drunken oblivion to which she had given herself over, and leads the dejected women in an extended ritual that enables their spiritual regeneration. After a "last supper" during which Consolata appropriates the authority and voice of Jesus, commanding the women to "follow me" (262), she oversees the drawing of templates of the women's bodies on the floor of the basement, where the women lie to share their devastation in a manner the narrator refers to as "loud dreaming": "Half-tales and the never-dreamed escaped from their lips to soar high above guttering candles, shifting dust from crates and bottles. And it was never important to know who said the dream or whether it had meaning" (264). Whether the ritual is read in terms of a return to an African religion, to a psychological process of reclaiming the self, to a Candomblé initiation, or to a Gnostic-infused take on mainstream Christianity, the result is the same. As Soane Morgan realizes, "the Convent women were no longer haunted" (266). The narrator speaks of "the rapture of holy women dancing in hot sweet rain" (283), a baptism that occurs on the morning of the slaughter. At that point, the narrative opens itself up to more questions than answers, as after the massacre none of the bodies of the five slain women are found and even their dilapidated old car has disappeared. While the residents of Ruby attempt to resolve their own questions of where the women went (and how), readers witness the women appear to family members as, presumably, ghosts. Tally suggests that we read the specters through the concept of the revenant, the spirit, in African tradition, "of someone who has been violently killed and returns to visit the living."[32] However, she also maintains that "There is, perhaps, an alternative interpretation: that these apparitions are, in fact, the creation of longing and desire, an attempt to fill the emptiness of loss."[33]

The novel's final scene also requires the reader to accommodate the theological in certain ways. Consolata, killed by a bullet to the brain, is lying in the arms of a woman "black as firewood" who is singing a song that "evoke[s] memories neither one has ever had." They await the arrival of a ship bearing "crew and passengers, lost and saved, atremble, for they have been disconsolate for some time. Now they will rest before shouldering the endless work they were created to do down here in paradise" (318). Missy Kubitschek emphasizes Morrison's reconceptualization of the traditional idea of paradise, claiming, "Dante's paradise transcends earth, whereas Morrison's shows earth and the spiritual world as inextricably mixed." She continues that in this novel, "certain human beings may be incarnations of eternal, divine energies."[34] The stunning conclusion of the novel accentuates the recurrence of events that cannot be explained through the premises of Western culture epistemology. While several other of Morrison's novels contain sections that can be read through the generic lens of magic realism, this novel all but requires the adoption of that lens. Mysterious figures appear and disappear, a house with no electricity contains a room that glows with a white radiance, and Consolata resurrects a young man who dies in an automobile accident. Bouson quotes Morrison as saying that in her approach to religion in the novel, she juxtaposed "organized religion and unorganized magic as two systems" and he goes on to maintain, "Even though the African-American Christianity of Ruby includes glimpses of the mysterious world of dreams and portents and walking men – that is, spiritual or ancestral guides – there is an inevitable clash between Ruby's organized religion and the unorganized magic practiced by the Convent women."[35]

While the novel's exploration of Christianity in contrast to some other form of spirituality that we might choose to call magic is hard to contest, Tally speculates that another form of religion may also be significant in reading the practices of the town of Ruby and the town's hostility to the Convent. Claiming that "Morrison's uppermost concern in *Paradise* is with the production of history and the ends to which it is pressed into service," Tally suggests that Morrison may be interrogating the religious beliefs and political practices of "the small but belligerent (and vocal) Nation of Islam (NOI), reinvigorated since the late 1970's by Louis Farrakhan." Tally cites the "obsession with the purity of the race and the absolute prohibition of marrying (or fornicating) outside the icons of blackness" as well as "the strictures of a self-sufficient life shut off from the outside (white) world."[36] That the women of Ruby live lives circumscribed by male authority is immediately evident. However, while these women are often praised for their beauty and their virtue by their husbands, it is equally apparent that they are expected to adhere to standards similar to those enforced upon woman in conservative versions of Islam. We are told, "The women of Ruby did not powder their faces and they wore no harlot's perfume" (143). The men also muse that "[c]ertainly there wasn't a slack or sloven woman anywhere in town," even as they grumble when their wives begin to plant flower gardens, "[complaining] of neglect and the disappointingly small harvest of radishes, or the too short rows of collards, beets" (89). Read in these terms, the threat the Convent women pose crystallizes, since the Convent has functioned as a safety valve for Ruby women frustrated by the restraints imposed upon them in the town. Soane Morgan has for years sought out Consolata for a herbal anti-depressant necessary for the woman whose life is so narrow that she "worked thread like a prisoner: daily, methodically, for free, producing more lace than could ever be practical" (53). Sweetie Fleetwood, worn down from years of tending her four damaged children, simply walks the seventeen miles in a trance, terrified of the Convent women but nevertheless needing to escape Ruby. Billie Delia takes refuge there after a quarrel in which her mother, "the gentlest of souls, missed killing her own daughter by inches" (203). The novel's feminist insight is perhaps articulated most clearly by Billie Delia, when she reflects, at Arnette's appalling wedding to K. D., "the real battle was not about an infant life or a bride's reputation but about disobedience, which meant, of course, the stallions were fighting about who controlled the mares and their foals" (150).

While in its outright condemnation of the forces of patriarchy *Paradise* may be seen as Morrison's cultivating a new terrain, the themes of interracial tension and the exploration of an unacknowledged Black presence in American history place it solidly in a milieu familiar to readers of Morrison. Similarly, the almost agonizing desire for the mother again haunts this text, as it did *Jazz* and other earlier works. Both in Ruby and in the Convent, characters are marred by a lack of mothering. K. D., for whose mother the town was named, bore "witness to his mother's name painted on signs and written on envelopes [while she herself] was displaced by these sad markings" (17). Mavis is betrayed by her mother after seeking sanctuary from her violent husband with her. Seneca, abandoned at age five by her young, single mother in a housing project, must fend for herself for several days until severe hunger forces her to abandon hope of reunion. Divine seeks refuge from her lonely, if wealthy, life only to discover her own sweetheart has become her mother's lover. Finally, Consolata's despair over Mary Magna leaving her is so intense that she uses her magical powers, which she herself believes are unholy, to keep the older woman alive against her will. Consolation comes only at the novel's end, when Consolata lies in the arms of Piedade (whose name means "compassion" in Portuguese). In death, Consolata experiences reunion with the mother, a fullness and a completion that are total. Bouson comments, "Countering the earlier troubling representations of abandoned and traumatized, or even dead, children, *Paradise* ends with a consoling image of divine maternal love in its depiction of the Black Madonna."[37] He continues, "Even as *Paradise* focuses on the horrific consequences of racial shaming . . . , the closure also presents the healing and redemptive gesture foreshadowed in the novel's epigraph . . . taken from the Gnostic writing

'Thunder, Perfect Mind': '*And they will find me there / and they will live / and they will not die again.*'"[38]

In many ways, *Jazz* and *Paradise* are vastly different novels, particularly in terms of style and narration. As I have indicated, Morrison uses *Jazz* as a vehicle to explore a bold form of narration that attempts to replicate the musical genre for which the novel is named, whereas *Paradise* is a more conventionally modernist narrative, with each of the nine sections of the novel named for one of the female characters in the work. In many instances, that character becomes the focalizer for significant parts of the chapter, although Morrison retains the use of an extra-diegetic, non-intrusive narrative voice throughout the work. Even so, the novels share themes that identify the works as part of Morrison's oeuvre. In each, the complexities and dangers of human love are explored unsentimentally with an acute awareness of the devastation and violence that often accompany the awe and reverence that love can inspire. Each text also falls in line with Morrison's agenda of writing African Americans into American history, hence her focus on less clichéd, more inclusive versions of the Harlem Renaissance, the Westward Expansion, and the Civil Rights movement. Finally, both novels reveal a pattern of growing sympathy for women's situatedness in patriarchal society, along with a growing willingness to critique men for their sense of entitlement and their use of violence as a mechanism of maintaining control. However, as always in Morrison's texts, in these works we are not confronted with heroes and villains, but with humans, all too flawed, yet resilient and capable of achieving self-knowledge and ultimately, in one sense or another, salvation.

NOTES

1. Gloria Naylor, "A Conversation: Gloria Naylor and Toni Morrison," *Conversations with Toni Morrison*, ed. Danille Taylor-Guthrie (Jackson: University Press of Mississippi, 1994), p. 207.
2. Toni Morrison, *The Bluest Eye* (New York: Washington Square Press, 1970), p. 159.
3. Toni Morrison, *Jazz* (New York: Plume, 1993), p. 179. All subsequent references will be documented internally.
4. Nancy J. Peterson, "'Say Make Me, Remake Me': Toni Morrison and the Reconstruction of African American History," *Toni Morrison: Critical and Theoretical Approaches*, ed. Nancy J. Peterson (Baltimore: Johns Hopkins University Press, 1997), p. 201.
5. Anne-Marie Paquet-Deyris, "Toni Morrison's *Jazz* and the City," *African American Review* 35 (Summer, 2001): 219.
6. Denise Heinze, *The Dilemma of "Double Consciousness": Toni Morrison's Novels* (Athens: University of Georgia Press, 1993), p. 117.

7. *Ibid.*, p. 97.
8. Peterson, "'Say Make Me,'" p. 208.
9. Jeremy Hawthorn, *A Glossary of Contemporary Literary Theory* (New York: Oxford University Press, 2000), p. 20.
10. Carolyn M. Jones, "Traces and Cracks: Identity and Narrative in Toni Morrison's *Jazz*," *African American Review* 31 (Fall, 1997): 483.
11. *Ibid.*, p. 484.
12. J. Brooks Bouson, *Quiet as It's Kept: Shame, Trauma, and Race in the Novels of Toni Morrison* (Albany: State University of New York Press, 2000), pp. 164–165.
13. *Ibid.*
14. Paula Gallant Eckard, "The Interplay of Music, Language, and Narrative in Toni Morrison's *Jazz*," *CLA Journal* 28 (September, 1994): 11.
15. *Ibid.*, p. 14.
16. Peterson, "'Say Make Me,'" p. 210.
17. *Ibid.*
18. *Ibid.*, p. 211.
19. Toni Morrison, *Beloved* (New York: Alfred A. Knopf, 1987), p. 172.
20. Peterson, "'Say Make Me,'" p. 211.
21. *Ibid.*, p. 215.
22. Jill Matus, *Toni Morrison* (Manchester University Press, 1998), p. 143.
23. Justine Tally, *Paradise Reconsidered: Toni Morrison's (Hi)stories and Truths* (Hamburg: Lit, 1999), p. 15.
24. Toni Morrison, *Paradise* (New York: Plume, 1999), p. 3. All subsequent references to this text will be documented internally.
25. Missy Dehn Kubitschek, *Toni Morrison: A Critical Companion* (Westport, CT: Greenwood Press, 1995), p. 179.
26. Matus, *Toni Morrison*, p. 154.
27. Richard L. Schur, "Locating *Paradise* in the Post-Civil Rights Era: Toni Morrison and Critical Race Theory," *Contemporary Literature* 45 (Summer, 2004): 285.
28. *Ibid.*, p. 289.
29. *Ibid.*, p. 290.
30. Quoted in Matus, *Toni Morrison* p. 157.
31. *Ibid.*
32. Tally, *Paradise Reconsidered*, p. 46.
33. *Ibid.*, p. 47.
34. Kubitschek, *Critical Companion*, p. 163.
35. Bouson, *Quiet as It's Kept*, p. 209.
36. Tally, *Paradise Reconsidered*, p. 71.
37. Bouson, *Quiet as It's Kept*, p. 213.
38. *Ibid.*, 215.

5

JUSTINE TALLY

The Morrison trilogy

Though critical evaluation of Morrison's novels *Beloved* (1987), *Jazz* (1992), and *Paradise* (1998)[1] has been copious (in descending order, respectively), there has been a curious critical silence concerning what the author herself has described as a trilogy. In spite of the author's indication that her editors imposed the break-up of her original project for *Beloved*, insisting that it was too long, certain critics have argued that the relationship among the resulting works is tenuous and that most readers are interested only in each individual novel – again in descending order.[2] This fact notwithstanding, there are many valid reasons for considering these three novels as a whole artistic endeavor. This essay intends to invigorate the discussion and point to ways in which critical inquiry might be expanded.

The most obvious and superficial links among the three novels concern the relationship between the temporal and spatial locus of each, what Mikhail Bakhtin would call the *chronotope*. *Beloved* is set during the 1870s in the rural area outside of Cincinnati, Ohio, with flashbacks to plantations in Kentucky and (probably) Carolina, and a chain gang in Alfred, Georgia, during slavery. The emphasis on the rural is exchanged for the urban beat of "the City" in the 1920s in *Jazz*, while the flashbacks are centered on the Reconstruction Era of the 1870s. *Paradise* moves the locus forward to the 1970s to a small-town setting in Ruby, but the memories that constantly surface concern the "Founding Fathers" of Haven in the 1870s after the political failure of Reconstruction, and the second migration during the 1920s to the "perfect" all-black town of Ruby in Oklahoma. The time frame thus set out spans one hundred years of black life in the United States, and the interrelated settings encompass black experience in the rural South, the urban North and the small-town (southern) Mid-West. Moreover, the immediate back-drop to each of these narratives is a major war, whose import mightily affected African Americans: the Civil War, with its short-lived promise of freedom and citizenship for the enslaved Africans; World War I, in which black soldiers had "proved" with their valor their right to full citizenship and had returned with the hope of acceptance, only to have their hopes and expectations dashed with intensified racism; and the Vietnam War, on whose memorial in Washington, DC, fully 60 percent of the names are African American, and whose legacy of lies and deception physically and psychologically takes its toll on the families of Ruby.

Thematically it is also viable to establish intimate links among these three quite different novels. John N. Duvall proposes that in the trilogy Morrison writes as a postmodern, understanding the term in Linda Hutcheon's definition as "historiographic metafiction," blending the reflexivity of metafiction with the post-structuralist recognition that "all attempts to construe the past are interpretive."[3] Beyond this question, however, lies a common thematic foundation to these narratives precisely arising from the concern with historiographic metafiction; that is, the underlying question of the relationship of history, memory, and story, both with each other and with their role in the survival of African Americans in the United States. Yet with each novel the focus changes to a different component of this tightly drawn triangle. No one reasonably doubts the crucial role of memory in *Beloved*, nor the emphasis on storytelling in *Jazz*, or even the challenges of establishing "true" history in *Paradise*; but memory and story become mutually dependent, and history must be nurtured in both.

In fact, each of these novels is built around an enigma that is never solved: Who is Beloved? Who is the narrator? And who is "the white girl"? And each of these enigmas foregrounds a different problematic of central concern to the postmoderns in the latter part of the twentieth century: in *Beloved*, the question of ontology – what is real? and, how do we know it is real?; in *Jazz*, the "linguistic turn" and the crucial role of language in any construction of "reality," historical or otherwise; in *Paradise*, the meanings of race and gender in the face of overt challenges to essentialism, and indeed the social construction of their value, beyond simple description, in any kind of personal understanding and interaction.

Moreover, both the structure and technique of each novel reinforce these themes. Each text is constructed over the "ghost text" of a popular fictional form, whose conventions Morrison uses initially, only to subvert the reader's expectations. *Beloved* obviously plays with the traditional ghost story, but this "ghost" has an independent history and enjoys its own internal monologues in the text. For a book largely concerned with ontology, what better choice? *Jazz*, on the other hand, is written like a hard-boiled detective novel (à la Raymond Chandler), yet both the crime and its resolution are set out on the first two pages; the mystery to resolve becomes not "who" and "how," but "why," or in Morrison's terms, not "what took place" but "what happened?" Its emphasis on stories, narrators (reliable or not), versions, and multiple interpretations, as well as its reliance on the past (in this case in the South) in order to make sense of the present, make the detective format novel an excellent vehicle for a novel concerned with language, storytelling and the search for meaning. The violent act which opens *Paradise* and the ensuing massacre call clearly to the genre of the western, while certain scenes echo the macho "home-on-the-range" style (see, for example, pages 12 and 13 which describe a scene right out of a "spaghetti western") and a "meanwhile-back-at-the-ranch" technique (particularly the scenes which alternate between the massacre at the Convent and the organization of the "posse" with which Lone tries to prevent it). Yet as exciting as is the women's resistance in the face of a preemptive attack (the men appropriately fortified with red meat), their murder dashes any expectations of the happy ending stipulated by the conventions of the *genre*, itself deeply associated and grounded in the mythical history of the American West.

From a formal point of view, the choices made emphasize the creativity and the discernible authorial intent underlying the writing. First, it is interesting to compare the author's selection of epigraphs. All three texts are "religious" in nature – the first taken from the Bible, and the second and the third from the allegedly Gnostic texts of *The Nag Hammadi*.[4] Yet the interpretation of each of these verses is far from stable. In *Beloved*, "I will call them my people, which were not my people, and her beloved which was not beloved" (Romans 9:25), understanding will turn on various readings: Is "beloved" here used as a noun, meaning we have a case of mistaken identity? Or is it rather intended as an adjective, meaning that rather than a beloved guest, the nature of the young woman is decidedly evil? Or both? Likewise the verses from "Thunder, Perfect Mind" (*Jazz*) read as a riddle –

> I am the name of the sound
> And the sound of the name
> I am the sign of the text
> And the designation of the division

– which can be credibly answered with "language,"[5] constituent *sine qua non* of storytelling. The epigraph from *Paradise* cites the final verses from "Thunder, Perfect Mind" –

> For many are the pleasant forms which exist in
>   numerous sins,
>   and incontinencies,
>   and disgraceful passions
>   and fleeting pleasures,
>   which (men) embrace until they become
>   sober
>   and go up to their resting place.

> And they will find me there,
> and they will live,
> and they will not die again.

– in which, and in light of the development of the novel, the "numerous sins," "incontinencies," and "disgraceful passions" come to signify not the "witches' coven" of the Convent, the feminist wilds on the outskirts of Ruby beyond the rule of the patriarchy, but the fathers of Ruby itself, hideously blown up with their own arrogance and self-aggrandizement. So concerned are they with the preservation of "their" idyllic (Our) Town of 8-rock citizens, that they violate their own founding codes by literally blowing up the women whom they perceive as a threat to their own position. Ironically, within the text, those who "will live" and "will not die again" turn out to be the murdered women – perhaps.

Secondly, the openings of all three novels are strikingly different from more "conventional" texts, yet all are strategically employed to reinforce the meaning(s) of the work. "124 was spiteful" in *Beloved* not only signals the supernatural quality of the text, but also has as its first "word" a number, whose symbolic import takes on more and more significance with each reading. *Jazz*, concerned as it is with language, opens with a sound, "Sth," also plying multiple interpretations, as it constitutes the consonants of both "Sethe" and "South." Moreover, its affirmation, "I know that woman," not only indicates the gossipy nature of the narrator, but also sets out its concern with *gnosis* (i.e., knowledge) as opposed to ontology, later qualified with the narrator's own admission of fallibility, which then entirely qualifies what can, in fact, be *known*, as opposed to *constructed* via storytelling. *Paradise*, however, opens with an action – riveting to be sure – but curiously employs a statement that starts with a personal pronoun, "They," the lack of any antecedent foregrounding precisely the *impersonal* nature of any categorization by race and gender.

While *Paradise* is divided into nine chapters enunciated with the names of different female characters (though not all are major protagonists, all contribute in very basic ways to the meaning of the text), both *Beloved* and *Jazz* are structured differently. In the former, the three major sections (all beginning with the number 124) are divided into smaller ones indicated not by name or number, but only by a break in the text. The fascinating numbers game is reinforced when the reader realizes that the first section – "124 was spiteful" – is comprised of eighteen subsections, feasibly corresponding to the eighteen years that have elapsed between the murder of Beloved and the temporal locus of the text, as they are filled with flashbacks and memories of times of slavery, escape, recapture, and the long (physical and psychological) road to freedom of the various characters. The second section – "124 was loud" – is divided into seven subsections, and given the magical properties of this number, the mathematical equation $1 + 2 + 4 = 7$, and this number's association with Beloved (the name itself has seven letters, as does, in fact, "slavery"), is appropriately given over to the increasing dominance of the eponymous character herself and the increase in "supernatural" phenomena, not to mention Beloved's own "rememory" of the Middle Passage. The third section has only three subsections, reinforcing the trinity (a traditionally holy number in both African and Western religions) of characters (either Sethe-Denver-Beloved, or Sethe-Denver-Paul D) and the "religious" incantations of the text: the final coda thrice repeats, "This is not a story to pass on" (or a variation). Moreover, as Wen-ching Ho has pointed out, the composition of that structure gives $18 + 7 + 3 = 1873$, the "present" of the story.[6]

Both the epigraph and the opening of *Jazz* signal the centrality of language, its multiplicity and multivocality, and the constitution of stories. Here again the chapters are not numbered nor titled, but just as in Chandler's novels, the sections flow into one another, the first line of the subsequent section picking up on the last line(s) of the former. In Morrison's work, however, the meaning of the words morphs to reflect a change in the narrative, often temporal, such that the relationship of the two is as often grounded in an association of ideas suggested by the *sound* of the word as it is its variation in semantics, i.e., the association of ideas through phonetic similarity. It is precisely the sound of the language in this text that reinforces the move from the rural South to the urban North, specifically "the City," as the lyrical cadence of nostalgia is replaced with the faster pace and heavier beat of the jazz age in Harlem. The sounds of the words, the quick pace of the syntax, and the punning and wordplay graphically enact the violent change in the lives of African Americans as they migrated north in search of better lives, carrying with them the "blackness" of their speech and stories and the music of their experience.

Dealing as it does with allusions to the afterlife and serious concern with the oral and the literary, the text of *Paradise* relies on stories told and retold, often in a biblical cadence, to constitute history, the master narrative in service of the masters. The most obvious example is the section given over to Pat Best's voice, specifically in her attempts to disentangle the kinships and blood ties of the families of Ruby. Heavily indebted to the style of the "Begats" from Genesis, the text elucidates the impossibility of certifying the supposed "purity" of blood lines together with hopelessly entangled familial relationships and foregrounds the ludicrousness (both in its sense of "playful" *and* "ridiculous") of establishing hierarchical power based on *any* family trees. The whole endeavor becomes a parody of itself. The clash between the oral and the literary for the construction of the "historical" is also on view here: Pat Best constructs her history of the families of Ruby partially through examining the family Bibles, but principally through the texts that she has her students write about their family history. The irony is, of course, that these written texts are based on the oral stories that the children hear from their parents and grandparents. Even in the case of the family Bibles, the blotting out of Coffee's brother's name, Tea, speaks to the intervention of (family) politics in (family) history. Moreover, the fight over the inscription of the oven ("Beware [or] Be the furrow of his brow") reinforces the malleability of language as a source of historical record: Arnold Fleetwood's aging mother-in-law, Miss Esther, who had traced the original words with her fingers when she was only five years old at the time of the writing of this "text," is called on by the elders of the community to verify the words inscribed there as "proof" of the intentions of the Founding Fathers, producing only derision among the young dissenters. For these would-be activists using the pre-literate oral to confirm the literate historical is laughable.

The use of the number nine as a structuring device in *Paradise* has many different manifestations: there are nine Founding Families (the Old Fathers), nine sections of the book, and nine gunmen who stalk the women at the Convent. First, the coupling of this number with female names in the chapter headings not only emphasizes the less privileged term of the male–female binary, but also calls to the religious use of numerology by the Nation of Islam (whose dogma is seriously critiqued in the novel) in which the number 19 is considered sacred, "one" being the sign for the masculine, and "nine" for the feminine. Historically (and ironically) speaking, there were "Nine Worthies of the World" as found in Medieval Literature,[7] all great warriors whose counterparts in the nine gunmen leave much to be desired. And then there is the obvious questioning of Dante's vision of the Christian afterlife: nine are not only the spheres of Paradise,[8] but also the circles of Hell. Yet the visitations of the revenants at the end of the novel and the final lyrically written "coda" make it clear that this vision of "paradise" is an earthly venture, one that endows the initial "supernatural" aspects set out in *Beloved* with the same viability and credibility as the "standard" religious dogma of the organized church. The reading of the trilogy as a whole piece at once provides a legitimization of Morrison's revisionist metahistorical project and, at the same time, makes the relationship among its thematic components absolutely clear: Memory is fickle, story is unreliable, and history is subject to manipulation.

What is repeatedly manifest in any analysis of the trilogy, however, is Morrison's concern with language, so clearly the center of her fascination as a writer and speaker, and exemplified in her acceptance address for the Nobel Prize for Literature. Be it biblical, dialogic, or semiotic, the Word takes center stage in all three of these novels, most particularly as it concerns power, performance, and patriarchy, the construction of narrative and the shaping of identity. And it is even more striking to discover that each of these three texts is an attempt to examine three different theories of discourse that came to the fore during the later decades of the twentieth century: Michel Foucault, Mikhail Bakhtin, and the "French Feminists." Indeed, what we find in these intricate stories is not only experimentation with historical metafiction, but, more profoundly, an *enactment* of literary theory. In effect, Morrison uses her literature to examine these theories: what exactly does a theory of discourse look like in narrative form?

Morrison has often mentioned that as an author she is constantly searching for "truth," and that she is not so much interested in the difference between fact and fiction, as between fact and truth.[9] For this author there is often more truth in fiction than in fact. Facts, according to Morrison, stand alone and independent, but truth must always be interpreted by human beings. It is hardly surprising, then, that she would be attracted to the theories of Michel Foucault, who asserted that "what was called truth was a combination of two practices, a discursive one called theory or philosophical speech or specialized knowledge or science, and a non-discursive one called power."[10] In his works entitled *The Order of Things* and *The Archaeology of Knowledge*, Foucault alleges that, "Every society has its regime of truth, its general politics of truth, that serves to regulate the production, distribution, functioning and circulation of some discourses and not of others."[11]

Foucault's particular point is the isolation and categorization of madness during the Enlightenment and the silencing of the voices of people who were not deemed "rational." It is crucial to remember, however, that fully 87 percent of all slaves brought to British North America arrived between 1701 and 1810,[12] and even "enlightened" philosophers such as "David Hume, Immanuel Kant and Thomas Jefferson . . . had documented their conclusions that blacks were incapable of intelligence."[13] African immigrants were therefore silenced as well as enslaved, and it is easy to see how Morrison appropriates Foucault's thesis, even to the point of adopting his working strategy of what he calls "archeology" in describing her own work on the recovery of memory for writing *Beloved* as "literary archeology . . . journey[ing] to a site to see what remains were left and to reconstruct the world that these remains imply."[14]

One of Foucault's key examples when substantiating his thesis in *Madness and Civilization*[15] is the case of Pierre Rivière, who murdered his mother, sister, and brother in the nineteenth century. Foucault related the notorious court case as a struggle between the discourses of the lawyers, who argued that Rivière was sane and therefore should be put to death for murder, and the psychiatrists, who argued that he was mad and therefore not responsible for his actions. But Pierre Rivière had written his *own* account of the murder[16] while he awaited trial, in which he explained that he wished to free his father from "the tyranny of a domineering wife; his siblings took their mother's side, so they had to be killed too." In fact, he writes of various plans of action to accomplish his objective. His final plan was to kill, give himself up, write about it, and die, fully understanding that by killing his mother, he was sacrificing himself for the sake of his father. Except for the twenty-nine days of flight, his plan transpired accordingly, but his testimony was suppressed, as only the "experts" could interpret the actions of peasants.

Although Morrison has repeatedly commented that the germ of *Beloved* comes from the true story of Margaret Garner, it is interesting to note just how closely Sethe's story follows Rivière's. After *twenty-eight* days of rest, community and peace, reunited with her children and with her mother-in-law, Baby Suggs, the posse comes looking for Sethe and her children to take them back to Sweet Home in Kentucky. In a passionate refusal to allow her children to be enslaved once more, Sethe tries to kill them, only succeeding with her crawling-already? baby, who will only be remembered as "Beloved." Sethe, still nursing Denver, is taken to jail. In the actual tragedy of Margaret Garner, abolitionists made much of the fact that this is what slavery did to people, caused them to commit "unnatural acts," appropriating her case for their own ends. The prosecutors, on the other hand, wanted to hang her, not for murder, but for the destruction of private property. These discourses effectively silenced the accused. Through Sethe, Morrison gives a voice and a story to the silenced "other." Later when Stamp Paid tries to show Paul D the newspaper story about the murder of the child, Paul D refuses to believe that the picture drawn there is of Sethe. "That ain't her mouth," he replies, mentioning her mouth in some form at least twelve times over five pages (154–158), i.e., this isn't her story. This is also the imposition of a discourse which has decided on the "truth" and meaning of the case without consulting the defendant. This silencing of the powerless pervades the novel: Mrs. Garner's inability to speak, the bit Paul D is forced to wear, and Halle's inarticulate madness, a consequence of his being unable to protect Sethe from abuse. Sethe's whipping for daring to speak results in her biting off the tip of her tongue, a graphic sign of the imposition of silence. And when she is later taken to jail by the white sheriff, the silence is total: "No words at all" (152).

Sethe's "truth" is inscribed by the discourse of the dominant not only in the newspaper and in the listing of her "human" and "animal characteristics" as instructed by Schoolteacher (and it is relevant to note that this character has no name other than that which denotes a "mastery" and "control of knowledge"), but also on her back. The punishment Sethe receives for daring to tell her own story is her "tree," inscribed by the whip. John Irwin reminds us that "perhaps because runes were first carved on trees or because writing was done on beech bark," the origin of our modern day *book* comes from *bec*, the Old English word for "beech tree."[17] This literal, visual inscription of the Word, powerfully used to classify human beings within the dominant ideology, will mark Sethe until the end of her days. Paul D is horrified that they whipped Sethe while she was pregnant; Sethe herself only insists on the fact that "they took my milk" (17).

Control of the Word, however, is contested by Baby Suggs's eloquent preaching in the Clearing, a triumph of orality in the reclamation of a body too long inscribed by the white patriarchy. Repeatedly identified with her "great heart," Baby appropriately culminates her reappropriation of individual body parts precisely with this organ: "More than lungs that have yet to draw free air. More than your life-holding womb and your life-giving private parts, hear me now, love your heart. For this is the prize" (89). Often interpreted as representing a love of community and of the self, the resonance of this metaphor is greatly magnified if read in the context of African cosmology. The knowledge of the great Thoth, scribe of the Egyptian gods and inventor of language, was thought to reside precisely in his heart. Baby Suggs's "prize," then, becomes intimately associated with the language that conceptualizes knowledge. Moreover, Thoth's "familiar" in Egyptian myth was the cock, a fact that casts a certain light on Paul D's confusion when he is being sold away from Sweet Home: "Then he saw Halle, then the rooster, smiling as if to say, You ain't seen nothing yet. How could a rooster *know* about Alfred, Georgia?" (229, emphasis added).

Alas, this battle for control of the discourse seems hopeless. Sixo makes a valiant attempt to modify the terms of his oppression in his famous argument with Schoolteacher over the meaning of his eating the shoat, an argument foreclosed by the latter's imposition of the whip to show that "definitions belong to the definers – not the defined" (190). After the child is murdered, Baby Suggs refuses to return to the Clearing, in spite of Stamp Paid's begging her to use her special gift, all to no avail:

"Say the Word!" . . . Bending low he whispered into her ear, "The Word. The Word."

"That's one other thing took away from me," she said . . .   (178)

In Morrison's enactment of Foucault's theory, domination through control of the Word is literally inscribed on Sethe's back; she must even proffer the use of her body in order to secure the only inscription she will ever have written on her murdered daughter's tombstone. The heavy weight of the discourse of an era seems to annul any agency on the part of the individual, any form of contesting the power from within the system, but in later developments Foucault incorporates the importance of human agency. If it is true that power relations are enacted on Sethe's body, it is equally true that Denver is granted the agency of a subject, and that the community of women will form a metaphorical "body" to oust Beloved.[18] Sethe herself claims agency to attack Bodwin, "mistaking" (?) him for Schoolteacher, but in effect lashing out at the entire elite white power system. Disconsolate over "losing" Beloved once again, she whimpers that Beloved was "her own best thing." But Paul D returns her subjectivity: "You your best thing, Sethe." "Me?" she replies. "Me?" (273).

Foucault's theory of discourse makes it more difficult to contest power from within the episteme, a crucial limitation if "others" are to challenge the existing power structures. For a theory of discourse that will constitute the subject as and through the other, Morrison turns in *Jazz* to Mikhail Bakhtin. While Foucault posits a theory of discourse that tries to suppress alternative voices, inscribe the will of power on the body, and negate the subject, Bakhtin situates alterity at the very crux of discourse and argues that the construction of the subject is found precisely in dialogue with the "not-me." He uses the concept of "carnival laughter" to explain that the monologic discourse of authority is constantly parodied and called into question by the popular voices of the marketplace. For Bakhtin, the carnivalesque (or "laughter") had three important characteristics: first, its "universalism," in that all were considered equal during Carnival; second, its "freedom," in that authority could be questioned and parodied; and third, "its relation to the people's unofficial truth."[19] The monologic discourse of Foucault's epistemes are rendered dialogic precisely because *any* statement can be ironized and undermined by changing its context, speaker, audience, or simply its intonation; hence the possibility of subversion and an opening for the voices of alterity.

However, Bakhtin's theory of the dialogic is not limited to the carnivalesque. For this theorist the intertextual references of an utterance may be manifold and are produced not only by the speaker/writer, but to a greater degree by the listener/reader. Discourse cannot be controlled. The centripetal forces that assign common means to words so that we can communicate with each other are directly counterbalanced by the centrifugal forces that constantly expand those meanings. Moreover, it is only through dialogue that the subject is constituted, through the production of utterance, which elicits a response from the not-me. Bakhtin labels this "response-ibility."[20]

Beginning with an epigraph and a sound, thereby indicating that language will be the subject of the novel, *Jazz* proceeds to narrativize Bakhtinian theory. In the first place, jazz music functions as a trope. Together with a southern black dialect, jazz traveled with African Americans on their great migration north during the later years of the nineteenth century and the first decades of the twentieth. Said to have originated in the Storyville area of New Orleans and associated with low life and prostitution, the music and the people who played it were associated with "life below the belt," somehow threatening the moral order. But apart from its threat to standard mores, its use as trope for dialogic discourse also resides in the nature of the music itself – its plan of call and response among instruments and vocalists, the on-going dialogue of music as process rather than product. Morrison adapts Bakhtin's theory of "response-ibility" to "response-ability," the power to respond to an instrument or an utterance.[21]

In addition to these two major indications, Morrison narrativizes aspects of Bakhtinian theory in each chapter of *Jazz*. For example, in chapter 3 she specifically looks at the multivocalic nature of the sign and the power of the word to elude a monologic interpretation. Perhaps the most obvious demonstration the author makes of this point is her explicit inclusion of street signs, playing specifically on the dialogic nature of the term itself. As Volosinov/Bakhtin writes, "[A] sign does not simply exist as a part of a reality – it reflects and refracts another reality . . . Wherever a sign is present, ideology is present, too. Everything ideological possesses semiotic value . . ."[22]

Morrison goes out of her way to indicate that the dialogic sign is indeed the crux of the matter in this chapter, first by capitalizing the letter in a seemingly incidental place ("The stomach-jump Dorcas and Felice have agreed is the Sign of real interest and possible love surfaces and spreads as Dorcas watches the brothers" [66]); secondly, by effectuating a change in Joe's perception through the teasing from Alice's friends ("But that day in Alice Manfred's house, as he listened to and returned their banter, something in the wordplay took on weight" [71]); and thirdly, and most explicitly, by including a specific section on actual signs found in the City –

> The City is smart at this: smelling good and looking raunchy; sending secret messages disguised as public signs: this way, open here, danger to let colored only single men on sale woman wanted private room stop dog on premises absolutely no money down fresh chicken free delivery fast. (64)

– in which, after the first two "signs," she deliberately drops the separating commas so that the ambiguity of their dialogic nature becomes even more transparent. Obviously, the reader is meant to toy with the alternatives in the messages.

Moreover, Bakhtin's concern with primary and secondary "speech genres" is everywhere. Within this chapter particularly one finds melded into the narrative music lyrics ("while a knowing woman sang ain't nobody going to keep me down you got the right key baby but the wrong keyhole you got to get it bring it and put it right here, or else" [60]), newspaper headlines ("Man kills wife. Eight accused of rape dismissed . . . Woman says man beat. In jealous rage man" [74]), radio serials [66–67], and folk sayings ("They know a badly dressed body is nobody at all" [65]).

Apart from an extensive interrogation of Bakhtin's concept of signs and speech genres in discourse, Morrison literally enacts his theory of the construction of the self via dialogue with the other in having Violet conceptualize "that other Violet" (whom the neighbors have dubbed "Violent") – her "other" who has somehow taken over her personality. She explains to Felice how she eliminated her:

> "How did you get rid of her?"
> "Killed her. Then I killed the me that killed her."
> "Who's left?"
> "Me." (209)

Subjectivity in Bakhtin is constructed through dialogues with the other. But apparently the theory as explored by Morrison in *Jazz* is not quite so neat or complete. Violet at times suffers from "cracks" in her discourse which neither she nor Joe can explain:

> Like the time Miss Haywood asked her what time could she do her granddaughter's hair and Violet said, "Two o'clock if the hearse is out of the way." (24)

And the last word on the subject, occurring right before the final coda calls up the discrepancy:

> Something is missing there. Something rogue. Something else you have to figure in before you can figure it out. (227–228)

And for this "something rogue," Morrison uses *Paradise* to examine the theory of the "French Feminists": Luce Irigaray, Hélène Cixous, and Julia Kristeva.

Unhappy especially with Freud, but also with Foucault, the French Feminists have modified theories of Lacan, who argued that it was not the actual phallus envied by the female child, but the power of the symbolic realm and the logos whose discourse authorizes the Father and relegates the Mother to silence. "Language, they argue, in privileging the phallus, suppresses what is feminine, subjecting it to the symbolization of a patriarchal system of naming and categorization."[23] Against this phallocentrism of the symbolic order, Irigaray and Cixous posit the pre-symbolic, or *semiotique*, or what Kristeva prefers to call the *chora*, the pre-symbolic communication with the Mother before the child enters into the realm of the Father.

For Cixous and Irigaray, in order to recover the lost Mother and the pre-symbolic, women must find and develop an *écriture féminine*, which for Cixous means "writing the body," "finding the mother's voice," and "writing in the mother's milk." While positing the *chora* as the site of the pre-symbolic and the necessity of recovering the Semiotic for women's voices to be heard, Kristeva expands, or rather adapts, Bakhtin's theory of "intertextuality" to include the exchange that is constantly going on between the symbolic and the pre-symbolic in all people, independently of gender. She surmises that this exchange will be manifest in the disruptions in discourse found in women's writing, which certainly seems to account for the "rogue," "irrational" comments Violet makes.

From the beginning *Paradise* sets the patriarchal town of Ruby against the feminine "wild zone" of the Convent. There are numerous references to the "Fathers" (Old and New) and even specifically to the "Law": "But a narrowly escaped treason against the fathers' law, the law of continuance and multiplication, was overwhelmed by the permanent threat to his cherished view of himself and his brother" (279), a view that will destroy the very notion of Ruby's *raison d'être*. It is precisely this calamity that is set out at the beginning of the trilogy: the wider context of Romans 9, from which the epigraph of *Beloved* is taken, makes clear that the intractability of the fathers is *not* the way to righteousness, because "they sought it not by faith, but as it were by the works of the law" (Romans 9:32). The women at the Convent, on the other hand, are atemporal and ahistorical, living outside the patriarchal law. The perceived affront to their sensibilities leads the men to use the Convent women as scapegoats, venting their fears and frustrations on what are clearly harmless females simply because they do not conform to their idea of a woman's place. The women themselves are "messy" human beings, all having been victimized by the patriarchal order. The Convent offers them a refuge of "blessed malelessness." Consolata (Connie), after Mother's death, is so "dis-Consolate" she retreats to live mainly in the cellar with no sense of self at all, until one afternoon, sitting alone at twilight, she encounters a male figure who is clearly the reflection of herself. Embodying the "bisexual self of the child," Connie is reunited with the wholeness that each child experiences in the pre-symbolic order. Taking charge of the four wayward young women who have found their way to the Convent, she explains the necessity of "wholeness," the unification of body and spirit: "Hear me, listen. Never break them [body and spirit] in two. Never put one over the other. Eve is Mary's mother. Mary is the daughter of Eve" (263).

Shirley A. Stave argues that in the extended passage Consolata's speech "disrupts accepted rules of grammar and syntax, once again pointing to the disruption of the symbolic order and gesturing in the direction of the Kristevian semiotique."[24] In fact, she actually takes the four young women into the cellar, a metaphorical descent into the *chora* of the semiotic. Here she has them lie on the floor in any position they choose and, when they are comfortable, draws their silhouette on the floor in chalk, a visceral enactment of Cixous's *écriture féminine*. When they have lain there until they are quite uncomfortable, Consolata begins to tell her story; she then has these women release their own trauma through projecting themselves onto and through their bodies in the silhouette drawn on the floor of the cellar-womb.

This attempted return to the semiotic is enacted as well by the men who have come to rout or murder the women. Stroking their representations of the phallus, they blast open a door that has never been locked, shooting one woman and tracking the others, understanding that their "guns are more than decoration, intimidation or comfort. They are meant" (185). As the men separate, some explore the rooms upstairs in which "[o]nly one mirror has not been covered with chalky paint and that one the man ignores. He does not want to see himself stalking females or their liquid" (9). In Kristeva's conception (following Lacan), passage into the symbolic is preceded by the "mirror" stage, which "opens the way for the constitution of all objects which from now on will be detached from the semiotic *chora*."[25] But a meaningful return to the semiotic is not possible for these men; once in the cellar they interpret the drawings in terms of the only discourse they now have available to them: "as defilement and violence and perversions beyond imagination. Lovingly drawn filth carpets the stone floor" (287). Unable to see the women as "women," nor understand their *écriture féminine*, the men shoulder their self-righteousness and eliminate the unruly females.

The women are murdered . . . aren't they? Before the final coda of the book the women have all appeared to loved ones – the irruption of the semiotic within the symbolic order. Billie Delia "knows" that they are out there, and will return. The semiotic will not be suppressed by the guns of the Fathers. "The material bodies of mothers, the relationship between mother and infant, create psychic, subjective images and rhythms which are never lost from our unconscious, although they may be forgotten."[26] Moreover, the final coda enacts the return to the Mother, with Piedade's song evoking "memories neither one has ever had; of reaching age in the company of the other; of speech shared and divided bread smoking from the fire" (318).

Though some critics have complained about the excess of Piedade's song, it is actually the author's enactment of the French Feminists' theory of feminine discourse: "a lyrical, euphoric evocation of the essential bond between feminine writing and the mother as source and origin of the voice to be heard in all female texts." Kristeva writes that

> [t]he voice in each woman, moreover, is not only her own, but springs from the deepest layers of her psyche: her own speech becomes the echo of the primeval song she once heard, the voice, the incarnation of the "first voice of love" which all women preserve alive . . . the Voice of the Mother, that omnipotent figure that dominates the fantasies of the pre-Oedipal baby.[27]

With the inclusion of the feminine voice within contemporary theories of discourse, Morrison brings her exploration in the trilogy full circle. The severing of the maternal bond with the child violently enacted in *Beloved* gives way to a female *pietà* and the "unambivalent bliss of going home to be at home – the ease of coming back to love begun" (318) at the end of the trilogy.

In summary, in addition to more easily recognizable links, underlying the Morrison trilogy is a concern for the theories of discourse that dominated the end of the twentieth century. Foucault insists that "truth" is only produced by those who are in power and can therefore control the discourse. Examples of this attempt to shut out alternative voices are everywhere narrativized in *Beloved*. Bakhtin posits that language cannot be controlled, that any utterance can be parodied, and that intertextual references can undermine the "official" meaning of words. *Jazz* is a study of the dialogic nature of language and how stories are told again and again, each time with additional meanings or interpretations. But even the unreliable narrator of *Jazz* wonders about "something rogue" in the language that cannot be accounted for. Hence, *Paradise* takes a narrative look at the French Feminists' theories of discourse, which incorporate the early "dialogue" between mother and infant in the *Semiotique* (the Realm of the Mother) – that phase before the child is initiated into symbolic language (the Realm of the Father). In the development of the novels of the trilogy Foucault's inscription *on* the body in *Beloved* becomes Cixous's writing *of* the body in *Paradise*. With a comprehensive reading of all three novels, Sethe's original lament can now be read as a loss of power, loss of story, loss of voice: "They took my milk!"

NOTES

1. Toni Morrison, *Beloved* (New York: Alfred A. Knopf, 1987); *Jazz* (London: Chatto & Windus, 1992); and *Paradise* (New York: Alfred A. Knopf, 1998). All references to these novels will be included within the text and refer to these editions.
2. John N. Duvall, in *The Identifying Fictions of Toni Morrison: Modernist Authenticity and Postmodern Blackness* (New York: Palgrave, 2000), acknowledges these works as a trilogy comprising a "distinct phase"; ". . . [Morrison's] work in the second phase suggests a more postmodern articulation of identity as a process plural and fluid" (p. 8).
3. *Ibid.*, p. 17.
4. Discovered only in 1945, hidden in earthen jars buried in upper Egypt, these texts are fourth-century copies of second- or third-century codices of Gnostic scriptures; declared heretical by Augustine, the Gnostics, followers of an early form of Christianity, held that "esoteric knowledge of spiritual truth" was essential to salvation (see *Merriam-Webster's Collegiate Dictionary* on-line at Encyclopaedia Brinannica 2006, www.britannica.com (Aug. 2, 2006).
5. See my discussion in *The Story of "Jazz"* (Hamburg: Lit, 2001), chapter 4.
6. "The Return of the Spirit – Toni Morrison's *Beloved*," Preface to *Beloved*, trans. Wen-ching Ho (Taipei: Commercial Press, 2003), p. iv.
7. "Three Paynims (pagans), three Jews, and three Christian men"; Sir Paul Harvey, ed., *The Oxford Companion to English Literature* (Oxford: Clarendon Press, 1981), p. 899.
8. The two signal numbers in Dante's "Paradise" are nine and three, the latter already mentioned above as a number with religious implications foregrounded in the structure of *Beloved*.
9. Toni Morrison, "The Site of Memory," *Inventing the Truth: The Art and Craft of Memoir,"* ed. William Zinsser (Boston and New York: Houghton Mifflin, 1988), p. 193.
10. Barry Cooper, *Michel Foucault: An Introduction to the Study of His Thought* (New York: Edwin Mellen Press, 1981), p. 7.
11. *Ibid.*, pp. 133, 134.
12. Roger Daniels, *Coming to America: A History of Immigration and Ethnicity in American Life* (Princeton, NJ: Harper Perennial, 1990), p. 48.
13. Morrison, "Memory," p. 189.
14. *Ibid.*, p. 191.
15. Michel Foucault, *Madness and Civilization: A History of Insanity in the Age of Reason,* (New York: Vintage, 1988).
16. *I, Pierre Rivière, Having Slaughtered my Mother, my Sister and my Brother: A Case of Parricide in the Nineteenth Century*, Michel Foucault (ed.), trans. of *Moi, Pierre Rivière, ayant égorgé ma mèma, soeur, mon frère* (1973) by F. Jellinek (Harmondsworth: Penguin, 1975).

17. John Irwin, *American Hieroglyphics* (New Haven: Yale University Press, 1980), pp. 32–33.
18. Interestingly, Harryette Mullen has described this scene in terms of Kristeva's *chora*, which, Duvall complains, leaves the ending of *Beloved* somehow dissatisfying (in Duvall, *Identifying Fictions*, p. 167, footnote 11). Yet considering the trilogy as a whole piece effectively validates this reading and provides another link among the novels. See below.
19. Mikhail Bakhtin, "Rabelais and His World," *The Bakhtin Reader: Selected Writings of Bakhtin, Medvedev, Voloshinov*, ed. Pam Morris (London: Edward Arnold: 1994, 1997), p. 209.
20. Mikhail Bakhtin, *Speech Genres and Other Late Essays*, ed. Caryl Emerson and Michael Holquist (Austin: University of Texas Press, 1986), p. 68.
21. Toni Morrison, *Playing in the Dark: Whiteness and the Literary Imagination* (Cambridge, MA: Harvard University Press, 1992), p. xi.
22. "Marxism," in *The Baktin Reader*, ed. Morris, p. 50.
23. Sara Mills, *et al.*, *Feminist Readings/Feminists Reading* (Hemel Hempstead: Harvester Wheatsheaf, 1989), p. 7.
24. Shirley A. Stave, "The Master's Tools: Morrison's *Paradise* and the Problem of Christianity," *Toni Morrison and the Bible: Contested Intertextualities*, ed. Shirley A. Stave (New York: Peter Lang Publishing, 2006), p. 224.
25. Kristeva, quoted in Toril Moi, *Sexual/Textual Politics* (London: Routledge, 1988), p. 162.
26. Maggie Humm, *Practising Feminist Criticism* (London: Prentice Hall & Harvester Wheatsheaf, 1995), p. 52.
27. Moi, *Sexual/Textual Politics*, p. 114.

6

MAR GALLEGO

Love and the survival of the black community

Toni Morrison's eighth novel, *Love* (2003),[1] foregrounds one of her most crucial concerns, a major theme recurrent in all her novels: how can love be defined, dissected, or accounted for? What are its multiple meanings and manifestations? In this her latest novel Morrison explicitly investigates the elusive nature of love in relation to heterosexual sex and pedophilia, but also to female friendship, mother–daughter and, especially, father–daughter relationships, and communal ties. As Morrison herself said in an interview with novelist Diane McKinney-Whetstone, "I was interested in the way in which sexual love and other kinds of love lend themselves to betrayal. How do ordinary people end up ruining the thing they most want to protect? And obviously the heart of that is really the effort to love."[2] In trying to answer these questions, Morrison tackles many key issues in her fiction: the empty category of "race" or the uselessness of racial boundaries, the rewriting of history from an African American standpoint, the importance of the survival of the community, the definition of black womanhood, and the crucial role of female bonding. This novel, therefore, becomes almost a compendium in which it is possible to see Morrison at her best, proving both her artistry as a gifted writer and her profound social commitment to the transmission of the values of the black community.

The novel recounts the story of Bill Cosey and the women who surround him, whose diverse stories center on their obsession with the patriarch of the family, defined as father, husband, lover, and, at times, friend. Twenty-five years after his death, his pervasive presence still shapes and conditions these women's responses to each other. But the central narrative focuses on the troubled relationship between Heed, Cosey's second wife, and Christine, his granddaughter – best friends until Cosey married Heed at age eleven – and their lifelong struggle over Cosey's inheritance. Back in the forties and fifties Cosey was the proud owner of one of the most popular resorts for blacks on the East Coast, where the upper-middle class could find "more than a playground; it was a school and a haven" (35). But the burgeoning Civil Rights movement and the end of segregation bring about the decline of the resort. When Cosey dies under very strange circumstances in 1971, his ambiguous will consolidates Heed and Christine's mutual hostility. Other women in the Cosey saga include May, Christine's mother and widow of Cosey's only son Billy Boy, also dead; Vida, formerly employed by Cosey in his resort and secretly infatuated with him; Celestial, Cosey's long-standing lover, who is also a prostitute; L, the resort's longtime cook and a ghostly witness to the Cosey saga; and Junior, who becomes an assistant to the aging Heed after being released from the Correctional.

Historically speaking, critics agree that the novel "explores the losses that went with the gains brought about by the Civil Rights era."[3] Morrison intentionally rewrites the legacy of the Civil Rights movement as a crucial chapter in African American history in order to foreground the contrast between the period before and after desegregation. Her imaginative reconstruction of a resort that catered exclusively to the black bourgeoisie reveals not only the dynamics of segregationist practices in the United States, but also gender and class politics within the black community. Resulting from Cosey's intention to build "a playground for folk who felt the way he did, who studied ways to contradict history" (103), the resort is a faithful representation of the racial and sexual restrictions circumscribing the black bourgeoisie at the time. The resort's success and especially its decline after desegregation are read by L as "a cautionary lesson in black history" (201). Indeed, this decay epitomizes the sense of loss that runs throughout the whole novel and effectively questions the actual "gains" of the Civil Rights movement. Reflecting on the ambiguous legacy of the movement, Morrison emphasizes once more the manifold ways in which the past determines the present and future of the black community, and how important it is to retell African American history from their own vantage point.

In the same vein, Morrison asserts the need for communal values in order to ensure the survival of the black community. She chronicles African Americans' pre- and post-Civil Rights efforts to keep their families and community together in a racist and sexist enviroment, one of the reasons why the resort is remembered by many characters as the paradise suggested by its motto: "The best good time" (33). However, L foresees its deterioration because it could not endure as a "showplace" (104), clearly signaling class barriers as an explanation for the resort's diminishing fortunes. The fact that the rest of the black community was not allowed into the resort also demonstrates a class consciousness among African Americans that repeatedly draws Morrison's reprobation. The author seems to reflect on how to create vital links within the community that help preserve their cultural uniqueness based on family and communal ties, while simultaneously rejecting the dominant American dogma of individualism. In this sense, the story of the warring Cosey family embodies the dangers of disunity and self-destruction that continue to plague the African American community. As she argues in her seminal essay "Rootedness: the Ancestor as Foundation," a key figure for nurturing a notion of community is the ancestor, who preserves black traditions and provides coherence to the other members: "there is always an elder there. And these ancestors are not just parents, they are a sort of timeless people whose relations to the characters are benevolent, instructive, and protective, and they provide a certain kind of wisdom."[4] In the novel there are two "ancestral" figures: Sandler Gibbons, Cosey's fishing partner and Vida's husband, who also worked in the resort for some time; and particularly L, who performs this function in the novel in her dual role as substitute mother–lover and as reliable commentator on the Coseys' tribulations and secrets.

In *Love* Morrison continues her critique of black patriarchy and unequal gender relations in the family. African Americans' adoption of a patriarchal model is reckoned as the greatest source of conflict in the text. The black notion of patriarchy personified by Cosey forecloses any idea of kinship and community because, as the head of the clan, he miserably fails to foster a sense of family and to guide and protect its members. On the contrary, he is at a loss as to how to act as Billy Boy's father or May's father-in-law. Moreover, his attitude toward his own granddaughter is ambivalent, and his relationship with his two wives, especially with Heed, can also seem quite puzzling. In addition, he constantly takes women as lovers, which foments the disintegration of the supposedly sacred vows of marriage. Finally, he allegedly leaves all his estate to his longtime lover, Celestial, clearly demonstrating his incapability of ensuring the preservation of the family.

Cosey's only son, Billy Boy, is never disciplined nor taught by his father, but acknowledges his authority by taking his advice "in everything, including marriage . . . So Billy Boy chose May, who . . . would neither disrupt nor rival the bond between father and son" (102). When Billy Boy dies of pneumonia, Cosey himself recognizes that he has made him his "shadow" (43), treating him more like a friend than an actual son. But Cosey as a father figure is also disappointing with respect to his daughter-in-law, May. More than an acquired daughter, she is literally described as his "slave" because "her whole life was making sure those Cosey men had what they wanted. The father more than the son; the father more than her own daughter" (102). Because of that complete devotion to her father-in-law, May is enraged by his marriage to Heed, apparently out of jealousy as well as class consciousness. May's unrelenting attack on Heed takes diverse forms, which include constant verbal abuse, threats, and intriguing plots, leading her to an obsessive, psychologically disturbed state. She takes to stealing and hiding things, ostensibly to preserve the family legacy in the uncertainty of the Civil Rights era, but actually as a way of preventing Cosey's wife from enjoying her husband's fortune. She even ignores her own daughter Christine, using her as a weapon against Heed and encouraging her to fight for her lawful share of the Cosey estate.

Christine's relationship with her grandfather Cosey is also quite problematic. On the one hand, he seems to act more like a father than a grandfather to her, given the absence of her real father, Billy Boy. But Cosey fails to act as a sustaining father figure when he self-centeredly decides to marry her childhood best friend without a second thought. As Christine puts it in her reconciliatory talk with Heed at the end of the novel, "he took all of you from me" (194). Even worse than that, Christine witnesses his lust for her friend when she sees him masturbating in her own room; this episode conditions her approach to men and sexuality from that point onwards: "The dirty one who introduced her to nasty and blamed it on her" (165). In addition to this phrase, there are other hints in the novel concerning the possibility of some kind of sexual understanding between Cosey and Christine herself before he married Heed. For instance, as a little girl she is told by her mother to change rooms "for her own protection" (95) on the pretext that "there are things she shouldn't see or hear or know about" (95). This sexual undercurrent may explain Christine's jealousy when her friend and her grandfather go on their honeymoon while she herself is immediately sent away to Maple Valley School for four years. After a disastrous party for Christine's sixteenth birthday and Heed's warning to stay away (setting her bed on fire), she is gone once more in what she herself terms as a "run for life" (85). Christine's view of the similarities between Cosey's resort, her school, and a whorehouse she recurs to in her desperate flight away from her family is revealing: "all three floated in sexual tension and resentment . . . and all were organized around the pressing needs of men" (92), acknowledging, thus, the dominance of the sexual component of her relationship to her grandfather. In fact, throughout her life she defines herself as a "displaced" or "replaced" woman, which can be understood not only as an allusion to her replacement in her grandfather's affection, but also as an intimation of an incestous relationship between them.

In light of this idea of deviant sexuality and the father figure, it is crucial to analyze Cosey's relationships with his two wives. Not much is known about his first wife Julia, except that he supposedly loved her very much and treated her with kindness and consideration. L's depiction of the first time she ever saw Cosey is quite telling:

> He was standing in the sea, holding Julia, his wife, in his arms . . . Her eyes were closed, head bobbing . . . She lifted an arm, touched his shoulder. He turned her to his chest and carried her ashore. I believed then it was the sunlight that brought those tears to my eyes – not the sight of all that tenderness coming out of the sea. (64)

From this descriptive passage it is clear that Cosey adored his first wife. Moreover, placing Cosey and Julia in the sea is a way of suggesting their sexual intimacy, as we are often told in the novel that Cosey likes making love on the beach. Nevertheless, when Julia found out that the family's fortune originated in his father's illegal transactions as a court informer, she withdrew her affection from him and died a few years later, leaving behind their twelve-year-old son for him to raise. Though the cause of her death is undisclosed, her last enigmatic whisper – "Is that my daddy?" (68) – signals the fusion of the roles of husband and father figure that Cosey constantly evokes in the novel. In this case, such association is perhaps more significant because he is still a young man (only twenty-four when they married) and their marriage is portrayed as one of the few instances of "normalized" heterosexual love. Later on in their marriage, however, their sexual life is not so satisfactory: "his adored first wife thought his interests tiresome, his appetite abusive" (110), which motivates his search for other lovers.

By far the most disturbing aspect of the novel is the relentless exploration of the sexual attraction Cosey feels for his second wife, Heed, who is only eleven years old at the time of the marriage. As a matter of fact, Cosey's questionable behavior in Christine's room is actually provoked by another upsetting incident: he intentionally caresses Heed's nipple while she is wearing Christine's bathing suit. That scene turns out to be the primeval source of tension between both friends: "that first lie, of many to follow, is born because Heed thinks Christine knows what happened and it made her vomit" (191). Cosey's sexual arousal over the incident, indicated by his subsequent masturbation in Christine's bedroom window, suggests an inclination toward pedophilia, which he then attempts to make more 'socially acceptable' by marrying the little girl thereafter. Throughout their married life, however, it is obvious that he acts as both her husband and her father. For instance, Heed always calls him "Papa," and there is a moment in which he even spanks her for misbehaving in front of Christine and May.[5] The novel offers several but quite divergent justifications for this scandalous marriage coming from the two seemingly reliable perspectives of the elder figures, Sandler and L.

Sandler recalls that Cosey hoped to end his "bachelor" behavior (meaning innumerable lovers) "by marrying a girl he could educate to his taste" (110). This idea is reiterated a few pages later (148), which evokes once more the fused roles of husband and father. Moreover, in the course of that conversation Sandler also remembers Cosey's vivid and detailed description of Heed's body when he saw her for the first time: "hips narrow, chest smooth as a plank, skin soft and damp, like a lip. Invisible navel above scant, newborn hair" (148). This depiction corresponds to any prepubescent child's body, which grounds a reading of Cosey's attraction for Heed as definitively bordering on, if not actual, pedophilic inclinations. However, L's own allegations about Cosey's marriage disclose his main motives from quite a different point of view. According to L, he wanted to have children to fill the void Billy Boy left at his departure and only a vigin would do for the mother of his descendants (104), basically adhering to the patriarchal requirement for female virginity. However, L articulates the underlying reason for this unfanthomable union: Cosey marries Heed as expiation for his father's betrayal of his own community. This view of their hideous marriage as an apology acquires deep resonances in the novel from a psychoanalytical approach, explaining, on the one hand, the enormous impact that his father's actions as a court informer had had on his own education and values, and on the other, his own perplexity about the proper behavior of a father figure. Finally, he also uses Heed to correct his mistakes with his first wife, because it was actually his father's misdoings that led to Julia's emotional detachment earlier. Be what it may, the truth is, as L affirms, that their marriage "laid the brickwork for ruination" (104) for each and every member of the clan and negated any possibility of family harmony.

All the women in Cosey's life are hurt by this untimely marriage, but Heed and Christine are particularly damaged because their resulting mutual hatred subsequently poisons their entire lives. Cosey's election of Heed as his child bride first prompts Christine to jealousy, but very soon those initial pangs are transformed into rancour and a misguided despisal of Heed. In turn, Heed's childish yearnings for her playmate and friend give way to a profound rage that erupts at the funeral, when the two of them start a fight that is only prevented by L's intervention. They spend the rest of their lives quarreling over the ambiguous words scribbled on a menu by Cosey, who has named his "sweet Cosey child" (88) as the only beneficiary of his will. In the closing chapter, they are finally able to blame the man, and not each other: "Poor us. What the hell was on his mind?" (188). In L's last monologue theirs is seen as the only loving relationship that actually matters in the whole novel, their "chosen love" is described with rapture and passion:

> If such children find each other before they know their own sex, or which one
> of them is starving, which well fed; before they know color from no color, kin
> from stranger, then they have found a mix of surrender and mutiny they can
> never live without. Heed and Christine found such a one.   (199)

This kind of love is thus seen as the perfect paradigm, transgressing racial, gender, or class barriers, and disregarding family and community restrictions. It is, perhaps, the purest form of love, which may elicit admiration but also envy. L stands for the former attitude, while Cosey – Dark as his father – personifies the latter because of his willingness to corrupt and annihilate that early female frienship with his patriarchal impositions.

Furthermore, concerning Cosey's role as a patriarch and his unusual sexual behavior, his need for other lovers reveals his endorsement of a patriarchal conception that deems it appropriate for a man to choose several sexual partners. But this profusion of lovers ironically seems also to imply his restless search for someone with whom to share his life. Apart from a number of nameless women, there are hints of possible affairs with L after his first wife's decease,[6] and even with Vida. However, the only woman that he is said to be truly enamored of is Celestial, whom he saved as a very small child and most probably initiated sexually. This idea can be inferred from a description of the woman he was looking at when his picture was taken (the photograph from which his portrait was painted): "the face had a look he [Sandler] would recognize anywhere . . . first ownership" (112). His deep commitment to this woman is summarized in a very telling sentence uttered by Cosey himself: "You can live with anything if you have what you can't live without" (112). And she is the only woman who is depicted as equal to him, powerful and self-confident, even dangerous. Morrison says that she "wanted the notion of a free female, or a licensed one."[7] Although she has no voice in the novel, Celestial plays a crucial role in its development because she is the indirect cause of Cosey's death. She constitutes his biggest mistake and where he fails as an accountable patriarch, as she takes precedence over his own blood ties. Upon discovering Cosey's testament that leaves practically everything to Celestial, L decides to exchange that "malicious thing" which contained his "vengeance" and "hatred" for the women of the family (201) for one scribbled on a menu. The will also seals his destiny, prompting L to poison him in order to make sure he cannot write a new version.

Finally, Cosey's last "lover" probably manifests the strangest form of attraction, as Junior seems to be infatuated by his portrait twenty-five years after his death. In her case, there is again the confusion between lover and father, since she calls him her "Good Man" (116). A fatherless child, Junior continually feels his ghostly omnipresence and hopes that, as a good father figure, he will protect her. After years of longing for her father, Junior believes she has definitively come "home" when she sees Romen, Sandler and Vida's nephew, who works part-time for the Cosey women, as a "gift" from Cosey (60). Moreover, she behaves according to what she thinks Cosey expects from her: "it pleased him to see her taking care of his wife; as it pleased him to watch her and Romen wrestle naked in the backseat of his twenty-five-year-old car" (124). With this Junior reinforces the idea of Cosey's penchant for pedophilia, but also adds a new layer of sexually perverse behavior when she pictures how he enjoys watching her trysts with Romen. In the end, however, her bewildered state leads her to fail him in two significant ways: first, she does not keep her promise to take care of his wife when she abandons Heed and Christine to their wrath in the dilapidated hotel. Second, she forgets about him while making love to Romen. As a consequence, she feels utterly forlorn and confused when she futilely tries to contact Cosey again and is unable to. As with all his previous women except Celestial, Cosey also forsakes her in the end, forcing her to face Christine alone after Heed's death in the hotel.

Cosey's failure to adapt to his multiple roles in the novel is ironically summed up on his tombstone: "Ideal husband. Perfect father" (301). Not only was he unable to fulfill any of these roles properly, but he was also unable to actually show any love either to his wives or to his own family. Moreover, he never cared for what any of the women in the family felt or needed, as he was only interested in satisfying his sexual drives and justifying himself by expiating his father's misdeeds. In fact, his supposedly deep commitment to Celestial is an illustration of his selfish interests and his lack of concern for the other family members. Evidently, a life like Cosey's should be read as a "cautionary lesson in black history," because he represents the far-reaching effects of African Americans' adoption of a dominant value system that systematically calls into question the very foundations of the black family and community. The only viable option to reconstruct those important foundations lies in the reestablishment of more equal gender roles and of cooperation within the family unit. This alternative might prevent the corruption of many types of loving relationships and nurture the "right" kind of love, especially an untarnished friendship like Heed and Christine's, which can in turn pave the way for a hopeful future in community.

NOTES

1. Toni Morrison, *Love* (Chatto & Windus, 2003). Further references will be cited in the text and refer to this edition.
2. Diane McKinney-Whetstone, "The Nature of Love," *Essence* 34.6 (October 2003): 206.

3. "Toni Morrison: Words of Love," CBS News (7 April, 2005).

4. Toni Morrison, "Rootedness: the Ancestor as Foundation," *Black Women Writers (1950–1980)*, ed. Mari Evans (New York: Anchor, 1984), p. 343.

5. This is another crucial scene in the text, because it shows Cosey's inner confusion about how to treat Heed as his wife. Indeed, this spanking drives Heed to set Christine's bed on fire as a way of affirming her authority and position in the family, which Cosey has undermined. Also interesting is Christine and May's reaction to the spanking, because they consider it a victory for them, the real family. Once more, L is the only one who really understands the deeper meaning of this episode and advises Cosey to apologize to Heed, which he never does, missing another opportunity to forge a more equal relationship with her (pp. 126; 134–135).

6. Despite the fact that L was only fourteen when Julia passed away, she decided to look after Billy Boy and Cosey as "the most *natural* thing in the world" for her (p. 100; my emphasis).

7. Barbara Lipkien Gershenbaum, "Review of *Love*," www.bookreporter.com (6 July, 2005).

7

ABENA P. A. BUSIA

The artistic impulse of Toni Morrison's shorter works

Toni Morrison is best known for her extraordinary novels and her influential essays. However, though less well known, her "shorter pieces"[1] are as remarkable as those, for they share that clear, visionary insight into the fate of Africans in the New World which is the guiding concern of all her work, whether as an editor, a writer, or a teacher. Her abiding artistic impulse is, in the words of one of her own songs, to "cut through the dark and get to the heart"[2] of the complex issues at stake. To date Morrison has produced four of these "shorter works": the unpublished songs and the story for *District Storyville*, a 1982 musical set in that district of New Orleans, choreographed by Donald McKayle and based on his 1962 dance of the same name; "Recitatif," a short story published in 1983 in *Confirmation: An Anthology of African American Women*, edited by Amiri and Amina Baraka; a play, *Dreaming Emmett*, written for and produced by the Albany Repertory Theater in celebration of Dr. Martin Luther King's birthday in January 1986; and the libretto for the opera, *Margaret Garner*, music by Richard Danielpour, commissioned and produced by the Detroit, Cincinnati, and Philadelphia Opera Houses which premiered at the Detroit Opera in May 2005.

Three of these four pieces are, at the time of writing, unpublished for different reasons,[3] and have received little critical attention. Thus, as indicated, my accounts of them are based primarily on a series of conversations with individuals involved in these collaborations; my sincere thanks to them all, in particular Ms. Morrison.[4]

Each of these works deals with some aspect of the social context in which we live, and love. Furthermore, though these pieces are all of different genres – songs, a short story, a play, and a libretto – they all also share that sense of the dramatic potential of vernacular language to uplift and instruct, that is, to enlighten, that is one of the hallmarks of Morrison's work. Finally, all of these works, even the short story, are experiments in collaboration; for an artist whose primary art form requires a solitary dedication, the potential and discipline of collaborative art forms has been an important aspect of Morrison's own artistic journey.

District Storyville

The first, little known collaboration was with the celebrated choreographer Donald McKayle, with whom she worked in turning his 1962 ballet *District Storyville* into a musical. This collaborative venture afforded Morrison the opportunity to write to create a language that evoked the moods and sensibilities, the feel of the district that had inspired both Bechet's music, to which her words were set, and the original ballet. "Storyville," the red-light district of New Orleans, was the only place in the United States where prostitution was legal. Created in 1897, it lasted until 1917, when it was officially closed down. In an attempt to obliterate it altogether, the area was razed in the 1940s to construct a public-housing complex. The district, acknowledged as being a place where jazz thrived in its early years, lived on in photographs, music, and memory. The musical is a tribute, a portrait of a district through the people who lived in it; thus the stage is peopled by brothel-house owners, prostitutes, and a young boy coming of age. What comes through is not degradation but the humanity within, the joy of living against the odds and the human dignity in despair that gave rise to the music the district inspired in the first place. Morrison set her lyrics to the music of Sidney Bechet, and managed to mirror it with such stirring sensitivity that twenty years later McKayle could recall and still sing the words to "First, I Found Love" faultlessly over the telephone.[5] Although the version to Bechet's music has not been recorded, those words were later set to original music by Andre Previn and can be found on his album *Honey and Rue*, where they form the first song in the cycle of other original songs written for Kathleen Battle. The musical itself has been performed in workshop only once, at the Michael Bennett Studios on Broadway in the summer of 1982.[6]

"Recitatif"

In her 1992 Preface to *Playing in the Dark* Toni Morrison states:

> Until very recently, and regardless of the race of the author, the readers of virtually all of American fiction have been positioned as white. I am interested to know what that assumption has meant to the literary imagination . . . How do embedded assumptions of racial (not racist) language work in the literary enterprise that hopes and sometimes claims to be "humanistic"?[7]

"Recitatif"[8] is one of Morrison's early attempts to address this question. This story demands of us as readers that we become conscious of our strategies of reading and our expectations of writing. It also exemplifies Morrison's abiding belief in reading as a collaborative art form; the act of reading the story dramatizes her belief that what we as readers get out of a text is informed, and indeed structured by, the values we bring in to it.[9]

"Recitatif" is about two eight-year-old girls, the narrator, who is "taken out of [her] own bed early in the morning . . . to be stuck in strange place with a girl from a whole other race," and the girl she meets in that shelter for orphaned and abandoned girls. The story is structured around their four subsequent random encounters over the next two decades. The tenuousness and turbulence of their relationship mirrors the nature of race relationships in the US during the decades in which the story is set, between the late fifties/early sixties and the late seventies/early eighties. This story has drawn critical attention because of Morrison's refusal to identify her characters by race, a gesture which, in the charged atmosphere of racial stereotyping and class classification that pervades the US, constitutes a radical act. A decade and a half later, Morrison would use the same strategy on a grander scale by opening her novel *Paradise* with the words "They shoot the white girl first" then refusing the easy identification of that "white girl" by color. Instead, by resisting the common assumptions designated by skin color, and withdrawing all obvious and loaded racialized physical descriptions, she liberates herself to explore what other racial, class, and cultural codes are available for character representation.

The result of this strategy is to create a particular kind of self-consciousness in her readers, for in the act of reading, the process of understanding depends on one's own prejudices, cultural memories, and expectations. To give one example of the way the story works, in the opening paragraphs that describe the first encounter, the narrator's mind goes first to her mother's contention that "they never washed their hair and they smelled funny." If you as a reader recognize (not to say accept) this as a racial stereotype that white people hold against Blacks, then what happens to embedded assumptions about relative class position when, in their next encounter eight years later it is the (presumably) white narrator who is working the night shift in the Howard Johnson's off the New York State throughway by a working-class town, serving the (by logical deduction) Black girl hippily mobile en route to find Hendrix in California?

Twelve years later still, at their next chance encounter, will the narrator's observation – "Shoes, dress, everything lovely and summery and rich. I was dying to know what happened to her, how she got from Jimi Hendrix to Annandale, a neighborhood full of doctors and IBM executives. Easy, I thought. Everything is so easy for them. They think they own the world" – convince you that you must have been wrong and the narrator must be the *Black* girl after all, because it is only white people who think they rule the world, or at least, only Black people who think white people think that? But then, would a white girl have gone chasing across the country with "two guys smothered in head and facial hair" to make an appointment with Hendrix? You may try to sort through a myriad of cultural codes of dress, language, music, even labor employment patterns and urban geography, but in the end what you truly confront is your own set of (race- and class-based) assumptions about race and class in the US. Though many critics read this work in the context of "passing" narratives, this concept implies some agency or desire to "pass for white" and there is absolutely no suggestion that the Black character in this story is doing anything of the kind. Rather, to read it as such is to fall into the very conventional clichés of reading that the story has been so very carefully crafted to challenge. More crucially, should the issue of tracking the race of the two central characters remain paramount, what then happens to an appreciation of the other issues raised in and by the story? The range of these issues includes the nature and power of memory and storytelling, the politics of contested memory, the politics of race and the possibilities of friendship, especially in a racially charged atmosphere, the claims of communal responsibility, not to speak of the need for love.

Dreaming Emmett

Toni Morrison consistently plays with cultural expectations, especially with expectations of words and the way language works. This is true even of the title of the play *Dreaming Emmett*, which would make most people focus on the word "Emmett," which since 1955 in the US has meant one person, the murdered teenager Emmett Till.[10] But the focus is as much on the word "dreaming," as a play between "dreaming of," that is, remembering Emmett, and, far more crucially, "Emmett dreaming," as, in the end, the play is the dream of a young man who everyone on stage believes to be Emmett, but who is instead an anonymous young man arbitrarily killed for wanting a kite.

Morrison wrote the play while at the State University of New York, for production at the Capital Repertory Theater, Albany, NY, to celebrate the birthday of Dr. Martin Luther King in January 1986. Thus the subject of civil rights came naturally to her, as did a drama centered around a Black teenager. Morrison is on record as saying that she was impelled to write her first novel *The Bluest Eye* because she needed to write a story which she would read, a story in which the world she knew, the world of little Black girls, was central. Could the interior lives, rather than only the external factors that circumscribed the lives of Black children, be taken seriously? The same impetus inspired her in the writing of this play; what forces shaped the world of this Black youth, what would he have to say, then or now, and when and by whom would his impulses and aspirations be taken seriously?

The issues that fueled the Till story were the issues that made it problematic for the collective psyche: race and sex, or rather the mere suggestion of interracial sex. In this context Morrison wished to see if the theater could be a venue in which her questions could be explored. The many aspects of the story of Emmett Till gave her much to explore, and she was particularly interested not in considering the aspects of the story that were shouted about, but in addressing the silences, particularly in the Black community. Her Emmett thus becomes iconographic, a figure through whom she could carry out the debates about race, gender, and in particular collective memory.

With *Dreaming Emmett* the process of bringing the drama to the stage was a truly collaborative effort. Both Toni Morrison, and Lorraine Toussaint who played Tamara, give credit to the director, the late Gilbert Moses. They both recalled his understanding of the project, his suggestion and staging of the use of masks, and his ability to empower the actors to embody and enact Morrison's words. Toussaint also recalled Morrison's engagement with the project, and the sympathy and time she committed to working with the actors to rewrite and edit the play to get the vision right, for though the premise of the play is simple, the execution proved complex.[11]

A young Black man appears on stage and begins to direct a film about "how I spent my summer, 1955," and summoning up his holiday friends, begins to recreate the summer as he would have had it. But the characters he summons, Black and white, resist his reverie, because they have changed, and because if they enter into his dream, as he is dead and they alive, they are subject to indictment. The trouble really erupts when a young Black girl comes out of the audience and disrupts the action, because she doesn't like the movie. When Emmett responds, "I'm doing this, girl. You ain't in my dream," the first act ends with her wonderful "Maybe that's the trouble with it. I'm not in it." This is a most argumentative play, and one of the central issues is precisely that, why was she not in it? Where is the Black woman in the lives and the fantasies of young Black men? Why was he so concerned about the presence of his white "Princess," then and now, but so little concerned about the Black mother in his drama, and doesn't want the Black girl there at all?

The drama is evoked through the quality of language. Toussaint, twenty years later, remembered it as a play written in poetry, though in actual fact it is not. She recognized that if you take away an actor's face, and you give him heightened language, behind the mask, what you do is spotlight the language, by removing the individual, and signaling the allegorical and representational. Her memory thus was a result of two aspects of the play, the lyrical quality of Toni Morrison's language, and the dramatic use of masks to convey the multi-layered nature of the representation on stage; part in the past, part in the present, part dream reverie, part relentless and unforgiving present. These requirements proved challenging to embody and to present on stage, and depended a great deal on the creative ability of the performers for interpretation.

An actor without a face must learn to communicate in other ways, and Morrison was interested in paring everything down in order to reach for the unspoken, and there were so many unspoken issues encircling this story. In addition to the role of the Black woman in peoples' lives, another issue was that there were innumerable "Emmetts," there were so many people with no *legend*, because their fates were not recorded, so to make masks of their faces was a way of emphasizing the repetitive nature of Emmett's fate, to focus on that story as iconic, because the real tragedy is that the story was not, and still is not, unusual. There is a multitude of unmemorialized Emmetts whose stolen lives litter the landscape of US history. In the end, as the details of the drama unfold, the play reaches through the anger and vengeance to a kind of reconciliation, an invitation to a collective truth.

Margaret Garner

With the opera *Margaret Garner*, Morrison returns to the historical story on which she had based her novel *Beloved*. The suggestion came from composer Richard Danielpour with whom she had already collaborated on two song cycles for Jessye Norman.[12] Morrison agreed to this project because she appreciated the opportunity to add this important story to the scarce repertoire of English-language opera. More particularly, she wanted her text to reveal the dignity and beauty of vernacular language, a project that has been dear to the heart of generations of African American writers. Morrison's own language reveals the quality she sees in African American vernacular; in her own words it is "exceptionally good at manipulating language and expressing the unspeakable." She continues, "I'm usually depressed at the way in which Black vernacular is handled in literature, and this was an opportunity to do what I had been doing in other ways throughout my writing life, to restore in language the beauty and the power of the spoken language and the music that already lies within it."[13] Thus her characters on stage are intelligent, introspective, and alive to the complexities of their situation, as when, in the opening scene, their auctioning off interrupted by the over-riding claims of ownership of Edward Gaines, they burst into a song of joyous reprieve celebrating "the gift of a little more time" with the people they love. The beauties, ironies, and subtleties of this are all brought out through the poetry of the language and the rich tapestry of the musical score.

Opera is a grandiose artistic form, far less nuanced than a novel, needing authentic, yet larger than life emotion and content. However, unlike in spoken drama, the grand sweep of operatic emotions is evoked through the music, rather than being the primary burden of the librettist. Nonetheless, Toni Morrison succeeded in projecting her concerns through a stunning libretto that carried the tensions of the story with poignant delicacy. The opera focuses on the slave community and its attempts to create a sense of family against the odds of brutality and communal insecurity that slavery brings. What matters are the relationships between husband and wife, mother and son, mother and daughter-in-law, the family and its community.

In returning to the story of Margaret Garner, Morrison's focus remains on the idea of family, in its affective nuclear, generational, and communal aspects, those aspects of the social and human story of Africans in America left out of historical narrative. The essential points about Margaret Garner's story are now well known: that she was a slave mother who escaped from Kentucky to Ohio for freedom, and, when recaptured, rather than return her children to slavery, tried instead to take their lives and succeeded in killing one of them. Morrison uses her libretto to raise the questions of agency and the creation of a moral community that issues of slavery provoke in American society. Garner's case, notorious in its day, became the most protracted slavery case in US history, lasting as it did for two weeks. Dramatic as this case was, however, the issues it raised were not unique, as the underlying causes, a direct consequence of the conditions of slavery in the United States, were shared with many others. The case before hers with which, in terms of the issues it raised for the larger community, it can best be compared is the 1855 case of *The State of Missouri vs. Celia: A Slave*.

In 1855, one year before the more celebrated and protracted case of Garner, the country was revisiting the Missouri Compromise of 1821, and what was at stake then was whether Ohio (the home state of both Margaret Garner and Toni Morrison) would be admitted into the Union as a slave or a free state. At this contentious moment the case of Celia became one in which, as with the Garner case, the tensions of legality, morality, gender, and "market transactions" all came into play. The legal issues revolved around the status of Celia as chattel, or as a human being with agency. In both historical instances, in cases ostensibly revolving around the legal status of female slaves who had taken a life (in Celia's case her abusive master who had raped her at puberty and fathered all her children), the unacknowledged and (legally) unspeakable subtext was the issue of the sexual rights claimed by slave masters, and the unbearable spotlight these cases shed on the moral violations of slavery. This is the darkness at the heart of the creation of the nation. Both cases highlight the compromises necessary, in law, to uphold those rights and violations in the creation of the Union. Both cases highlight the extent to which the domestic tranquility for peoples of all races, as well as the moral fate of the nation, would founder on the issue of the status of sexualized Black women before the law.[14]

The circumstances of the Garner story that came out in the trial make this clear. The ending of that story is known: after escaping with her family including her "mulatto" children, being captured, and surviving a river-boat accident which claimed the life of a second daughter on the journey back south into slavery, Garner died of typhus fever two years later on a southern plantation. Following the break-up of the family, the husband raised the two remaining children, fought in the Civil War, and lived a long time after abolition. What Morrison has kept intact is the detail of the story that makes it such an important one: that she was a slave mother who preferred to try to kill her children rather than have them returned to slavery. Beyond that, Morrison was not concerned about recreating historical accuracy. She was more concerned, once again, in exploring the story to create art, an art in which the slaves and their community could finally live on their own terms. She wanted her art to examine the least understood aspects of what the Margaret Garner story represents. As with the story of Emmett Till, history is littered with a lot of Margaret Garners whose stories are untold. What can we come to understand when we focus on their stories and their humanity?

For instance, one of the most dramatic scenes of tension in the opera occurs at the wedding feast of Caroline, the daughter of Margaret's master, a scene which exposes the contested ideologies within the slave-holding community as well. Caroline, a liberal young woman of northern sensibilities wants to assert the humanity of all people by insisting that slaves are human and also know about love. Yet in asking Margaret to speak on the subject in such a public forum, she at one and the same time exposes rather than defends Margaret, and offends the sensibilities of her neighbors, thereby destroying her father's attempt to establish himself as legitimate in that slave community. The scene, rather than empowering the more subjugated Margaret, disempowers them all as they cannot withstand the immediate and disruptive consequences of the entrenched nature of the "peculiar institution." The wedding party breaks up in a polite, yet acrimonious shambles. Yet even here what Morrison chooses to emphasize on the emptying stage is Margaret's compassionate humanity. Through her sorrowful aria "only unharnessed hearts can survive a locked-down life," she asserts the power of the secret soul to keep its quality love.

How to stage the opera to signal this unbreakable humanity was an issue of paramount concern. Thus the opera begins with the chorus of slaves declaiming the words: "No, No, No, No More" as the opera opens on a slave auction. For Toni Morrison, this collective resistance of the slave community was crucial, for she wished to establish from the start, and incontrovertibly, the long-denied humanity of these "chattel goods." Morrison and Danielpour worked with the director Kenny Leon to find ways of staging slavery without the easy references of "bales of hay and bags of cotton." For example, for a story centered on slavery, for the most part the brutality is suggested through sign, costume, and gesture, not dramatized openly on stage; the rape of Margaret Garner is superbly staged so that she is physically cornered while trying, verbally through her aria, to escape, and as her master corrals her, the curtain falls on the first act.

When the curtain rises on the final act, it is the date which calls attention to the most important deviation from the historical story (and there are many). Morrison takes artistic license concerning the historical timing of Garner's flight for freedom, the events of her trial and the staging of the final act of the opera. The actual trial of the historical Margaret Garner in 1856 proved to be a crucial one, as it took place in the Free State of Ohio, about slaves who had escaped from Kentucky after the passage of the Fugitive Slave Act. Thus, for the state of Ohio, the issue was whether or not to comply with federal law, which would make her subject to a return to Kentucky, where she could be tried for the destruction of property and hanged. The alternative was to appeal to a higher law, establish her rights as a human being and citizen in Ohio, and thereby make her subject to a trial for *murder*, which would then allow for an appeal for clemency under the laws of this Free State.[15] In the end federal law was upheld, and she was returned to Kentucky. Morrison condenses the drama and has her captured and tried in Kentucky, making that slave state the sole arbiter of her fate.

Morrison changes the date of the trial from 1856 to February 24, 1861, symbolically placing her trial amidst the immediate events leading to the outbreak of Civil War, midway between the inauguration of Jefferson Davis as President of the Confederate States and Abraham Lincoln as President of the Union. This shift dramatizes the integral relationship between the status of the African population and the fate of the Union, emphasizing how the outcome of a myriad of such cases determined the legal and moral history of the United States.

In staging the final scene, a scene in which Garner is to be hanged for the destruction of property (the murder of her child), the creative team worked and reworked the staging to evoke a pietà and thus make visually clear the notion of a sacrificial death. Having been condemned to death, Garner asserts her right to agency, and thus her humanity, by choosing to hang herself at the very moment of being pardoned. A scene of degradation and despair is ultimately transformed into one of poignant resistance and a death of chosen dignity. This search for dignity, for a recognition of the common humanity that binds us in our awful histories, and ennobles us to face and even transcend them, can be seen as the hallmark of Toni Morrison's many and diverse works.

NOTES

1. In addition to the works discussed here, Toni Morrison has also written the pictorial narrative *Remember: The Journey to School Integration* (2004), as well as five children's books in conjunction with her son Slade Morrison: *The Big Box*, 1999; *The Book of Mean People*, 2002; *The Lion or the Mouse*, 2003; *The Ant or the Grasshopper*, 2003; and *The Poppy or the Snake*, 2004. She is also the author of the lyrics for André Previn's *Honey and Rue*, 1992, and *Four Songs*, 1995, as well as Richard Danielpour's *Sweet Talk: Four Songs*, 1996, and *Spirits in the Well*, 1998.

2. This is a line from "The Town is Lit," the third of the songs from *Honey and Rue*.

3. The musical and the play exist only in manuscript. A manuscript of lyrics for *District Storyville* can be found in Mr. McKayle's papers in the archives at the University of California, Irvine. Ms. Morrison's only copy of the play *Dreaming Emmett* was destroyed by fire about twenty years ago, and, after many years of searching, she only recently received a working manuscript fortuitously preserved by one of the production stage managers. Ms. Morrison sent me a copy of this document shortly after receiving it. At the time of writing, the libretto of Margaret Garner is available on the website of the North Carolina Opera House though the full opera has as yet not been published. Only the short story "Recitatif" has been published.

4. Personal interview at Princeton University on September 21, 2005. This chapter would not have been possible without Ms. Morrison's generosity in giving her time, and sharing her recollections about the impetus behind all these works.

5. For additional insight into this work I spoke with Mr. McKayle (director and choreographer) and Charlayne Woodard (Knockout) over the telephone on March 20 and April 4, 2006, respectively.

6. The stellar cast included Carmen DeLavallade, Anne Duquesne, Jacquee Harry, Odetta, Lynne Thigpen, Tico Wells, and Charlayne Woodard.

7. Toni Morrison, *Playing in the Dark: Whiteness and the Literary Imagination* (Cambridge, MA: Harvard University Press, 1992), p. xii.

8. Amiri Baraka and Amina Baraka, eds., *Confirmation: An Anthology of African American Women* (New York: Quill, 1983), pp. 243–261.

9. "Recitatif" has garnered a small, but important corpus of criticism: see for instance Elizabeth Abel, "Black Writing, White Reading: Race and the

Politics of Feminist Interpretation," *Female Subjects in Black and White* (Berkley University of California Press, 1997), pp. 102–131; and David Goldstein-Shirley, "Race/[Gender]: Toni Morrison's "Recitatif," *Women on the Edge*, ed. Corinne H. Dale and J. H. E. Paine (New York: Garland, 1999), pp. 97–110. Both critics, in their very different ways, highlight the imbrications of gendered racial, sexual, and class politics, not only in the act of reading the story, but even in the act of writing textual criticism about it.

10. Emmett Louis Till, born July 1941, Chicago, Illinois, died August 1955, Money, Mississippi; the Black teenager whose "wolf whistle" at Carolyn Bryant, a white store-keeper, was considered sufficient excuse for his lynching by her husband and brother-in-law. The discovery of his body in the Tallahatchie River, and the subsequent acquittal of his alleged murderers, caused national outrage. Together with the Montgomery Bus Boycott started later the same year, these two incidents are celebrated for triggering the mass protests of the Civil Rights movement of the 1950s and 60s.

11. I had two interviews with Lorraine Toussaint (Tamara), one over the telephone, and the other face to face in her home in Mt. Washington, Los Angeles, five weeks later on October 23, 2005.

12. Richard Danielpour allowed me, in preparation for writing this piece, to read an early copy of the libretto to *Margaret Garner*, and shared his insights in a series of informal conversations between August 2002 and October 2004. In addition I saw the Detroit and Philadelphia productions of the opera in May 2005 and February 2006.

13. Quoted in Janelle Gelfand, "Morrison Contributes to Diversity in Opera," *Cincinnati Enquirer* Music Section (May 8, 2005), www.enquirer.com (accessed June 3, 2005). This article has now been archived and is available for purchase online, article ID: cin86109748.

14. See Melton A. McLaurin, *Celia: A Slave* (Athens and London: University of Georgia Press, 1991).

15. See Steven Weisenburger, *A Modern Medea* (New York: Hill & Wang, 1998), and his article "A Historical Margaret Garner" on the website of the Michigan Opera theatre: www.motopera.org (accessed June 3, 2005). At the time of writing, this article remains online through the link to the educational section of the website.

PART TWO

Toni Morrison's criticism and editing

8

HANNA WALLINGER

Toni Morrison's literary criticism

In "Unspeakable Things Unspoken: The Afro-American Presence in American Literature" and *Playing in the Dark: Whiteness and the Literary Imagination*, Toni Morrison contributes significantly to the debate about the canon of American literature in general and, in particular, its underlying discourse of what she calls the "dark, abiding, signing Africanist presence."[1] She uses 'Africanism' as a term for denoting the undercurrent of blackness in American literature and culture, on the one hand, and as a term for designating the unspeakable in discourses about class, sexuality, issues of power and domination, on the other. The metaphor she employs most prominently is that of the map that needs to be redrawn in order to lay bare the intellectual legacy of the African American in the United States, an endeavor that she compares to "the original charting of the New World" (*Playing*, 3). The earlier article and the volume are dazzling pieces of scholarship, thoughtful and provocative analyses of the presence of African American characters, themes, language, and structure in American literature. They are grounded in African American criticism and have turned out to be a persistent call to arms answered by an array of scholars. In the following my analysis will be divided into a discussion of the content and main points of Morrison's critical theory, then an investigation of its theoretical background, and, as a third part, recent scholarly responses.

Both pieces of criticism foreground Morrison the scholar, the Professor of the Humanities, with training and various teaching experiences in departments of English and the Humanities, and demonstrate, as Nancy J. Peterson says, her high stature as a writer and her "prominence as a cultural commentator."[2] The 1989 essay, published in the *Michigan Quarterly Review*, was the Hector Tanner Lecture on Human Values at the University of Michigan. *Playing in the Dark* (1992), a slender volume of some ninety pages, is the published version of the William E. Massey Sr. Lectures in the History of American Civilization at Harvard University. The Tanner Lecture was given after she had received the Pulitzer Prize for Fiction and the Robert

F. Kennedy Award for *Beloved* (both in 1988); the lectures at Harvard were delivered after she had accepted the Robert F. Goheen Professorship of the Humanities at Princeton University and were published in the same year as *Jazz*, just one year short of her receiving the Nobel Prize for Literature.

In "Unspeakable Things Unspoken" Morrison propagates a three-fold strategy of literary theory. First of all, she says there is a need for a conceptual model "that truly accommodates Afro-American literature,"[3] which means one that is based on African American culture, history, and artistic production. The second strategy is to examine and reinterpret the canon for "the unspeakable things unspoken," which is a search for the ways in which African Americans have been represented, depicted, and used in American literature, and the ways in which they have influenced the language and structure of this literature. It is a search "for the ghost in the machine" (210), as Morrison calls it. This awareness leads to the third point: relying on a close analysis of language, critics should examine contemporary literature for African American traces, which is a task that includes an examination of the particularly black features in African American literature itself. In *Playing in the Dark* her emphasis on this second goal is clearly stated:

> I wanted to identify those moments when American literature was complicit in the fabrication of racism, but equally important, I wanted to see when literature exploded and undermined it . . . Much more important was to contemplate how Africanist personae, narrative, and idiom moved and enriched the text in self-conscious ways, to consider what the engagement meant for the work of the writer's imagination. (*Playing*, 16)

She finds evidence of this American Africanism in such texts as Willa Cather's *Sapphira and the Slave Girl*, Poe's *The Narrative of Arthur Gordon Pym*, Twain's *Huckleberry Finn*, Hemingway's *To Have and Have Not*, and his *Garden of Eden*.

Morrison's literary criticism can be seen as a contribution to the debate over the revision of the canon that dominated much of the scholarship of the 1980s and 1990s, many aspects of which she specifically references in her work. Unhappy with the school of New Criticism, which prevailed in the 1950s, she struggles with the use of "quality" as the "only criterion for greatness" ("Unspeakable Things," 202), because it is usually tied up with the superiority of Western culture, which claims the prerogative of defining the norms that underlie qualifying statements. Morrison here takes up an issue – the "aesthetic value" as the sole criterion for what is usually called "great literature" – that is not new, of course, and has come under attack ever since New Criticism began to give way to theories of cultural studies, feminist scholarship, postcolonial revisions, and investigations of race and ethnicity.

Morrison's contribution, however, gained significance because her status as a widely acclaimed author gave her access to the public limelight, while her status as a professor of American literature gave her the academic credibility that allowed her to be persuasive, provocative, and polemic at the same time. Specifically referencing the ground-breaking work by Henry Louis Gates, Jr., Edward Said, Ivan van Sertima, and Martin Bernal,[4] she raised her voice with theirs and those of many other scholars of her time in the passionate and urgent realization that the accepted canon of literature taught at school, marketed by publishing houses, and thus consumed by the reading public had a decisive influence on shaping the collective mind of a nation. "Canon building is Empire building," she says, and "race" (a term which she often puts in quotation marks) clamors for attention with its potential to challenge the bias of Western civilization ("Unspeakable Things," 207).

In "Unspeakable Things Unspoken," Morrison is concerned with the definition of American literature and whether it reflects "an eternal, universal or transcending paradigm," a paradigm that separates it clearly and unequivocally from Chicano or African American or Asian American or Native American literature, and one that defines it, as she says, as "the protected preserve of the thoughts and works and analytical strategies of whitemen" (202). She sees evidence of an "incursion of third-world or so-called minority literature into a Eurocentric stronghold" (205), which threatens power structures and leads to an upheaval of existing norms. This is why she says, "Canon defense is national defense. Canon debate, whatever the terrain, nature and range . . . is the clash of cultures" (207). Her example for this canon debate about the deeper significance of race and color is Herman Melville's *Moby-Dick*, in which she traces the moment of recognition in America "when whiteness became ideology" (214). Morrison sees Captain Ahab's madness resulting in large part from his doomed awareness that the concept of whiteness was inhuman. This also made him "the only white male American heroic enough to try to slay the monster that was devouring the world as he knew it" (215).

Morrison also engages in the difficult question of whether the black presence is automatically visible in works written by African American writers. The third part of her "Unspeakable Things Unspoken" essay focuses on "the art of the black writer" (217), on the difficult task of defining what may make a writer black. She illuminates her point by referring to the first sentences of her first five novels, in order to demonstrate that a full understanding of these opening lines relies on the reader's comprehension of the "codes embedded in black culture" (221): "Quiet as it's kept, there were no marigolds in the fall of 1941" (opening of *The Bluest Eye*), or "He believed he was safe" (opening of *Tar Baby*) or "124 was spiteful. Full of a baby's venom" (opening of *Beloved*). In this rare instance in which a writer becomes her own informed reader and expert critic, Morrison offers a model for the search in the textual silences and voids that speak of a racial as well as female subtext through language. In this part of her essay Morrison also details her development as a writer, conveys a sense of how she struggles with every word, dismisses, as she did with *Sula*, an original opening sentence and then is dissatisfied with the alternative she decided on. Using elements of structuralism (careful analysis of opposites, close attention to words as signs), narratology, and reader-response criticism, she combines her roles as writer, reader, and critic.

Playing in the Dark is divided into a preface and three chapters. The Preface starts with a reference to one of the widely read autobiographical novels of the 1980s, Marie Cardinal's *The Words to Say It*, a book that details the author's descent into madness and her process of healing. One of the crucial experiences in this book was triggered by her hearing Louis Armstrong in concert. While Cardinal, Morrison argues, is profoundly moved by this music, which leads her to question the deep side of her psyche, Morrison interrogates the "dark" side of Cardinal's psyche, the black music and her past in Algeria, and sees them as metaphorical associations with the power of blackness. This reading of Cardinal's book encouraged Morrison to carry out a project she had long been interested in, namely to explore "the sources of these images and the effect they have on the literary imagination and its product" (x).

The first chapter is entitled "Black Matters," with the deliberate ambiguity of "matters" as a verb or a noun. Morrison draws upon a wide range of literature from classical to contemporary times to arrive at a definition of the main themes of American literature: "individualism, masculinity, social engagement versus historical isolation; acute and ambiguous moral problematics; the thematics of innocence coupled with an obsession with figurations of death and hell" (5). Morrison wants to call attention to the racial and racist discourse behind these themes, how, for example, racism not only exposes the victim, but also how racial hierarchies and exclusions have an impact on those who perpetuate them. Literature has to be cured, she says in drastic terms, of this "trembling hypochondria" so that surgery can be carried out on assumedly race-free, "lobotomized" literature (12). Readers and critics have to be cured of a "willful critical blindness" (18) so that they see the hidden sides in works by such writers as Edgar Allan Poe, Henry James, Gertrude Stein, or Flannery O'Connor. Morrison then concentrates on Willa Cather's novel *Sapphira and the Slave Girl* and explains the racial forces behind the power structure between white mistress and black slave, as well as between slave mother and slave daughter.

The chapter entitled "Romancing the Shadow" analyzes Poe's *Narrative of Arthur Gordon Pym* and its Old World realities and New World dreams, the haunting worlds of the Gothic, Romantic, and Puritan. Most remarkably, Morrison endorses a reevaluation of the term Romance not as an escape from reality, but as a useful genre to include symbols of absence, loneliness, aggression, opportunity, morality, and violence. Since romances most often embrace the outcast, the broken, or the downtrodden, the slave population serves as a natural means for mediating between the dreams of freedom and the reality of powerlessness. "Nothing highlighted freedom," Morrison insists, "like slavery" (38). This paradox explains why the most inherently American feature of American literature, its "fabricated brew of darkness, otherness, alarm, and desire" (38), relies on the presence of the dark "other." To illuminate her point, Morrison provides a long quotation from Bernard Bailyn's *Voyagers to the West* that contains the story of William Dunbar, an eighteenth-century immigrant from Scotland and early slave-holder. Morrison sees his background in European enlightenment and his New World endorsement of slavery as a portrayal of the "process by which the American as new, white, and male was constituted" (43). "He is backgrounded by savagery," Morrison puns (44) before she challenges the prototypical depiction of Americans as innocent, alienated, and different. Race is an integral part of American literature, often implicitly as metaphor and symbol, often explicitly as shadows and silences. Using Poe's narrative as an illustration, Morrison then writes about the Africanist character as a surrogate for the writer him- or herself; about an Africanist idiom signaling modernity; about the body disguising sexuality, vulnerability, and anarchy in black and white terms; and about the manipulations of language disguising the underlying ethical and ethnic discourses of civilization and reason. A discussion of the controversial ending of *Huckleberry Finn* then exemplifies the techniques of "othering" found so often in American literature, "estranging language, metaphoric condensation, fetishizing strategies, the economy of stereotype, allegorical foreclosure" (58).

In "Disturbing Nurses and the Kindness of Sharks" Morrison resumes the central argument of freedom set off most clearly when compared to the bound and unfree. Her example of the taboo subject and the forbidden subtext is Hemingway, who provides her with examples of stereotypes, metonymic displacement, metaphysical condensation, fetishization, dehistoricizing allegory, and explosive language. Critics should look below the white surface, excavate the Africanist properties, and investigate the ways "in which a nonwhite, Africanist presence and personae have been constructed – invented – in the United States, and of the literary uses this fabricated presence has served" (90).

With her emphasis on American Africanism Morrison enters an old debate about the legacy of slavery and the dark side of standard white American literature. With the benefit of a good hundred years of freedom, struggle, and racism, she can now ascertain that slavery "enriched the country's creative possibilities" (*Playing*, 38), joining a similar trend in African American criticism to attribute the uniqueness of American culture to its infusion of African American culture, topics, and symbols. The writer Morrison is most often associated with in this theory is Ralph Ellison. In "What America Would Be like without Blacks" (included in *Going to the Territory*), Ellison argues persuasively that African Americans have always contributed to the American cultural mainstream. He names Faulkner, Stephen Crane, Hemingway, and Twain as some of the major writers using and exploiting the Africanist presence in American life. Ellison thinks that African Americans have tested American ideals, cultural stereotypes, and social conditions, but they always promise a better future of human freedom. In "Twentieth-Century Fiction and the Black Mask of Humanity" (in *Shadow and Act*), Ellison selects Twain, Hemingway, and Faulkner for a scrutiny of African American presence in their works.[5]

Morrison was not, however, the first African American woman to claim an Africanist presence in American literature. It is less well known that a generation of African American intellectual, politically active, and artistic women from roughly 1880 to 1920 defined race literature by the choice of the African American as subject. For Pauline E. Hopkins, Victoria Earle Matthews, Gertrude Bustill Mossell, Anna Julia Cooper, and others race literature was an imaginative record of the past and a true record of the many facets of contemporary African American life. On the one hand, they proclaimed their own distinctive and recognizable contribution to this race literature. Anna Julia Cooper, for example, claimed that literature, in order to gain the "distinction of individuality" and an "appreciative hearing" (176), had to contain something "characteristic and *sui generis*" (175). She firmly believed that only by presenting themes that resulted from American realities could American literature become distinctive: "And 'twas not till the pen of our writers was dipped in the life blood of their own nation and pictured out its own peculiar heart throbs and agonies that the world cared to listen."[6] On the other hand, these writers were concerned with finding the African American as subject, inspiration, and distinguishing topic – or, as Cooper phrases it, the "great *silent* factor" (178) – so long unacknowledged in mainstream American life and literature. Whereas the first object corresponds quite well to Morrison's own practice as a writer who is concerned with African American topics, history, and culture, the second goal can be seen as an early manifestation of Morrison's search for the Africanist presence. It is interesting to find that the earlier writers, particularly Cooper in the essays collected as *A Voice from the South*, and Matthews in "The Value of Race Literature," focused on certain representative white American writers and criticized their disregard and misrepresentation of African American characters. Cooper's indignation is roused by William Dean Howells, the eminent Boston scholar, writer, and editor, because of his racial generalizations and superficial presentation of a character like Rhoda Aldgate in *An Imperative Duty*. The authors Matthews selects for display of stereotypes about black people are Washington Irving, Mark Twain, John Ridpath, William Dean Howells, and Arthur Conan Doyle. Like Morrison, Cooper, Matthews, Mossell, and Hopkins pointed out the undercurrent of African American topics, characters, and plots that influenced the writing of their white contemporaries but which usually went unrecognized in critical discourse.[7]

The response to Morrison's literary criticism has triggered a number of interesting projects. The direct and immediate impact of *Playing in the Dark* can be traced, for example, in the treatment of *Sapphira and the Slave Girl*, Willa Cather's last and for a long time least acknowledged novel. Morrison is interested in "the interdependent working of power, race, and sexuality in a white woman's battle for coherence" (10) and offers a subtle and fresh reading of this novel. Ann Romines, editor of *Willa Cather's Southern Connections: New Essays on Cather and the South*, credits Morrison with turning the interest to *Sapphira* because of her "incisive and highly influential reading of the charged dynamics."[8] Romines sees the reason for the timeliness of Morrison's interpretation in "a climate of cultural studies, interdisciplinary scholarship, and new- and posthistoricist reading,"[9] all of which led to the most provocative session of the Cather conference on which this volume is based. In the volume, Marilyn Mobley McKenzie even sees Morrison's reading as dangerous, "for it calls into question the author's narrative intentions and exposes the contradictions between art and life, between the writer's expressed intentions and the ways in which language betrays and deconstructs those intentions to tell a national narrative America has not yet allowed itself to read or hear."[10]

In a similar vein, Betina Entzminger has applied Morrison's model to Eudora Welty, Michael Nowlin has applied it to her own novel *Jazz*, Dwight A. McBride presents her literary theory as evidence of a "racialized discourse,"[11] and Andrea Dimino analyzes her various roles as a critic of white literature as "an impassioned, often sardonic critique of the blindness of some of the people who help to make the canon."[12] Patrick O'Donnell reads passages of Faulkner's *Light in August* as if Faulkner "were working under the influence of *Playing in the Dark*,"[13] which is a kind of reversed intertextuality, and Katherine Clay Bassard sees Harriet E. Wilson, author of

Our Nig, at the beginning of a tradition of African American novelists and Morrison at the end of this lineage.[14] Richard C. Moreland reads Huck Finn as playing in the dark and puts Twain's novel into a cross-cultural dialogue with *Beloved*. *Playing in the Dark* can also be credited with initiating or influencing a recent line of research called "whiteness studies," concerned with the visibility, meaning, symbolic implications, representation, and concept of whiteness. Both Richard Dyer in *White* and Valerie Babb in *Whiteness Visible: The Meaning of Whiteness in American Literature and Culture* refer to Morrison's book as provocative and thought-provoking.[15]

In the field of African American studies, Morrison's legacy is wide and diverse. Kenneth Warren signals Morrison's notion of the unspeakable as his point of departure in *Black and White Strangers: Race and American Literary Realism* (1993). Eric Sundquist refers to Morrison in his introduction to *To Wake the Nations: Race in the Making of American Literature* (1993), a book in which he redefines the premises and significance of central American texts. Henry B. Wonham reprints the first two parts of "Unspeakable Things Unspoken" in his edited volume *Criticism and the Color Line: Desegregating American Literary Studies* (1996) and gives an overview of the central question of whether American literature would have been American without its African American people. This volume also contains a bibliographical essay by Shelley Fisher Fishkin with an overview of more than one hundred books and articles in the years 1990 to 1995 alone which challenge the traditional understanding of American culture.[16]

The great value of Morrison's literary criticism lies in its playfulness. She draws upon all registers of her writerly skills to combine persuasive argumentation with often graphic, sometimes drastic metaphors. "I am made melancholy when I consider that the act of defending the Eurocentric Western posture in literature as not only 'universal' but also 'race-free' may have resulted in lobotomizing that literature, and in diminishing both the art and the artist. Like the surgical removal of legs so that the body can remain enthroned, immobile, static – under house arrest, so to speak" ("Unspeakable Things," 212). Her playfulness disguises an undercurrent of anger and sadness; she is acutely aware that the unspeakable things she examines in American literature have always permeated the everyday reality of non-white peoples. Her literary criticism highlights the continued relevance of these hidden linguistic elements for a new generation of readers and reveals Morrison's own abiding concerns with racial and racist phenomena. Toni Morrison's main argument that American identity could only be defined as white and free because of, and not despite, the visibility of the non-white and non-free has led her to devise a new hermeneutics for the evaluation of literary texts. A talented teacher, an outstanding editor, and a gifted author, her incursions into the world of literary theory and powerful new readings of classic American texts have confirmed her yet again as one of the outstanding intellectuals of the contemporary United States.

NOTES

1. Toni Morrison, *Playing in the Dark: Whitness and the Literary Imagination* (Cambridge, MA: Harvard University Press, 1992), p. 5. All further references will be included in the text.
2. Nancy J. Peterson, "Introduction: Reading Toni Morrison – from the Seventies to the Nineties," *Toni Morrison: Critical and Theoretical Approaches*, ed. Nancy J. Peterson (Baltimore: Johns Hopkins University Press, 1997), p. 13, fn. 9.
3. Toni Morrison, "Unspeakable Things Unspoken: the Afro-American Presence in American Literature," *Toni Morrison*, ed. Harold Bloom (Philadelphia: Chelsea House, 1999), p. 210. All further references will be included in the text.
4. Morrison makes particular reference to Gates's volume entitled *"Race," Writing and Difference*, to the scholarship by Edward Said on *Orientalism* (New York: Vintage, 1979), to Van Sertima's literary, linguistic, and anthropological study, *They Came Before Columbus: The African Presence in Ancient America* (New York: Random House, 1987), and to Bernal's scholarship on *Black Athena: The Afroasiatic Roots of Classical Civilization* (The Fabrication of Ancient Greece 1785–1985), vol. 1 (New Brunswick, NJ: Rutgers University Press, 1987).
5. Ralph Ellison, "What America Would Be like without Blacks," *Going to the Territory* (New York: Random House, 1986), pp. 104–112; and "Twentieth-Century Fiction and the Mask of Humanity," *Shadow and Act* (New York: Random House, 1964), pp. 24–44.
6. Anna Julia Cooper, *A Voice from the South* (New York: Oxford University Press, 1988), p. 175.
7. See Victoria Earle Matthews, "The Value of Race Literature," *With Pen and Voice: A Critical Anthology of Nineteenth-Century African-American Women*, ed. Shirley Wilson Logan (Carbondale: Southern Illinois University Press, 1995), pp. 126–148.
8. Ann Romines, ed., *Willa Cather's Southern Connection: New Essays on Cather and the South* (Charlottesville: University Press of Virginia, 2000), p. 4.
9. *Ibid.*, pp. 4–5.
10. Marilyn Mobley McKenzie, "'The Dangerous Journey': Toni Morrison's Reading of *Sapphira and the Slave Girl*," in *Willa Cather's Southern Connection*, ed. Romines, p. 85.
11. See Betina Entzminger, "Playing in the Dark with Welty: the Symbolic Role of African Americans in *Delta Wedding*," *College Literature* 30.3 (2003): 52–67; Michael Nowlin, "Toni Morrison's *Jazz* and the Racial Dream of the American Writer," *American Literature* 71.1 (1999): 151–174; Dwight A. McBride, "Speaking the Unspeakable: On Toni Morrison, African American Intellectuals and the Uses of Essentialist Rhetoric," *Modern Fiction Studies* 39 (1993): 764.
12. Andrea Dimino, "Toni Morrison and William Faulkner: Remapping Culture," *Unflinching Gaze: Morrison and Faulkner Re-Envisioned*, ed. Carol A. Kolmerton, *et al.* (Jackson: University Press of Mississippi, 1997), p. 41.

13. Patrick O'Donnell, "Faulkner in Light of Morrison," in *Unflinching Gaze*, ed. Kolmerton, p. 225.
14. Katherine Clay Bassard, "'Beyond Mortal Vision': Harriet E. Wilson's *Our Nig* and the American Racial Dream-Text," *Female Subjects in Black and White: Race, Psychoanalysis, Feminism*, ed. Elizabeth Abel *et al.* (Berkeley: University of California Press, 1997), p. 188.
15. See Richard C. Moreland, *Learning from Difference: Teaching Morrison, Twain, Ellison, and Eliot* (Columbus: Ohio State University Press, 1999); Richard Dyer, *White* (London: Routledge, 1997); Valerie Babb, *Whiteness Visible: The Meaning of Whiteness in American Literature and Culture* (New York: New York University Press, 1998).
16. See Kenneth Warren, *Black and White Strangers: Race and American Literary Realism* (Chicago: University of Chicago Press, 1993); Eric Sundquist, *To Wake the Nations: Race in the Making of American Literature* (Cambridge, MA: Harvard University Press, 1993); Henry B. Wonham, ed., *Criticism and the Color Line: Desegregating American Literary Studies* (New Brunswick, NJ: Rutgers University Press, 1996); Shelley Fisher Fishkin, "Interrogating 'Whiteness,' Complicating 'Blackness': Remapping American Culture," in *Criticism and the Color Line*, ed. Wonham, pp. 251–290.

9

SÄMI LUDWIG

Toni Morrison's social criticism

"But we *do* language."[1]

"Being a writer, she [the *griot*] thinks of language partly as a system, partly as a living thing over which one has control, but mostly as agency – as an act with consequences."
(Toni Morrison, "Nobel Lecture" 13)

". . . lethal discourses of exclusion blocking access to cognition for both the excluder and the excluded."
(Toni Morrison, "Nobel Lecture" 19)

Though much less widely recognized or acclaimed than her fiction, or even her work in the field of literary theory, Toni Morrison's social criticism specifically elaborates on discussions raised elsewhere in her oeuvre. As in her other work, it contains a strong cognitive element, in the sense that she is primarily preoccupied with the way in which language is used by human beings and how it shapes what she calls the "construction of social reality."[2] Much of this is dealt with in her fiction, which is often fairly straightforward about the social conditions of African Americans, as, for example, in the episode in *Song of Solomon*, when in a "lecture" dominated by the word *not*, Railroad Tommy lists many of the things that a black person cannot have.[3]

Nevertheless, Morrison's criticism goes beyond the mere representation of facts. Using the label "cognitive" can take much of the mystery out of the so-called "magic realism" of her work and place it in a context of pragmatics, of a discourse that connects language and the human beings who use it in a framework which puts at the center of intellectual activity embodied minds[4] rather than some kind of textualist grammatology.[5] Language is something that people "do"; it is a part of human behavior and therefore intrinsically of social relevance.

This "realistic" involvement in her fiction may be one reason why the corpus of Morrison's social criticism in essay form is relatively slim. She has edited two volumes on very topical issues: first, *Race-ing Justice, En-gendering Power. Essays on Anita Hill, Clarence Thomas, and the Construction of Social Reality* (1992) on the Clarence Thomas hearings before his Supreme Court appointment, and secondly, *Birth of a Nation'hood: Gaze, Script, and Spectacle in the O. J. Simpson Case* (1997). For both books she has written introductions that engage in the language politics of these very public issues. There is no mistaking these texts for anything else than straightforward social criticism, and they provide a good opportunity to pinpoint some of Morrison's cognitive concerns. Once we better understand the nature of some of these representational issues, we can easily connect them to three of Morrison's other essays that are more focused on the intricacies of writing as an interactive process negotiating inside and outside, the private and the public, namely her brilliant lecture upon the award of the Nobel Prize for Literature (1993), then her equally impressive speech upon the acceptance of the National Book Foundation Medal for Distinguished Contribution to American Letters, "The Dancing Mind" (1996), and finally, "Home" (1997), the introductory piece to a volume of contributions at a conference in Princeton inspired by her colleague Cornel West's seminal book *Race Matters*.[6]

"Friday on the Potomac"

In her introduction to *Race-ing Justice, En-gendering Power*, entitled "Friday on the Potomac,"[7] Morrison shares some of her ideas on the construction of an "official story" of the Clarence Thomas hearings and the desire of the public to receive the "ultimate historical account" or "last word" (x). Significantly, she turns this end into a beginning and meaning into a matter of process: "For the kind of insight that invites reflection, language must be critiqued" (xi). She demonstrates in an almost haunting way how the language used to characterize the black nominee was motivated by racist stereotypes, reducing him to his laughter, his body, and his sexuality (xii–xiv). Similarly, the descriptions of Anita Hill deprived her of a rational self:

> Since neither the press nor the Senate Judiciary Committee would entertain seriously or exhaustively the truth of her accusations, she could be called any number or pair of discrediting terms and the contradictions would never be called into question, because, as a black woman, she was contradiction itself, irrationality in the flesh. She was portrayed as a lesbian who hated men *and* a vamp who could be ensnared and painfully rejected by them. She was a mixture heretofore not recognized in the glossary of racial tropes: an *intellectual* daughter of black *farmers*; a *black* female taking *offence*; a black *lady* repeating *dirty words*. Anita Hill's description of Thomas's behavior toward her did not ignite a careful search for the truth: her testimony simply produced an exchange of racial tropes. (xvi, original emphases)

The hearings were reduced to "an exchange of racial tropes," Morrison concludes; the "official story" found no consistent motivation in her accusations that made sense. In both cases, Thomas *and* Hill, the black human beings are eclipsed by a language that completely controls them: "The participants were black and therefore 'known,' serviceable, expendable in the interest of limning out one or the other of two mutually antagonistic fabulations" (xvii). Morrison puts her finger on these projections of "voyeuristic desire, fueled by mythologies that render blacks publicly serviceable instruments of private dread and longing" (xvii–xviii). This is, of course, a classical case of "othering," but the crucial point is that Morrison takes the binary out of the realm of mere language structure and contextualizes it in a historical realm of human interaction. The crux of the matter is the denial of motivation, of rational intentionality, to the people concerned – which is simply a denial of their humanity, of their right to think for themselves and make sense of their cognitive agency.

"Friday on the Potomac" is mainly about the dehumanizing nature of racial stereotypes – which is why Morrison's main intertextual reference is to the colonizing narrative of *Robinson Crusoe*: the foot on Friday's head, learning the master's language, the subaltern script. It is interesting, however, to look at the details of Morrison's criticism. Though the "internalization" of the master's language "is complete" in the case of Friday ([xxvii] and implicitly Clarence Thomas), she insists on the cognitive implausibility of his case:

> During the time in which he knows no other English, one has to assume he thinks in his own language, cogitates in it, explains stimuli and phenomena in the language he was born to. But Crusoe's account suggests otherwise, suggests that before his rescue Friday had no language, and even if he did, there was nothing to say in it. (xxiv)

Morrison wonders: "Did Friday forget completely the language he dreamed in?" (xxv). Though she is strongly aware of the influence of the colonizing discourse and of the inevitability of the master's language, she signals its incompleteness. Rather than lamenting the "official story" and narratives of self-destructive black irrationality, her introduction ends on notions of "conversation," "serious exchange," "intense debates" and "new conversations" (xxx). The way out of victimization involves a dynamics of multiple agency – the recognition of "people [talking] to one another" (viii), of a plurality of voices behind language, i.e., of cognitive empowering, of language motivated by individual lives.

Such a cognitive model of language is very different from a textualist one because it focuses on people speaking rather than on interacting texts only (how can texts "interact" all by themselves anyway?). Language is two-tiered: it is only meaningful as a symptom of human behavior; it is not the mere product of some generative grammar or structuralist synchronicity. Thus the circularity involved is one of the *feedback loop* of a learning mind (which involves a causality of people creating concepts) rather than a *hermeneutic circle* of conceptualist referral (which would limit itself to a grammatological interaction of signs).[8] When Morrison talks of a "new arena" (xxx) of debate, the realm of symbols is opened up to the world of human interaction.

"Dead Man Golfing"

Morrison's contribution to her edited volume on the O. J. Simpson trial[9] is again concerned with the denial of black cognition by the "official story." The press and the public are shocked about their own delusion: "We thought he loved us" (vii). The black subject is defined by mutually exclusive frames of "puppy" and "monster," which can only be reconciled at the price of "incoherence": "incoherence and emotional disorder 'fit' when the subject is black . . . Difficult explanations are folded into the general miasma of black incoherence" (ix). Morrison observes that the prosecution "needed a coherent case, not a coherent defendant. 'Senseless' is the term most often applied to crime (and criminals) anyway" (ix). The price for a coherent narrative that explains reality is the irrationality of "the other," of blacks, and, as Morrison suggests, even of devious "criminals" in general.

Morrison draws a historical analogy to Melville's "Benito Cereno," a story that she had previously made reference to in her piece on Clarence Thomas:

> Like Captain Delano in *Benito Cereno*, the racist thinker can jump from the view of the slave, Babo, as "naturally docile, made for servitude" to "savage cannibal" without any gesture towards what may lie in between the two conclusions, or any explanation of the jump from puppy to monster, so the truth of Babo's situation – that he is leading a surreptitious rebellion aboard the slave ship, that he is a clever man who wants to be free – never enters the equation.   ("Friday," xv)

The denial of intelligence ("that he is a clever man") is demonstrated to be part of an old story that refuses to acknowledge the black mind. Melville is important for Morrison because he exposes the nature of that self-deception and emphasizes the instantaneous change of perception in the Captain's mind from "dog" to "snake," the "abrupt switch of the Senegalese from one kind of animal to another" ("Dead Man," x). She calls this an "epiphany" of American reframing: "[T]he reversal is played out with and on a black man" (x). And she makes clear that this projective imposition is also a denial of humanity:

> Even when permitted conceptually to enter the kingdom of *Homo sapiens*, blacks have historically been viewed as either submissive children, violent ones, or both at once . . . What might be illogical for a white is easily possible for a black who has never been required to make, assumed to make, or described as making "sense." (xi)

Equally frightening is the analogy that Morrison finds of this framework with the description of criminals as "psychotics" and scapegoats within public reasoning, as "the perfect marriage of Jekyll and Hyde" (xii). There is an "absence of a rational analysis of behavior." She uses this expression twice because it provides a common denominator for all three contexts: Simpson, the slave, the criminal. When she herself tries to build a case and "construct a plot any reader would accept," she fails (xii). She cannot write a coherent narrative of O. J. Simpson's behavior that would satisfy the "standards of believability": "All my efforts collapsed into non-sense. Without the support of black irrationality . . . the fictional case not only could not be made, it was silly" (xiii). This is why the "official story" of the media again resorts to old underlying narratives of lynching, a "symbolic language . . . already scripted, fully spectacularized and riveting in its gazeability" (xvi). Morrison observes a precession (as Baudrillard would have it)[10] of given representations over reality – but at the same time, crucially, she puts her finger on what is precisely excluded by such a postmodernist semiotics: "[T]he dialogue is confined to the terms the spectacle has set" (xvii). The racism is contextualized by a framework of imposition and non-interaction that excludes causality in the sense of human agency by the object concerned.

Morrison's point is that the "real lives" remain "largely unimagined" and feed no input into the "official story," which "is already in gear to protect itself" (xviii). In cognitive terms this means that in order to keep the schemata intact, the media limit themselves to active gestures of *assimilation*, of appropriating lived experience to the already given public representation, thereby avoiding *accommodation*, i.e., a readjustment (or *adaptation*) of the given schemata to reality – which is nothing less than a refusal of learning on their part.[11] What stays intact therefore are the racist stereotypes and the given intractability of policing power: "It would take the whole department to effect such a conspiracy, wouldn't it?" (xxii). This way difficult issues can be avoided and their complexity can be ignored – Morrison also regrets that, for example, there is no "domestic abuse dialogue" and that the complexity of race *and* gender issues combined remains unpacked (xxii–xxiv). She demonstrates how "the grammar of the meta-narrative" (xxiv) imposes its simplistic binary ("guilty or innocent") on the case, "dismissing or trivializing all counternarratives" (xxv).

Because of the commercial "gigantism" of the case (xvii) the given "grammar" is applied to Simpson and at the same time (naturally) reflected back unto its origin as a projection, i.e., "the black individual is forced to stand in for the entire race" (xxviii). For Morrison this "official story" marks the "longing for a living black man repeating forever a narrative of black inferiority" (xxvi), a tendency which she associates with the "post-Civil Rights discourse on black deviance" (xxvii). In the end the real Mr. Simpson is reduced to a "disembodied voice, a phantom. A social cadaver and a minor irritant in the official gaze, which cracks occasionally to expose him golfing. A 'dead' man arrogantly alive" (xxv). Morrison shows how through the imposition of "the will of the dominant culture" (xxviii) Simpson becomes a ghost, a disembodied conceptual haunt exemplifying the alienation of the black minority. It is probably no coincidence that she is hinting at traditional black imagery of *duppies* and *zombies*, in which the body is severed from the mind and concepts deny the lived experience.

Nobel Lecture

In the other three texts discussed here, Morrison moves from specific political arenas into her own domain of writing and shows how this struggle for a cognitive dimension of acknowledged humanity translates into a pragmatic approach to language when it comes to the life of books. In her Nobel Lecture she makes clear that the example of her old and blind griot applies to the "lore of several cultures" (9) – it applies to all human societies. Being "both the law and its transgression" (10), this woman is the keeper of a tradition to which she at the same time contributes what T. S. Eliot would call her "individual talent."[12] She preserves and she makes new in order for the heritage to survive. Her blindness is only at first sight a "profound disability" – it also stands for the "clairvoyance" of the traditional *seer* (10). Cognizant of history and the past, she is not distracted by the perceptualist logic[13] of what Morrison terms "spectacle" or "gazeability" in the Simpson piece. Her vision is one of *knowledge*, i.e., it is precisely a cognitive one. The old woman's treatment of language is not phenomenological; it does not follow the logic of phenomena but engages in human behavior.

"It is in your hands," is what she says about the children's bird (11). Language depends on responsible agency: "Being a writer, she thinks of language partly as a system, partly as a living thing over which one has control, but mostly as agency – as an act with consequences" (13). This is why she argues against the irresponsibility of a "dead language," what she calls a "statist language" (13) because it "suppresses human potential" (14). The fact that such language can do "violence" implies an intimate connection with the extra-linguistic world – language is always part of a process of human interaction at its origin: "Sexist language, racist language, theistic language – all are typical of the policing languages of mastery, and cannot, do not, permit new knowledge or encourage the mutual exchange of ideas" (16–17). Hence, language that is severed from its living use is deadly.

Like many critics today, Morrison acknowledges the grammatological powers of structure, but her main aim is to expose this aspect as a problem rather than as an epistemological origin. She regrets the "lethal discourses of exclusion blocking access to cognition for both the excluder and the excluded" (19). Her language is a door to the mind, and the reason why a monolithic language fails (Morrison uses the example of the Tower of Babel) is the simple fact that "heaven," the superstructure, must be imagined at one's "feet": "Perhaps the achievement of Paradise was premature, a little hasty if no one could take the time to understand other languages, other views, other narratives" (19). When she suggests "a view of heaven as life," she implies biology as a crucial ingredient of language. "The vitality of language" means that it can "limn the actual, imagined and possible lives of its speakers, readers, writers" (20). Though "displacing experience," it cannot be "a substitute for it" (20). Though acknowledging what deconstructionists would consider "deferral," Morrison rather points beyond language as a hermeneutic chain of signifiers and suggests that linguistic incompleteness be complemented by the user – in a model that corresponds to a feedback loop.

Morrison's example of such language use is Lincoln's "Gettysburg Address," in which he states that the world will not "remember what we say here" but "what they did here." "Language can never 'pin down' slavery, genocide, war," says Morrison. "Nor should it yearn for the arrogance to do so. Its force, its felicity, is in its reach towards the ineffable" (20–21). And this "ineffable" is inevitably cognitive. Morrison suggests deference rather than deferral, respect for the other subjectivity in language, for the intentionality, the motivation, the knowledge described. The "generative" element in word-work is not found in its grammar but in its securing of our "difference, our human difference" (22). Language is something that "we do," Morrison insists – this is why it "may be the measure of our lives" (22). It is about concepts measuring life, not concepts measuring concepts only.

In the second part of her Nobel Lecture, Morrison changes to the perspective of the children, testing the relevance of such a live heritage. They have a right to question their elders: "You trivialize us and trivialize the bird that is not in our hands" (27). There is a receiving end in Morrison's narrative, i.e., her model of understanding is personified: "Think of our lives and tell us your particularized world" (27). They do not want the closure of a blueprint, but rather want to be shown "belief's wide skirt and the stitch that unravels fear's caul" (28), which is why they insist that her blindness is a blessing: she can "speak the language that tells us what only language can: how to see without pictures. Language alone protects us from the scariness of things with no names. Language alone is meditation" (28). Language can free us from the powerful onslaught of visual totalizing because it can register things not seen, such as the knowledge of the past, and it makes possible "mediation," i.e., a negotiation of multiple influences, reflection, control over one's experience.

Morrison ends this dense text with the epiphanic scene of "a wagonload of slaves" arriving at an inn in a winter environment reminiscent of Eliot's "Journey of the Magi."[14] It exorcises Faulkner's image in an encounter of the slaves with a girl and a boy who offer them food and drink, "and something more: a glance into the eyes of the one she serves" (30). Morrison emphasizes that "look" and the "look back," which "warm" their stop. The final episode in this essay about language insists on its social nature. It is about interaction, recognition, respect,[15] striving for a redeeming communion of equals. Similarly, the moment of encounter between the *griot* and the children means that they have "truly caught" the bird – this encounter is what the ineffable of language refers to.

The Dancing Mind

In *The Dancing Mind*[16] Morrison again uses this fundamentally egalitarian and empowering image of dialogic interaction, a behavioral model of human encounter, and applies it to both the acts of writing and of reading. "There is a certain kind of peace," she writes, "that is not merely the absence of war" (7). Thus we see her break out of a given binary (war vs. peace) and looking for an alternative: "The peace I am thinking of is the dance of an open mind when it engages another equally open one" (7). She liberates the notion of peace from its supplementary position as absence of activity and redefines it as an alternative activity of dancing, a pleasurable agency of interaction and cooperation.

Morrison's conceptual alternative is not based on "active negation" but on "passive negation."[17] An active negation would be defined by its opposition to what it stands against – "peace" as the other of "war," the dominant concept to which it is functionally attached and on which it is dependent. Passive negation conversely does not let itself be defined by what it opposes – the oppositional aspect is not part of the alternative; it is merely perceived as such when the two notions are compared. Rather than opposition, we have difference – thus passive negation is actually a positive "affirmation" in its own right. Whereas active negation is the product of a closed gestalt of conceptualist logic,[18] passive negation is a matter of pragmatics and language use. It simply stands for the open possibilities of variety, of multiple positivity.

This does, of course, involve agency on all sides and therefore moves beyond representational structures into cognitive processes. The stress is not on language determining behavior but on behavior within language. Thus even writing and reading, the interior moments when a human being is together with a text, are defined as dialogic. Morrison regrets that "to be alone with a book" is a lost "skill" (10). She attributes this to an educational system of top-down discursive control that she calls "the terror of growing up vacuum-pressured in this country" and sees as a danger "even to the entitled" (13). She rather wants textual encounters to be encounters of minds, "that intimate, sustained surrender to the company of my own mind while it touches another's – which is reading" (15). Note that this is "surrender" to company (personification) and interaction (dialogue).

It is significantly different from, say, the experience described in George Poulet's classical description of the "Phenomenology of Reading":

> As soon as I replace my direct perception of reality by the words of a book, I deliver myself, bound hand and foot, to the omnipotence of fiction . . . I become the prey of language. There is no escaping this take-over. Language surrounds me with its unreality . . . I am the subject of thoughts other than my own. My consciousness behaves as though it were the consciousness of another.
>
> This is mere reflection. In a sense I must recognize that no idea really belongs to me. Ideas belong to no one. They pass from one mind to another as coins pass from hand to hand.[19]

This is no experience of dialogue but an experience of possession by another. Morrison is unwilling to submit to such a format. She knows that ideas are not a matter of mere neutral *exchange value* ("coins") but always belong to the person whose ideology they reflect. Moreover, as an African American she is wary[20] of the controlling power of ideas. In the black animist tradition, ideas behave like the "invisibles," the selfish *loas*, when the Voodoo gods, or "laws," try to control people in acts of literal physical "possession." These ideas must be negotiated with by the *houngan* or *mamba*, the priest or priestess, whose medicine is precisely powerful because they can stand up to these possessive voices with their *connaissance*, i.e., with their knowledge of ideologies and their ability to negotiate (this is also implied by the griot of her Nobel Lecture). Hence the art of Morrison's "surrender" in the act of reading is to let it happen while not letting it become overwhelming.

In this speech to the National Book Foundation Morrison emphasizes "the seriousness of the industry" (15). She makes clear that there is a political responsibility in the encounter of reader and writer in the text, i.e., in "the life of the book world": "Its real life is about creating and producing and distributing knowledge; about making it possible for the entitled as well as the dispossessed to experience one's own mind dancing with another's; about making sure that the environment in which this work is done is welcoming, supportive" (16). This pledge can be read as a reminder to the publishing world to make the encounter of minds possible, to secure cognitive agency: "Securing that kind of peace – the peace of the dancing mind – is our work" (17). As Lakoff and Johnson argue in their cognitive linguistics manifesto, we "live by" metaphorical concepts, and there is a crucial difference whether we define our arguments in terms of war (and peace) or as a matter of "dance."[21]

"Home"

The essay "Home"[22] both confirms many of the observations already made above and adds to them by clarifying some of the political dimensions in the context of "race." Morrison tries to imagine "a-world-in-which-race-does-not-matter" (3), and the metaphor she comes up with is a "home" rather than a "house." She likes the term "home" because it helps her "domesticate" the racial issue and turns the utopian project into "a manageable, doable, modern human activity" (4). Morrison has no delusions about "agency," "sovereignty," or "authority":

> As an already- and always-raced writer, I knew from the very beginning that I could not, would not, reproduce the master's voice and its assumption of the all-knowing law of the white father. Nor would I substitute his voice with that of his fawning mistress or his worthy opponent, for both of these positions (mistress or opponent) seemed to confine me to his terrain, in his arena, accepting the house rules in the dominance game. (4)

Note Morrison's preoccupation with the problem of gestalt logic in a spatial environment, one that would force her into active negation: "In short, wasn't I (wouldn't I always be) tethered to a death-dealing ideology even (and especially) when I honed all my intelligence toward subverting it?" (4–5). She is afraid of being merely reactive in her intellectual enterprise, and of becoming the victim of an active negation that eclipses her own self. Or, to express this in the terminology of postcolonial theory: Morrison does not want to "write back" to the colonizing discourse and then find herself victimized by a theory that locates, once again, the colonizer at the center of an inverted map![23] It is crucial that this gesture of active negation be avoided.

"Home" means that she wants to have her written encounters on her own territory, to be her own mind rather than the supplement of somebody else's. In that sense, Morrison is a Bakhtinian, as Justine Tally has suggested.[24] Bakhtin's arguments for the cognitive humanism of the dialogic and against the logical abstractions of the dialectic[25] are also hers, and that precisely because Morrison wants to avoid the pitfalls of active negation, which is dehumanizing and depriving the "other" of his or her own cognitive agency. An example of this kind of problem in the imagination of what she calls "Western hegemony" (11) can be found at the *Negerball* of a European carnival. We will not learn much about blacks there: we will merely learn about "the other" as a carnivalesque projection of disguises. Though we may encounter some African stereotypes, the *Neger* part of the event will include men dressed up as ladies, cowboys, Chinese, beggars, animals, and generally symbols of otherness. This kind of negativity is already conceptualized; these figures are not concept-making – they have no mind of their own. My point is that in their negativity such projections merely reflect the cognitive agency of one side – hence the "incoherence" of the other side. The "black irrationality" Morrison found in the "official" stories of the Clarence Thomas hearings and the O. J. Simpson trial is informed by *Negerball* semiotics. Rather than *represent* the other, one should *talk to* "them" in order to learn about their inside, the reasonings of their mind – which involves a framework of personifying dialogue.

Morrison's example of cross-influence in "Home" is how she changed one word in the last sentence of *Beloved* at the suggestion of her editor. This triggers a process of reflection in which she states: "My efforts were to carve away the accretions of deceit, blindness, ignorance, paralysis, and sheer malevolence embedded in raced language so that other kinds of perception were not only available but were inevitable" (7). Writing in a non-racial language is impossible: this "register of permanently unrealizable dream" would allow "racism an intellectual weight to which it has absolutely no claim" (8). Hence the ultimate political gesture is to voice the other as a self.

This is why "home" is more important than "theory": "We need to think about how invested some of the best theoretical work may be in clinging to the house's redesign as simulacrum" (8). Theory means following the logic of your premises when they no longer refer to reality. The need for a "nonmessianic language" (11) opposes the dialectical mode of a totalizing gestalt. Submitting theory to the dialogue of a conference may even, as she insists, "save our lives" (11). Because we "live by" these terms, as Lakoff and Johnson would have it, we have to discuss them, negotiate them, remake them within a pragmatic context.

I find Morrison here in the tradition of the pragmatist philosopher and cognitive psychologist William James, who insists that theory cannot match experience. A cognitive model is human, conversational, but not limited to logic: "Reality, life, experience, concreteness, immediacy, use what word you will, exceeds our logic, overflows and surrounds it."[26] Tracing experience, language is used and at the same time overcome: "I want to inhabit, walk around, a site clear of racist detritus, a place where race both matters and is rendered impotent" (9). This is her vision of a "social space that is psychically and physically safe" (10). And, most important, this "new space" is "formed by the inwardness of the outside, the interiority of the 'othered,' the personal that is always embedded in the public" (12). The "safety without walls" Morrison envisages is one of interaction between the personal and the public, where the personal may not be primary, but it is priority, a place "both snug and wide open" – "home" as a comfortable space of encounter, beyond alienation.

At the core of Morrison's concerns in her social criticism are logical snares of representation. They have to be pointed out because they dominate the media, the political debates and agendas, and they are abused for reasons of power, racism, and, sometimes, sheer ignorance. Moreover, many of these images also determine our internalized discourses, our own thinking, writing, reading. It is at this cognitive core of mental human agency where Morrison is most political, when she unpacks the modalities, incompatibilities, the contradictions, and the injustices, and effectively demonstrates how exactly they "measure" our lives (*Nobel Lecture*, 22).

NOTES

1. Toni Morrison, *The Nobel Lecture in Literature*, 1993 (London: Chatto & Windus, 1994), p. 22 (original italics). All other references to this essay will be included within the text.
2. See the subtitle of Morrison's book on the Clarence Thomas hearing (note 7 below).
3. See Toni Morrison, *Song of Solomon* (London: Chatto & Windus, 1978), pp. 59–60.
4. I am borrowing this notion from George Lakoff and Mark Johnson, *Philosophy in the Flesh: The Embodied Mind and Its Challenge to Western Thought* (New York: Basic Books, 1999).
5. Here I am borrowing from Jacques Derrida, *Of Grammatology* (1967), trans. Gayatri Chakravorty Spivak (Baltimore: Johns Hopkins University Press, 1974).
6. Cornel West, *Race Matters* (Boston: Beacon Press, 1993).
7. Toni Morrison, "Introduction: Friday on the Potomac," *Race-ing Justice, Engendering Power. Essays on Anita Hill, Clarence Thomas, and the Construction of Social Reality*, ed. Toni Morrison (London: Chatto & Windus, 1993), pp. vii–xxx. All other references to this essay will be included within the text.

8. See my definition of these two concepts in Sämi Ludwig, *Pragmatist Realism: the Cognitive Paradigm in American Realist Texts* (Madison: University of Wisconsin Press, 2002), pp. 3–4.

9. Toni Morrison, "The Official Story: Dead Man Golfing," *Birth of a Nation'hood: Gaze, Script, and Spectacle in the O. J. Simpson Case*, ed. Toni Morrison and Claudia Brodsky Lacour (New York: Pantheon Books, 1997), pp. vii–xxviii. All other references to this essay will be included within the text.

10. See Jean Baudrillard, "The Precession of Simulacra" (1981), *Simulacra and Simulation*, trans. Sheila Faria Glaser (Ann Arbor: University of Michigan Press, 1994), pp. 1–42.

11. The origin of this terminology can be found in Jean Piaget's cognitive psychology, which has revolutionized the modern psychology of learning; see Dorothy G. Singer and Tracy A. Revenson, *A Piaget Primer: How a Child Thinks* (New York: Plume, 1996), p. 15. Piaget's operational cognitive model is based on the interaction of a living organism within the environment.

12. See T. S. Eliot, "Tradition and the Individual Talent" (1919), *Selected Essays* (London: Faber & Faber, 1951), pp. 13–22.

13. See my discussion of pictorial conceptualizing in *Pragmatist Realism*, "Beyond Binary Perceptualism," pp. 37–39.

14. T. S. Eliot, "Journey of the Magi" (1927), *Collected Poems, 1909–1962* (London: Faber & Faber, 1963), pp. 109–110.

15. The "look back" is an important image here; also see the photograph of an Igorot man used by James Clifford in order to demonstrate a notion of ethnographic *égalité* in his discussion of Victor Segalen. James Clifford, *The Predicament of Culture. Twentieth-Century Ethnography, Literature, and Art* (Cambridge, MA: Harvard University Press, 1988), p. 164.

16. Toni Morrison, *The Dancing Mind: Speech Upon Acceptance of the National Book Foundation Medal for Distinguished Contribution to American Letters* (New York: Alfred A. Knopf, 1996). All other references to this essay will be included within the text.

17. I am borrowing this terminology from John Elster, "Active and Passive Negation: an Essay in Ibanskian Sociology," *The Invented Reality: How Do We Know What We Believe We Know? (Contributions to Constructivism)*, ed. Paul Watzlawick (New York: Norton, 1984), pp. 175–206.

18. Like the "ground" in a gestalt, active negation is determined by the foregrounded shape of a predominant "figure." It merely traces an argument given by the preceding part.

19. George Poulet, "Phenomenology of Reading," *New Literary History* 1 (1969): 55–56.

20. She uses the word "vigilance" (7).

21. George Lakoff and Mark Johnson, *Metaphors We Live By* (Chicago and London: University of Chicago Press, 1980).

22. Toni Morrision, "Home," *The House That Race Built: Original Essays by Toni Morrison, Angela Y. Davis, Cornel West, and Others on Black Americans and Politics in America Today*, ed. Wahneema Lubiano (New York: Vintage, 1998), pp. 3–12. All other references to this essay will be included within the text.

23. My example for this fallacy is the seminal text in postcolonial theory by Bill Ashcroft, Gareth Griffiths, and Helen Tiffin, *The Empire Writes Back*.

Theory and Practice in Post-Colonial Literatures (London, New York: Routledge, 1989).

24. See Justine Tally, *The Story of "Jazz" : Toni Morrison's Dialogic Imagination* (Hamburg: Lit, 2001).

25. See M. M. Bakhtin, *Speech Genres and Other Late Essays*, trans. Vern W. McGee, ed. Caryl Emerson and Michael Holquist (Austin: University of Texas Press, 1986), p. 147.

26. William James, *A Pluralistic Universe* (1909), ed. Fredson Bowers and Ignas K. Skrupskelis (Cambridge, MA: Harvard University Press, 1977), p. 96. This is why James even warns of "intellectualism" as "vicious" (p. 99).

10

CHERYL A. WALL

Toni Morrison, editor and teacher

Toni Morrison has described writing as the work she could not live without, but she has also expressed the "*huge* joy" she took in her work as an editor.[1] She edited a range of books, fiction and non-fiction, poetry and prose, on subjects ranging from abortion rights to reparations. But she took particular pride in what she called her contribution to "the shelf," that is, to the tradition of African American literature. She believed that her presence in the offices of Random House, where she served as senior editor from 1970 to 1988, assured the black author who walked through the door "that he doesn't have to explain everything – somebody is going to understand what he's trying to do, in his terms, not in somebody else's, but in his."[2] Among the writers to whom she conveyed this assurance were Toni Cade Bambara, Wesley Brown, Lucille Clifton, Leon Forrest, Gayl Jones, Nettie Jones, June Jordan, John McCluskey, and Quincy Troupe. No other editor before Morrison or since has boasted a comparable list of African American writers. As an editor, she helped to define two decades of African American literary history.

Although they do not share a common aesthetics the writers on Morrison's roster share a common sensibility which is preoccupied with "the kind of information you can find between the lines of history. It sort of falls off the page, or it's a glance and a reference. It's right there in the intersection where an institution becomes personal, where the historical becomes people with names."[3] Whether it is Bambara's description of the Harlem woman who arranges a field trip for the children on her block to the Fifth Avenue toy store F. A. O. Schwarz to teach them a lesson about race and class, or Brown's account of the "tragic magic," the cool machismo of young black urban men that both preserves their selfhood and dooms them to violent deaths, they reveal cultures and communities observed with care from the inside.[4]

One of the first titles on Morrison's list was Toni Cade Bambara's now classic book of short stories, *Gorilla, My Love* (1972). The girls who move through the pages of these stories are a new kind of female protagonist:

fearless and bold, feisty and articulate. Under various aliases (Scout, Peaches, and Badbird), Hazel appears in four stories, including the one that gives the volume its title. In each story, Hazel refuses to yield her sense of right and wrong even when – or especially when – her views are challenged by those in authority. Her moral vision is the source of her self-confidence. Her disgust with the adult world stems from the failure of adults to live up to the standards of honesty, integrity, and self-respect that Hazel demands of herself. In the sharpness of her social critique, Hazel is sister to Claudia, the sometimes narrator of Morrison's *The Bluest Eye*. Yet Hazel's voice is distinctively her own; Bambara has perfect pitch for the edgy urban idiom she gives her characters.

Morrison edited a second volume of Bambara's short stories, *The Sea Birds Are Still Alive* (1977), as well as her two novels, *The Salt Eaters* (1980) and *Those Bones Are Not My Child*, published posthumously in 1999. *The Salt Eaters* is a dazzlingly dense novel that many regard as Bambara's artistic triumph; it achieves "the boldness and design" that Bambara defines as "black genius." Musicians are the exemplars of genius as they perform "on the stand with no luggage and no maps and ready to go anywhere in the universe together on just sheer holy boldness."[5] Structured like a jazz fugue, *The Salt Eaters* begins with a question, "Are you sure, sweetheart, that you want to be well?" The cure fuses politics and spirituality. Challenging in its themes and experimental in form, *The Salt Eaters* was a commercial failure. But its impact on subsequent black writing is significant.

After Bambara's death in 1995, Morrison called her work "absolutely critical to twentieth-century literature."[6] She acted on those words when she edited *Those Bones*, an epic novel that represents the rash of child murders in Atlanta that occurred in the 1980s. Although her style is realist and almost documentary in its depiction of the range of residents that people the city, Bambara approaches the subject by imagining the most intimate details of a fictional family whose son is caught up in the terror. As editor, Morrison culled the novel from eighteen hundred pages of manuscript.

Like Bambara, Leon Forrest might be described as a writer's writer. His novels are set in the fictional counterpart of Chicago that he calls Forest County. Rooted equally in history and myth, they focus on specific incidents in the life of Nathaniel Turner Witherspoon, for example the death of his mother in *There is a Tree More Ancient than Eden* (1973) and his discovery of the family's history of enslavement in *The Bloodworth Orphans* (1977). Like Morrison's, these narratives draw from a deep well of literary traditions. In a chorus of voices and through multi-layered perspectives – shifting among dreams, nightmares, legends, sermons, and monologues – Forrest's novels explore a complex past with a technique as intricate as their subject. Forrest, who credits Morrison with suggesting titles for his novels, admired her work as editor. "She was an excellent line editor," because "she, too, is very much caught up in language." Remembering what a "tough fight" it was to get his books published, he conceded that "at the time I could not have done it without Morrison's help. She was indispensable."[7]

Lucille Clifton, who met Morrison when they were both undergraduates at Howard University, published *Good Times*, her first volume of poetry, in 1969. In spare, blues-inflected lines, her lyrics evoked life "in the inner city." Sharply observed portraits of Clifton's parents, of the bag lady "Miss Rosie," and of Buffalo soldiers – the young men standing idly on the street corners of the post-industrial city with no war to fight – recall the vignettes of Gwendolyn Brooks's 1945 classic, *A Street in Bronzeville*. But unlike Brooks's sonnets and ballads, Clifton's free verse stylizes 1960s' black vernacular speech. Morrison edited two other volumes of Clifton's poetry, *Good News About the Earth* (1972) and *An Ordinary Woman* (1974). However, like most poetry published in the United States, they did not sell. Morrison urged Clifton to try her hand at prose. To begin the project Clifton envisioned, Morrison suggested she tape-record the family stories she remembered.[8] The result was the stunning 1976 memoir, *Generations*. Charting the genealogy of her family back to her African foremother, *Generations* recuperates memories in words and photographs. The language of the text draws on a range of influences from the King James Bible to Walt Whitman's *Song of Myself*, as well as the rhythms and repetitions of black oral tradition. *Generations* anticipates the intensifying impulse among African American writers to reconnect with an African heritage undocumented in written history. That impulse animated many signal novels of the 1970s and 1980s, including Morrison's own *Song of Solomon* and *Beloved*.

Poet June Jordan, known for passionate, polemical, and oracular verse, reveals a more intimate side in the volume, *Things that I Do in the Dark: Selected Poems*. Dedicated to "the liberation of all my love" and to the memories of her parents, the volume selects poems inspired by their lives and meditative lyrics reflecting Jordan's sabbatical in Rome as well as poems responding to the Watergate scandals and the assassination of Martin Luther King. The acknowledgment reads in part "with gratitude for the beautiful work of the writer Toni Morrison, who as my editor, kept on believing this book into print."[9]

Morrison believed that African American writers could and should be read in multiple contexts, as the five-hundred-page volume, *Giant Talk: An Anthology of Third World Writing*, affirmed. Edited by African American poet Quincy Troupe and the German-born poet and translator Rainer Schulte, the volume defined Third World writers in terms of consciousness rather than race, class, geography, or nation. These writers identify with "the historically exploited segment of mankind, and confront the establishment on their behalf."[10] Men and women from almost every continent who write in diverse languages and various genres are represented. *Giant Talk* is divided into sections that designate what Troupe and Schulte call the "phases" through which Third World writing developed. Beginning with the oppression and protest that are the initial impetus for the writing, the phases move through the violence that is the consequence; a crisis of identity; the exploration of music, language and rhythm; an ironic humor that distance provides, ritual and magic, and conceptualization and abstraction. *Giant Talk* includes a particularly rich sampling of African American writers, including almost all of those on Morrison's list. Selections from Bambara, Clifton, Forrest, and Jones appear alongside those from Pablo Neruda, Wole Soyinka, Derek Walcott, and May Wong.

Morrison was a hands-on editor who was closely involved with every step of the publishing process from acquisition to marketing. Not only did she feel herself to be a kindred spirit to other artists, she believed her perspective as an editor gave her a privileged vantage point from which to appreciate both the author and the text. For example, she worked closely with Gayl Jones to bring her first novel *Corregidora* to print. In an interview with Michael Harper, Jones remembered how Morrison urged her to "clarify the relationships between Ursa and her mother and between Ursa and Mutt."[11] In the process of writing, Jones read Morrison's *Sula*, a novel that opened the path for Jones to complete her own. In subsequent interviews, Morrison analyzes the achievement of *Corregidora*, by suggesting that Jones took "a large idea," the history of slavery, and "brought it down small, and at home, which gives it a universality and a particularity which makes it extraordinary."[12]

Not all of Morrison's important editing projects were literary; she made other key interventions in African American intellectual history. As one might expect, *Angela Davis: An Autobiography* chronicles the allegations of conspiracy against the activist, her flight, capture, arrest, trial, and eventual acquittal. But it gives equal weight to a careful exposition of the professor's political philosophy. Davis's *Women, Race, and Class* is a foundational work of feminist scholarship that deploys race, class, and gender as interlocking factors in the history of black women; it also develops a comparative analysis of black and white women's experiences. Ivan Van Sertima's controversial book *They Came Before Columbus* argues that Africans traveled to the Western Hemisphere before the age of European exploration.

The book that attracted the most publicity and generated the best sales was, appropriately enough, Muhammad Ali, *The Greatest, My Own Story* (1975), written with Richard Durham. After being barred from the ring for draft evasion, the boxer had regained the world heavyweight championship in October 1974, with an eighth-round knockout of George Foreman in Kinshasa, Zaire. Riding an ever-higher crest of fame, Ali made international appearances on behalf of the book, including one at the Frankfurt Book Fair.

Perhaps the most singular project that Morrison undertook was *The Black Book*, published in 1974. In an article for the *New York Times Magazine*, she outlined the vision that inspired it:

> Like every other book, it would be confined by a cover and limited to type. Nevertheless, it had to have – for want of a better word – a sound, a very special sound. A sound made up of all the elements that distinguished black life (its peculiar brand of irony, oppression, versatility, madness, joy, strength, shame, honor, triumph, grace and stillness) as well as those qualities that identified it with all of mankind (compassion, anger, foolishness, courage, self-deception and vision). And it must concentrate on life as lived – not as imagined – by the people: the anonymous men and women who speak in conventional histories only through their leaders. The people who had always been viewed only as percentages would come alive in "The Black Book."[13]

Many commentators and the author herself have characterized Morrison's greatest novel in quite similar terms.

The Black Book is a source for *Beloved* in a very specific sense. It reprints an article titled "A Visit to the Slave Mother Who Killed Her Child," a contemporary account of Margaret Garner's crime and punishment, the historical event that is the kernel of the plot of *Beloved*. In "Rediscovering Black History," Morrison recounts her response to the article: "I . . . lived through a despair quite new to me but so deep it had no passion at all and elicited no tears."[14]

But beyond its specific allusion, *The Black Book* represents a model for reconstructing the past that is topological, interactive, and communal. A fictional reimagining rather than a historical reconstruction, *Beloved* shares these same qualities. Both challenge conventional, historical discourse. Both determine to excavate the lives of the anonymous black folk who have been "disremembered and unaccounted for."[15] Both reflect what Morrison views as the necessity for black people "to find some way to hold on to the useful past without blocking off the possibilities of the future."[16]

Published after the Civil Rights movement had gone into eclipse and in the waning years of the Black Power movement, *The Black Book* was intended in part as a corrective, particularly to rhetoric that had grown more and more disparaging of "the Negro" and his history. It sought to bring honor to those whose courage and bravery had been dismissed, overlooked, or misunderstood. It sought, moreover, to honor those who had not perceived themselves to be heroic. Their self-understanding could be summed up in the words of an epigraph to a photograph of a black cowboy, "we was mostly 'bout survival / 'Bout living anyhow."[17] Although it included artifacts belonging to the famous (such as a handwritten letter from Frederick Douglass to an acquaintance who wished him well on the occasion of his controversial second marriage to a white woman, and a letter to W. E. B. Du Bois from a white academic who inquired whether the Negro sheds tears), its focus was on those whose lives and deeds had been lost to history. To its readers, *The Black Book* was a call to remember.

Generically, *The Black Book* can be described as a scrapbook; it documents the history of African Americans through posters, newspaper articles, letters, speeches, bills of sale, spirituals and blues, work songs and folktales, children's rhymes, drawings, advertisements, photographs (both family pictures and documentary photographs of quilts, tools, furniture, and other artifacts), recipes, patent applications, sheet music, playbills and movie stills, formulas for conjure, and dream interpretations. In a Whitmanesque conceit, *The Black Book* subsumes the experience of the group in a collective "I." Neither a vehicle of social protest nor a compilation of individual achievement, the volume announces itself on the back jacket as "everything I have hated . . . , all the ways I have failed . . . , all the ways I have survived . . . , all the things I have seen . . . , and all the things I have ever loved." It becomes, in other words, a "memory book" for African Americans.[18]

If it documents the creativity of black Americans as expressed through story and song, *The Black Book* also records their victimization during and after slavery. If it celebrates African American ingenuity as documented by patents filed for the fountain pen, clothes-drier, airship, lawn-sprinkler, eggbeater, hot comb, and corn-harvester, it also documents the ways in which African American bodies and personae were debased and caricatured to sell products from Sunlight soap to Aunt Jemima pancakes. If it documents political resistance in black communities from nineteenth-century slave uprisings to abolitionism to twentieth-century Civil Rights activism, it also reproduces pages from the family Bible of black slave owners. The evidence of self-hatred and betrayal it offers intensifies the power of the final selection of photographs and drawings of individuals and groups of individuals, a gallery of family pictures, as it were, that signify love and kinship.

Significantly, as Morrison emphasizes in the *Times* article, "Rediscovering Black History," *The Black Book* "was not a book to be put together by writers," but by "collectors – people who had the original raw material documenting our life" (16). Authorial credit for *The Black Book* went to Middleton Harris, "with the assistance of Morris Levitt, Roger Furman, and Ernest Smith." Morrison was the in-house editor. Despite the fact that it does not carry her signature, Toni Morrison's engagement with *The Black Book* was intense. She told one newspaper reporter that "nothing could have interfered with my putting this book together."[19] In "Rediscovering Black History," she begins a passage describing in the first person the need to recover a usable past and the genesis of the project ("Because of the work I do, my thoughts turned naturally to a book. But a book with a difference"). Then she shifts pronouns: "We called it 'The Black Book'" (16). The "we" included the authors, the designer, the production manager, and Morrison, who "built the book, item by item," producing in the end "an organic book which made up its own rules" (16).

Those "rules" complemented the aesthetic that Morrison was shaping in her fiction. Like Langston Hughes, Zora Neale Hurston, Ralph Ellison, and Amiri Baraka before her, Morrison formulated a literary aesthetic from her study of and appreciation for African American art in general and African American music in particular. Her formulations, shared mainly in interviews, have been remarkably consistent for three decades. In one statement, she averred, "If my work is faithfully to reflect the aesthetic tradition of Afro-American culture, it must make conscious use of the characteristics of its art forms and translate them into print: antiphony, the group nature of art, its functionality, its improvisational nature, its relationship to audience performance."[20] To achieve the last and, "having at my disposal only the letters of the alphabet and some punctuation," she explained on another occasion, "I have to provide places and spaces so that the reader can partic-ipate. Because it is the affective and participatory relationship between the artist or the speaker and the audience that is of primary importance, as it is in these other art forms that I have described."[21] *The Black Book* aspires to the same standard. Indeed, its accretion of facts and images does not constitute a narrative; instead it invites readers to construct narratives of their own.

The published book contains traces of Morrison's personal investment. Her parents, Ramah and George Carl Wofford, are among those acknowl-edged for their contributions to the text "with stories, pictures, recollections and general aid." A small oval photograph of her mother appears on the cover, surrounded by a playbill from a show starring Ethel Waters and two other images of Waters from early and late in her career as well as a Sambo doll; Ramah Wofford's photograph is also among the family pictures repro-duced on the closing pages.

The Black Book was marketed to a mass audience: the paperback edition was priced at $5.95, and the book contained an introduction, conversational in tone, by television star Bill Cosby. Cosby began with a conceit of his own: "suppose a three-hundred-year-old black man had decided, oh, say, when he was about ten, to keep a scrapbook . . ." His description of the book as "a folk journey of Black America" underscored its non-academic appeal. "Folk" also suggested that the book was more than merely a commercial venture; it hoped to reach an audience beyond the traditional book-buying public. Finally, the adjective "folk" aptly conveyed the sense that this book not only documented a shared experience, it could be read as one. Even the dimensions of the book (8 ¼ by 11 ½ inches) welcomed more than one reader at a time. Rather than encouraging reading as a solitary practice, *The Black Book* was designed to replicate the interactive dynamic of storytelling. This dynamic is, of course, evident throughout *Beloved*. As she relates the narrative of her birth, Denver, who is one of the novel's finest storytellers, enacts the process: "Denver was seeing it now and feeling it – through Beloved. Feeling how it must have felt to her mother. Seeing how it must have looked. And the more fine points she made, the more detail she provided, the more Beloved liked it. So she anticipated the questions by giving blood to the *scraps* [emphasis added] her mother and grandmother had told her – and a heartbeat. The monologue became, in fact, a duet" (*Beloved*, 78). If its producers were collectors, readers of *The Black Book* were invited to recollect, to give "blood to the scraps" it contained. They could fill in the gaps, add fine points, and provide details that were part of no official history, the details to which only they and their relatives were privy. Told in response to a book that provided countless occasions for recollections of kin, their narratives become the book's "heartbeat."

In addition to her careers as novelist and editor, Morrison has also been an influential teacher. After earning the MA at Cornell University, she taught for two years at Texas Southern University in Houston and then for five years at her alma mater, Howard University. Her classes at Howard included the freshman humanities course that surveyed the masterpieces of Western literature from Greek and Roman mythology to the King James Bible to twentieth-century novels. Her students included future autobiographer Claude Brown and Student Non-Violent Coordinating Committee leader Stokely Carmichael. Philosophical questions of freedom and love raised by the literature resonated in the context of the Civil Rights movement, questions Morrison would eventually explore in her fiction.

Yet she never left the classroom. In the 1970s she started teaching black women writers and creative writing at Yale. During the next decade, she also taught at the State University of New York at Purchase, Bard College, and the State University of New York at Albany. In 1989 she became the Robert F. Goheen Professor of Humanities at Princeton. There, after teaching African American literature, she tried out the ideas of the Africanist presence in American literature that became the core of her influential volume, *Playing in the Dark*. Her abiding curiosity about the creative process led her in 1994 to develop the Atelier Project that brought together guest artists from different media on campus for an intensive, in-residence collaborative effort with each other and with faculty and students. The focus of the Atelier is on the process of creating a work of art rather than on the finished product, and guest artists must bring to campus an idea they want to create, explore, and develop. Participants have included choreographer Jacques d'Amboises, cellist Yo-Yo Ma, composer Richard Danielpour, filmmaker Louis Massiah, and novelists A. S. Byatt and Gabriel Garcia Marquez. In June 2006, Morrison retired from the faculty at Princeton.

As a teacher as well as a public intellectual, Morrison speaks eloquently in support of the role of higher education in a democratic culture. She recognizes how embattled that role now is, when she poses this challenge: "If the university does not take seriously and rigorously its role as guardian of wider civic freedoms, as interrogator of more and more complex ethical problems, as servant and preserver of deeper democratic practices, then some other regime or ménage of regimes will do it for us, in spite of us, and without us."[22] Given the rise of reactionary politics in the United States at the turn of the twenty-first century, the mission of the university has become even more urgent. But the response to Morrison's clarion call is as yet unclear.

Reflecting on her multi-faceted career, Morrison has mused, "I know it seems like a lot . . . But I really only do one thing. I read books. I teach books. I think about books. It's one job."[23] Through that one job, Morrison has transformed the literary and intellectual culture of her time.

NOTES

1. Robert Stepto, "'Intimate Things in Place': a Conversation with Toni Morrison," *Chant of Saints*, ed. Michael Harper and Robert Stepto (Urbana: University of Illinois Press, 1979), pp. 224, 229.
2. *Ibid.*, p. 229.
3. Toni Morrison, "The Art of Fiction CXXXIV," *Paris Review*, 128 (Fall 1993):105.
4. See Toni Cade Bambara, "The Lesson," *Gorilla, My Love* (New York: Random House, 1972); and Wesley Brown, *Tragic Magic* (New York: Random House, 1978).
5. Toni Cade Bambara, *The Salt Eaters* (1980. New York: Vintage Contemporaries Edition, 1992), p. 265.
6. Valerie Boyd, "'She Was Outrageously Brilliant': Toni Morrison Remembers Toni Cade Bambara," *Savoring the Salt: The Legacy of Toni Cade Bambara*, ed. Linda J. Holmes and Cheryl A. Wall (Philadelphia: Temple University Press, 2008).
7. John G. Cawleti, ed., *Leon Forrest: Introductions and Interpretations* (Bowling Green, OH: Bowling Green University Popular Press, 1997), pp. 289, 288.
8. Charles Rowell, "An Interview with Lucille Clifton," *Callaloo*, 22.1 (1999): 56.

9. June Jordan, *Things that I Do in the Dark* (New York: Random House, 1977), p. xi.

10. Quincy Troupe and Rainer Schulte, eds., *Giant Talk: An Anthology of Third World Writing* (New York: Random House, 1975), p. xxiii.

11. Michael Harper, "Gayl Jones: an Interview," in *Chant of Saints*, ed. Harper and Stepto, p. 360.

12. Stepto, "Intimate Things," p. 229.

13. Toni Morrison, "Rediscovering Black History," *New York Times Magazine* (August 11, 1974): 16.

14. *Ibid.*

15. Toni Morrison, *Beloved* (New York: Knopf, 1987), p. 274.

16. Morrison, "Rediscovering," p. 14.

17. Middleton Harris, Morris Levitt, Roger Furman, and Ernest Smith, eds., *The Black Book* (New York: Random House, 1974), p. 49. Further references to this edition will be cited in the text.

18. The *OED* defines "memory book" (US) as a blank book in which cuttings from newspapers and the like are pasted for preservation; a scrapbook.

19. Barbara Campbell, "New Book Bridges Gap in Black History," *New York Times* (March 5, 1974).

20. Toni Morrison, "Memory, Creation and Writing," *Thought* 59 (1984): 388–389.

21. Toni Morrison, "Rootedness: the Ancestor as Foundation," *Black Women Writers (1950–1980): A Critical Evaluation*, ed. Mari Evans (New York: Anchor Books, 1980), p. 341.

22. Toni Morrison, "How Can Values Be Taught in the University?" *Michigan Quarterly Review* 40.2 (2001): 278.

23. Hilton Als, "Ghosts in the House: How Toni Morrison Fostered a Generation of Black Writers," *New Yorker* (October 27, 2003): 66.

PART THREE

Essays

11

JUDYLYN S. RYAN

Language and narrative technique in Toni Morrison's novels

It would be difficult, and perhaps counterproductive, to discuss Toni Morrison's language and narrative technique without examining the social vision, reimagined relationships, and redirected gaze they are designed to support. For, as feminist narratologist Susan Lanser notes in *Fictions of Authority*, "Narration entails social relationships and thus involves far more than the technical imperatives for getting a story told."[1] The notion that extra-textual relationships can motivate, inform, illuminate, or even confound the narrative project has particular significance for an understanding of Toni Morrison's choice of literary techniques.

In "Rootedness: the Ancestor as Foundation," an essay published in the early 1980s, Morrison clarified the social and political vision informing her writing, stating that:

> If anything I do, in the way of writing novels (or whatever I write) isn't about the village or the community or about you, then it is not about anything. I am not interested in indulging myself in some private, closed exercise of my imagination that fulfills only the obligation of my personal dreams – which is to say yes, the work must be political.[2]

At a time when the dictum of art for art's sake had not yet been stripped of its disguise, Morrison was adamant in asserting that a socio-political function neither detracted from, nor conflicted with, aesthetic worth. Equally important, she revealed that this socio-political function was inextricably connected to her relationship to the society-as-readers she called "the village." In "Home," an essay published in 1997 that explores contemporary cultural and social contestations around "race," she offered a more pointed description of the "manageable, doable, modern human activity" her fiction performs, that is, creating "a-world-in-which-race-does-*not*-matter."[3]

Morrison's view of the role of the artist in community is connected to several objectives shaped by a determination "to teach the habit of exercising interpretive agency."[4] Her teacherly vision is a conscious response to the racialized gaze that has informed the discursive practices, interpretive habits, and moral competence of the society-as-readers, and that has been the root cause of particular failures of democracy. At the heart of Morrison's teacherly vision is a concern for the relationship between interpretation and ethics, or, more specifically, for the ways in which interpretive competence increases ethical competence and supports ethical agency. In her fiction, language and narrative technique provide the scaffold on which Morrison constructs her role as artist–teacher.

In the following discussion, I suggest some of the ways in which Morrison's concern for social relationships – those outside the text as well as those implicated in the production and publication of literary works – has engendered particular narrative choices. I examine the ways in which ideological (and philosophical) objectives shape language, particular narrative choices, and/or reconfigure standard narratological conventions. I argue first that the traditional positioning of the readers of American literature as white, coupled with the historical positioning of the Black speaker as unreliable narrator, impose a reciprocal and troubled positioning from which Black women writers have had to extricate themselves in order to express their own epistemological standpoint. Second, that Morrison uses particular textual strategies to claim discursive authority and, thereby, to respond to the needs of a society of deficient readers, while avoiding the constraints of this troubled relationship and racialized gaze. The most significant textual strategies she uses are extra-representational acts, the deployment of an ideal narrative audience, and recursion. Third, that Morrison's fashioning of language and narrative techniques supports both literary and extra-literary objectives. It supports a proactive commitment to constructing and advancing what I have called a democracy of narrative participation – a project that combines both narratological and ideological aspects. In fact, Morrison's response to the needs of a nation of readers and misreaders – her focus on expanding representation, participation, and interpretive competence – expresses her commitment to democracy and to the type of social relationships it predicates. The language and narrative techniques used to achieve these effects are all introduced in her first novel, *The Bluest Eye*, and amplified, revised, and reiterated in each subsequent novel.

Social vision

In her non-fiction writings and in several interviews, Toni Morrison has been explicit in describing the ways in which social relationships have been reflected in, and informed, American literature, and of the ways in which that tradition has affected her own fiction. Her most extensive analysis of this intersection appeared in the 1989 essay, "Unspeakable Things Unspoken." In that essay Morrison examines the history of racialized thought and its impact on American literature and on literary criticism. Based on that analysis, she recommends three foci for literary study, illustrating these in the subsequent sections of the essay, with examples drawn from her first five novels.[5] In *Playing in the Dark*, a collection of critical essays published in 1992, Morrison revisits and elaborates upon her earlier analysis, showing how "race" figures in both the artist's consciousness and in the reader's consciousness. She observes that "until very recently, and regardless of the race of the author, the readers of virtually all of American fiction have been positioned as white."[6] Morrison also alludes to the fact that the racialized positioning of her society-as-readers has had a significant impact on her own literary imagination. She notes, for example, "The only short story I have ever written, 'Recitatif,' was an experiment in the removal of all racial codes from a narrative about two characters of different races for whom racial identity is crucial" (xi). Language, she argues, has been used in much of American literature to "powerfully evoke and enforce hidden signs of racial superiority, cultural hegemony, and dismissive 'othering' of people" (x).

Morrison's comments on the racialized position assigned to American readers closely resemble and recall analyses of the racialized and gendered position – the white male gaze – assigned to film spectators. In fact, the title *Playing in the Dark* signifies on both the mode and space of engagement reserved for the classical Hollywood film spectator. In *Inside the Gaze*, film theorist Francesco Casetti describes this mode of engagement as one in which the "film 'inscribes' or 'posits' its spectator and guides that spectator along a 'path'."[7] As Morrison observes, this positioning was often reproduced in literature, conditioning similar responses from readers and viewers alike. It undermined interpretive competence, constricted and systematically impoverished the gaze of the viewer, the reader, and ultimately the society. Several symptoms mark this impoverished gaze: a lack of recognition of, an absence of curiosity about, and a failure of inquiry into, the human landscape it surveys.

Pecola's encounter with Mr. Yacobowski, the shopkeeper, in *The Bluest Eye*, provides a typical example of this impoverished gaze.

> The gray head of Mr. Yacobowski looms up over the counter. He urges his eyes out of his thoughts to encounter her. Blue eyes. Blear-dropped. Slowly, like Indian summer moving imperceptibly toward fall, he looks toward her. Somewhere between retina and object, between vision and view, his eyes draw back, hesitate, and hover. At some fixed point in time and space he senses that he need not waste the effort of a glance.[8]

Mr. Yacobowski's gaze enunciates both dominance and dismissal. Yet, as Morrison explores his gaze, she also exposes its deficiency. Mr. Yacobowski's blindness, his inability to "see" Pecola, points to both the hegemony and the weakened state of the male White gaze. It is both debilitating *and* debilitated.

> He does not see her, because for him there is nothing to see. How can a fifty-two-year-old white immigrant store-keeper with the taste of potatoes and beer in his mouth, his mind honed on the doe-eyed Virgin Mary, his sensibilities blunted by a permanent awareness of loss, *see* a little black girl? Nothing in his life even suggested that the feat was possible, not to say desirable or necessary. (48)

Here, Morrison responds to and revises what she describes as a "pattern of thinking about racialism in terms of its consequences on the victim – of always defining it asymmetrically" (11). She demonstrates that, whether hierarchical or not, looking relations are always already reciprocal. Pecola apprehends Mr. Yacobowski's gaze; she *sees* him unseeing her:

> She looks up at him and sees the vacuum where curiosity ought to lodge. And something more. The total absence of human recognition – the glazed separateness. She does not know what keeps this glance suspended . . . Yet this vacuum is not new to her . . . She has seen it lurking in the eyes of all white people. (48–49)

Throughout her fiction, Morrison crafts language and narrative technique to explore and reconfigure the looking relations unveiled in this encounter.

Morrison's fiction inscribes enlarged parameters of reader positioning and agency. As she notes in "Rootedness," "to have the reader work *with* the author in the construction of the book – is what's important" (341). This involves the deployment of language and narrative techniques that unveil her own authorial presence, and that call attention to her role in scripting the reader's position so that she or he consciously experiences her/his position as scripted, as part of a collaborative relationship, as an exchange of gazes. Her description of Black women's gaze is self-revealing: "Your gaze, so lovingly unforgiving, stills, agitates, and stills again."[9] Morrison's gaze is attentive to the reader's *needs* (not demands) and is *responsive* (not indulgent) in seeking to increase the reader's competence. Her novels inscribe a reader who is neither a consumer nor a decoder, but a co-creator of the text. Not only does she anticipate that the reader possesses certain (perhaps diminished) competencies but she assists the reader in *reclaiming and strengthening* these. This teacherly role transcends her academic career. In fact, it derives from and reflects an expansive vision of the role of the artist in a democratic society. Morrison's teacherly disposition toward readers – not just readers of her fiction but toward the society-as-readers – forms a pattern of looking relations that are enunciated, mapped, remapped, and democratized in her novels.

Teacherly vision

The teacherly vision that informs Morrison's oeuvre can be traced to the preacherly model that Marcellus Blount outlines in "The Preacherly Text: African American Poetry and Vernacular Performance." In that essay, Blount defines the preacherly text as part of a tradition that "stretches back to the eighteenth and nineteenth century African American sermons" and that is informed by the preacherly performances of literary artists such as James Weldon Johnson. According to Blount, the preacherly text is one in which the artist is able to "establish the grounds of their literate and poetic authority" in the "continuum of African American expressive culture." What these artists borrowed from the vernacular sermon was not only certain "recurring aesthetic and ideological tendencies."[10] More importantly, they appropriated and extended the model of discursive authority founded on the audience's conscious acceptance of the preacher's leadership and their confidence in her/his ability to give voice to their inner strivings and lived experiences. In sum, "The relations of preachers and their congregations . . . provided African American poets with a model for what Barbara Bowen has called 'untroubled voice': the performance of perfect community between artist and audience."[11] Given Morrison's assessment of the historical positioning of the readers of American fiction, the achievement of untroubled voice reflects a successful repositioning of both the racially privileged authorial audience and the ideologically constructed unreliable [Black] narrator.

The performance of untroubled voice is a central pillar on which Morrison constructs her teacherly role and claims narrative authority. Deploying and refashioning narrative techniques allows Morrison to claim the discursive authority necessary for her teacherly role. In her several novels, Morrison adapts and extends both conventional *and* African American narrative poetics in order to create the framework for this role. In *The Bluest Eye*, the novel that inaugurated her literary career, Morrison refashioned particular techniques of African American literature and simultaneously created a new ur-text for the literary tradition. As described by Robert Stepto, Frederick Douglass's 1845 *Narrative* provided an ur-text for African American narrative. It represented the first instance in which a text achieved narrative autonomy instead of being dominated by authenticating devices designed to certify the narrator's credibility and humanity.[12]

Like Douglass's writing, Morrison's fiction provides a new model for African American literature, in part by mimicking Douglass's use of an ideal narrative audience as a mechanism for accruing discursive authority. Morrison has signaled the strategies developed by Douglass and other early African American writers to effectively negotiate the challenge of writing for a racially privileged authorial audience: "As determined as these black writers were to persuade the reader of the evil of slavery, they also complimented him by assuming his nobility of heart and his high-mindedness. They tried to summon up his finer nature in order to encourage him to employ it."[13] This strategy – of assigning to the narrative audience a degree of ethical consciousness and maturity that was not reflected in nineteenth-century public attitudes toward race and Blackness – enabled Douglass and his contemporaries to reposition their authorial audience. While Douglass was able to construct a narrative audience that was "ideal" in the sense that it was both in need of persuasion and persuadable, Morrison frequently constructs an ideal narrative audience that is teachable, that is, positioned to accept the narrator's knowledge, intellectual and ethical judgments, in sum, her discursive authority. In Morrison's fiction, however, this is only one of several pillars supporting discursive authority.

Discursive authority and perfect community

In her discussion of the "Feminist Poetics of Narrative Voice," Lanser argues that "discursive authority – by which I mean here the intellectual credibility, ideological validity, and aesthetic value claimed by or conferred upon a work, author, narrator, character, or textual practice – is produced interactively." Furthermore, "[i]n Western literary systems . . . discursive authority has attached itself most readily to white, educated men of hegemonic ideology. One major constituent of narrative authority, therefore, is the extent to which a narrator's status conforms to this dominant social power."[14] For Morrison – as for other Black women writers – claiming discursive authority is both complicated and necessitated by her impoverished positioning within this racialized and gendered economy. This process is further complicated by the historical positioning of the Black (woman) as unreliable narrator – someone whose credibility (intellectual, moral, aesthetic) the reader should not, need not, credit.

From the perspective of conventional narratology, the "unreliable narrator" is usually the character narrator whose statements and judgments are internally contradictory. Although unreliable narration is typically viewed as an aspect of narrative fiction, recent analyses have identified other contexts in which this dynamic can be observed. Ansgar Nünning notes that "unreliable narration as a phenomenon is, of course, not confined to narrative fiction, but can be found in a wide range of narratives across the genres, the media, and different disciplines."[15] Nünning also notes that "ascriptions of unreliability involve a tripartite structure that consists of an authorial agency, textual phenomena (including a personalized narrator and signals of unreliability), and reader response."[16] While narratology has traditionally defined unreliable narration as the product of rhetorical effects, Nünning's analysis expands the list of possible causes to include ideological effects such as the reader's judgments and frame of reference, making it easy to appreciate how ideologically motivated and race-inflected ascriptions of unreliability have shaped the Black woman narrator's positioning within dominant social narratives.

Despite the Black woman's discredited positioning as unreliable narrator, and notwithstanding the hegemony of the racialized and gendered semiotics of authority she describes, Lanser asserts that "narrative authority can also be constituted through . . . textual strategies that even socially unauthorized writers can appropriate."[17] Extra-representational acts, those that "are not strictly required for telling a tale," include "reflections, judgments, generalizations about the world 'beyond' the fiction, direct addresses to the narratee, comments on the narrative process, allusions to other writers and texts."[18] According to Lanser, these acts "expand the sphere of fictional authority to 'nonfictional' referents and allow the writer to engage, from 'within' the fiction, in a culture's literary, social, and intellectual debates." Narrators who undertake "extra-representational acts" have the most significant degrees of discursive authority.

Not surprisingly, extra-representational acts appear throughout Morrison's fiction. In fact, she frequently reserves both the opening and closing paragraphs of her novels for striking displays of extra-representational acts that consolidate her discursive authority, accentuate her role as artist–teacher, and enter various contemporary debates. Her first novel, *The Bluest Eye*, for example, opens with a primer narrative that pointedly critiques idealized fictions of domesticity, foregrounds and engages ongoing debates on (the representation of) the American family. In describing Pauline's "education in the movies" and the ways in which the ideas she acquired there – romantic love and physical beauty – destroyed her self-esteem, the narrator pauses to offer her own judgment. Her assertion that these are "[p]robably the most destructive ideas in the history of human thought" (122) is striking in its self-assured authority. Her closing critique of the social environment responsible for Pecola's collapse is equally so: "This soil is bad for certain kinds of flowers. Certain seeds it will not nurture, certain fruit it will not bear, and when the land kills of its own volition, we acquiesce and say the victim had no right to live" (206). This is not the muted tone of Ralph Ellison's narrator who, on a lower frequency, "may be speaking for you." Here, instead, the narrator offers a sweeping indictment that attests to her own moral and intellectual authority. As an extra-representational act, the adult Claudia's closing critique of "this soil" bridges the gap between the fictional universe and the social universe in which the novel exists, effectively consolidating Morrison's authority.

Yet this closing gesture undoes the novel in some significant ways. Although *The Bluest Eye* sets out to explore the causes underlying Pecola's descent into alienation, Claudia's journey toward self-consciousness and self-possession stands in dramatic – and unspoken – counterpoint to Pecola's journey. The authoritativeness of her final pronouncement calls attention to and seems to contradict the pronouncement itself. By leaving the narrative of Claudia's journey unspoken but evident, Morrison provides readers with a narrator whose stability and self-possession are so definite that they enable a degree and type of authority rarely displayed in African American literature. Yet, the fact of her self-possession contradicts the certainty of her assessment that the soil will not nurture certain seeds. This doubt seeps into her second pronouncement that for Pecola "it's much, much, much too late" (206). If Claudia is, like Pecola, one of the "seeds" that this soil will not nurture, how do we account for her survival, her intellectual and ethical stature? Significantly, the finality of this first novel's closing pronouncement never recurs in Morrison's fiction. To the contrary, Morrison goes to great lengths to ensure that new choices, new avenues remain available to her characters and to her readers. The open-endedness of her subsequent novels suggests that Morrison too has benefited from the recursions that are mapped throughout her fiction.

In addition to extra-representational acts, Morrison also deploys an ideal narrative audience as a mechanism for constructing narrative authority, thereby repositioning actual and authorial audiences. Peter Rabinowitz argues that "there are at least four audiences implied in any narrative literary text."[19] In addition to the traditional categories of actual, authorial, and narrative audiences, Rabinowitz identifies the "ideal narrative audience" as an audience that is "ideal . . . from the narrator's point of view" because that audience "believes the narrator, accepts his judgments, sympathizes with his plight, laughs at his jokes even when they are bad" (134). In the context of Black women's literature – and, specifically, Morrison's fiction – however, an ideal narrative audience is one that accepts the Black woman's epistemological standpoint, and credits her intellectual, moral, and discursive authority. The engagement with such an audience liberates the literary imagination from the ideological demands of the (racially) privileged/positioned reader.

Through this technique, Morrison positions the authorial audience to accept her credibility and authority regarding both intra-textual and extra-textual matters.

Thus, in *Beloved*, Morrison creates a work of realist fiction – not, as some scholars have alleged, of magical realism – that coheres around modes of spiritual agency that the dominant society views as unthinkable, and does so without catering to the authorial audience's predictable expectations of narrative justification. That Beloved, the "ghost," is not simply a figment of Sethe's imagination but also the titular protagonist further attests to the freedom Morrison attains from successfully repositioning the authorial audience through the device of an ideal narrative audience. This repositioning is part of a comprehensive agenda aimed at restructuring social relations outside the text and at fostering the reader's interpretive competence. In fact, Morrison's choice of narrative technique and narrative construction are designed to reveal that interpretive competence is a prerequisite for ethical competence.

One of the strategies used to expand the reader's interpretive competence is what one might call a "democracy of narrative participation."[20] As a literary technique, democracy of narrative participation dismantles the "binary casting of central and marginal characters" and "enables the artist to expand the narrative to reveal that even individuals whose presence is temporally or socially limited have full personalities and unlimited human agency."[21]

In each of her novels Morrison creates a fictional universe populated with both major and minor characters who are all allowed to occupy the narrative spotlight. As an example, the narrator uses a single-sentence brush stroke to draw attention to the complexity of Mr. Yacobowski's character. By describing him as a "fifty-two-year-old white immigrant store-keeper with . . . sensibilities blunted by a permanent awareness of loss" (48), the narrator prompts the reader to see Mr. Yacobowski as a person with his own complex psychology and humanity.

For a society of readers conditioned by literary, cinematic, social, and political practices to accept the "convenience" of "major" characters portrayed with complex humanity and "minor" characters diminished and flattened, entering Morrison's populous and democratic narrative universe is both demanding and (initially) disorienting. Nevertheless, the technique creates several important effects. First, it avoids the danger of "othering," by having the narrative consciousness enter the interior world of "major" as well as "minor" characters. Second, it generates an epistemology that enables readers to know each character from within his/her own particularized psychological universe. Third, it allows for an exchange of multiple gazes among the characters and readers. In sum, these effects add complexity to the reader's interrogation and interpretation of motivation.

Consistent with the goals informing her fiction, Morrison uses recursion as a technique for promoting specific literary, pedagogical, and ideological objectives. Significantly, she likens her artistic/intellectual process to archeological investigation, using fragments to uncover buried sites. Her gaze continuously returns to specific thematic sites in a process of deepening excavation. In *Jazz* (1992) and in *Love* (2003), for example, she returns to the investigation of women's friendships begun in *Sula* (1973). In *Paradise* (1998), she enlarges the exploration of an unwitting mimicry of oppressive, anti-human behaviors on the part of separatist Black communities begun in *Song of Solomon* (1977). And in *Tar Baby* (1981) she elaborates upon the focus of *The Bluest Eye* (1970) in the expanded depiction of the psychological impact of competing cultural worldviews. Indeed, Morrison's later novels are recursive variations on the thematic and technical explorations initiated in her three early novels.

In a conversation with Gail Caldwell in 1987, Morrison noted that "[t]he past, until you confront it, until you live through it, keeps coming back in other forms. The shapes redesign themselves in other constellations, until you get a chance to play it over again."[22] Her use of the word "chance" suggests that, for Morrison's characters and readers, this recursive tendency is more blessing than burden. The opportunity to analytically unmake and remake the past is an unfailing ideology in Morrison's fiction. The past (including past works – not the future – is treated as unfinished and continuously unfolding. By revisiting specific themes, techniques, and textual strategies, Morrison positions her characters, her readers, and the society-as-readers to discover that the (recurring) past is a reservoir from which the future can be drawn and redrawn in more expansive and enabling ways.

In her fiction – as in her literary criticism and cultural/social criticism – Morrison reveals the world as it is with such clarity that readers are prompted to consider what needs doing, what must be done. Typically, she follows the disclosure of truths that are staggering with a steadying reassurance that some agency – critical, intellectual, political, artistic – can be directed toward transforming the revealed world. In her role as artist–teacher, Morrison directs a steadying gaze toward her readers, a gaze whose primary objective is to prompt and/or assist the reader in attaining a balanced, accurate, unwavering, multi-faceted, and independent focus – a teacherly role for a democratic vision.

NOTES

1. Susan Lanser, *Fictions of Authority: Women Writers and Narrative Voice* (Ithaca: Cornell University Press, 1992), p. 4.

2. Toni Morrison, "Rootedness: the Ancestor as Foundation," *Black Women Writers (1950–1980): A Critical Evaluation*, ed. Mari Evans (New York: Anchor/Doubleday, 1984), p. 344.
3. Toni Morrison, "Home," *The House that Race Built*, ed. Wahneema Lubiano (New York: Random House, 1997), p. 4.
4. Judylyn S. Ryan and Estella Conwill Májozo, "*Jazz* . . . On 'The Site of Memory'," *Studies in the Literary Imagination* 31.2 (Fall 1998): 126.
5. Toni Morrison, "Unspeakable Things Unspoken: the Afro-American Presence in American Literature," *Michigan Quarterly Review* 28.1 (1989): 1–34.
6. Toni Morrison, *Playing in the Dark: Whiteness and the Literary Imagination* (Cambridge, MA: Harvard University Press, 1992), p. xii.
7. Francesco Casetti, *Inside the Gaze: The Fiction Film and Its Spectator*, trans. Nell Andrews and Charles O'Brien (Bloomington: Indiana University Press, 1998), p. xvii.
8. Toni Morrison, *The Bluest Eye* (New York: Penguin, 1994), p. 48.
9. Toni Morrison, "A Knowing So Deep," *Essence* (May 1985): 230.
10. Marcellus Blount, "The Preacherly Text: African American Poetry and Vernacular Performance," *PMLA* 107.3 (1992): 584.
11. Barbara Bowen, "Untroubled Voice: Call and Response in *Cane*," *Black Literature and Literary Theory*, ed. Henry Louis Gates, Jr. (New York: Methuen, 1984), pp. 187–203.
12. See Robert Stepto's *From Behind the Veil: A Study of Afro-American Narrative* (Urbana: University of Illinois Press, 1979).
13. Toni Morrison, "The Site of Memory," *Inventing the Truth: The Art and Craft of Memoir*, ed. William Zinnser (Boston: Houghton Mifflin, 1987), pp. 106–107.
14. Lanser, *Fictions of Authority*, p. 6.
15. Ansgar Nünning, "Reconceptualizing Unreliable Narration: Synthesizing Cognitive and Rhetorical Approaches," *A Companion to Narrative Theory*, ed. James Phelan and Peter J. Rabinowitz (Oxford: Blackwell, 2005), p. 90.
16. *Ibid.*, pp. 90–91.
17. Lanser, *Fictions of Authority*, pp. 6–7.
18. *Ibid.*, p. 16.
19. Peter Rabinowitz, "Truth in Fiction: a Reexamination of Audiences," *Critical Inquiry* 4 (Autumn 1977): 125.
20. Judylyn S. Ryan, *Spirituality as Ideology in Black Women's Film and Literature* (Charlottesville: University of Virginia Press, 2005), p. 18.
21. *Ibid.*
22. "Interview with Gail Caldwell," *Conversations with Toni Morrison*, ed. Danille Taylor-Guthrie (Jackson: University Press of Mississippi, 1994), p. 241.

12

DWIGHT McBRIDE

Morrison, intellectual

A dead language is not only one no longer spoken or written, it is unyielding language content to admire its own paralysis. Like statist language, censored and censoring. Ruthless in its policing duties, it has no desire or purpose other than maintaining the free range of its own narcotic narcissism, its own exclusivity and dominance.

The systematic looting of language can be recognized by the tendency of its users to forgo its nuanced, complex, mid-wifery properties for menace and subjugation. Oppressive language does more than represent violence; it is violence; does more than represent the limits of knowledge; it limits knowledge . . . Sexist language, racist language, theistic language – all are typical of the policing languages of mastery, and cannot, do not permit new knowledge or encourage the mutual exchange of ideas.[1]

Nobel Lecture, 268, 269

Though perhaps best known to most as the first African American Nobel laureate in literature, it would be short-sighted – as evidenced by the other essays in this volume – to limit Toni Morrison's incredible contributions to the world of arts and letters to her achievements as a novelist alone. The author of scores of critical essays and articles, published speeches, book reviews, interviews, opinion pieces; author of *Playing in the Dark: Whiteness and the Literary Imagination*; editor of both *Race-ing Justice, En-Gendering Power: Essays on Anita Hill, Clarence Thomas, and the Construction of Social Reality* and *Birth of a Nation'hood: Gaze, Script, and Spectacle in the O. J. Simpson Case*; and a professor of writing and literature for decades, Morrison's record, role, and influence as an intellectual are by any measure extraordinary. Indeed, it could be argued that Morrison's corpus is best understood when read as a broad, far-reaching intellectual contribution that defies our contemporary artist–scholar divide with which we have become increasingly comfortable in the academy.

Author-ization

Morrison has a keen interest in what she calls the academy's contrived barriers between critic–scholar and artist. In fact, much of her own distinguished career as a writer, teacher, and editor – not to mention her forays into criticism – throw such easy divisions into doubt.[2] Even in one of her most oft-cited critical essays, "Unspeakable Things Unspoken," Morrison seems invested in collapsing these barriers in statements like: "Certainly a sharp alertness as to *why* a work is or is not worthy is the legitimate occupation of the critic, the pedagogue and the artist."[3] Consider also the essay's closing paragraph:

> For an author, regarding canons, it is very simple: in fifty, a hundred or more years his or her work may be relished for its beauty or its insights or its power; or it may be condemned for its vacuousness and pretension – and junked. Or in fifty or a hundred years the critic (as canon builder) may be applauded for his or her intelligent scholarship and powers of critical inquiry. Or laughed at for ignorance and shabbily disguised assertions of power – and junked. It is possible that the reputations of both will thrive, or that both will decay. In any case, as far as the future is concerned, when one writes, as critic or as author, all necks are on the line. ("Unspeakable Things," 33–34)

Here Morrison makes it clear that, "regarding canons," time will tell not only the story of the reception of the artist, but of the critic as well. By equating the risks of historical permanence involved for writers with the (all-too-often unspoken) risks involved for critics, Morrison issues an equalizing blow to the power of the critic in his or her relationship to writers. The final example of Morrison's deconstruction of the artist–critic dichotomy comes in her discussions of Kundera's *The Art of the Novel* and Terrence Rafferty's review of the same in the *New Yorker*. She writes:

> Kundera's views, obliterating American writers (with the exception of William Faulkner) from his own canon, are relegated to a "smugness" that Terrence Rafferty disassociates from Kundera's imaginative work and applies to the "sublime confidence" of his critical prose. The confidence of an exile who has the sentimental education of, and the choice to become, a European. ("Unspeakable Things," 5–6)

The amalgamation of this statement with the preceding one accomplishes several things, not the least of which is that it invites us to take seriously the rhetorical strategies and subtext of Morrison's discourse. For if Rafferty can distinguish the character of Kundera's imaginative work from his critical prose, we are certainly invited to determine how to negotiate the same issue in the case of Morrison. By challenging the boundary between artist and critic, Morrison creates a legitimate place in critical literary discourse for her own voice. She resists the kind of facile distinction Rafferty makes with Kundera, and, in fact, depends upon the critic–artist dichotomy for her rhetorical positionality in this essay. Nowhere is this more clearly demonstrated than in the essay's equalizing final paragraph. I argue later that Morrison is negotiating two kinds of "otherness" – the otherness of "artist" in the academy and the otherness of "race" in America. In this way, the rhetorical gesture of challenging the artist–critic dichotomy becomes a crucial move for Morrison in order to enshrine herself (as much of this essay arguably does) as a legitimate critical voice.

This serves as one example of how Morrison's rhetoric seems to learn from, or be informed by, her critical project as she proceeds. The shrewd enshrining of self here is not unlike the academy's enshrining of traditional canonical text that Morrison is questioning. That is, if Morrison deconstructs the artist–critic dichotomy to legitimize her critical voice, then academic traditionalists challenge the inclusion of women and "people of color" in the canon to maintain the status of white male domination that obtains in the curriculum and in the membership of the academy as well. While Morrison's rhetorical strategies here seem deconstructive, they still rely on a kind of thinking that essentializes "artist," "critic," and "American literary canon." This may speak to Diana Fuss's larger claim that constructionism really operates as a more sophisticated form of essentialism.[4] Whatever the case, Morrison is not beyond using the "master's" rhetorical process, which has obviously worked so well for him, to perform the same kind of legitimizing function for herself.

But let me return for a moment to Morrison's discussion of Rafferty's review of Kundera, in order to concentrate on how Morrison's rhetorical strategies function in that instance. Rafferty writes that

> Kundera's polemical fervor in *The Art of the Novel* annoys us, as American readers, because we feel defensive, excluded from the transcendent "idea of the novel" that for him seems simply to have been there for the taking. (If only he had cited, in his redeeming version of the novel's history, a few more heroes from the New World's culture.) Our novelists don't discover cultural values within themselves; they invent them.　(Quoted in "Unspeakable Things," 5)

Now consider Morrison's response to this statement:

> I was refreshed by Rafferty's comments. With the substitution of certain phrases, his observations and the justifiable umbrage he takes can be appropriated entirely by Afro-American writers regarding their own exclusion from the "transcendent 'idea of the novel.'" For the present turbulence seems not to be about the flexibility of a canon, its range among and between Western countries, but about its miscegenation.　("Unspeakable Things," 6)

Here Morrison positions herself as a mediating door between the competing forces of the defenders of the canonical faith and the more insurgent intellectual voices involved in the present canon polemic. She makes the discussion slightly more palatable (or in her words "not endangering" [4]) for the more conservative interlocutors who may be reluctant to enter this debate. She places all of her readers at ease by creating, via the figure of Rafferty, a sympathy for American literature against European arrogance and European exclusion of American literature from its definition of canonical texts (here represented by Kundera). It is a swift, unifying, and almost patriotic "call to arms." It enlists our sympathies as Americans, and we feel slighted. The crucial move comes, however, at the close of her discussion of Kundera when Morrison draws the parallel that what Kundera (Europe) is doing to American literature is like what American literature is doing to African American literature. It is an established rhetorical tactic (initially putting the reader at ease only to make more stark the realization to which you want him/her to come) that proves effective here. I am thinking here particularly of the rhetorical tactics of Phillis Wheatley and of the many nineteenth-century slave narrators' direct addresses to their readers.

Consider also that Morrison's position in this essay by way of audience is complicated in much the same way that the position of the authors of these slave narratives was. If she is to be heard she must negotiate the right amount of courting of her traditionalist audience without appearing sycophantic and overly accommodationist to her more progressive audience. The way this rhetorical gesture functions at the level of racial and cultural identity politics should not go unmentioned here either. By establishing herself, in the eyes of her American reading audience, as the critical voice that points out Kundera's Eurocentrism to the detriment of American literature, Morrison also positions herself to be the recipient of the admiration that this critical "call to arms" creates. This then allows her to metonymically enlist those same sympathies for the ways African American literature may suffer from the exclusion of the traditional American literary canon. It is, after all, Morrison (as African American artist–critic) who is able to read the connection between European literature and American literature that Rafferty makes for its applicability to the relationship between American literature and African American literature.

The kind of analysis Morrison performs on white American literature in *Playing in the Dark* (via the issue of the serviceability of black bodies) suggests a way of reading the similar rhetorical moves she makes in "Unspeakable Things Unspoken" in "writing" the figure of Rafferty. If white American writers – and in some cases their white characters – enlist black bodies to economize stereotype and to "imaginatively act out the forbidden in American culture," then Morrison makes use of Rafferty's rhetorical serviceability in "Unspeakable Things Unspoken" to legitimize her critical voice in an academy where the artist–critic dichotomy has been concretizing for quite some time.

Commitment

If any one theme might be said to characterize the primary intellectual commitment of Toni Morrison's work, even across genres of fiction and non-fiction, it would be the pursuit of freedom. Like her friend and contemporary, James Baldwin, Morrison is everywhere obsessed with freedom: political freedom from labels and "-isms" (her consistent resistance to "feminism"), linguistic freedom from the limits of language (as in her Nobel speech); conceptual freedom from concrete ideas like corporeality, for example (*Beloved* and *Jazz*); and artistic and intellectual freedom from being pigeonholed as either artist or intellectual (as I have just been arguing). Before turning to her fiction in this regard, specifically to *Beloved* and *Jazz*, it remains to say a word about another non-fiction example in Morrison's work – the epigraph to this paper taken from the Nobel acceptance speech.

At the center of the Nobel acceptance speech is a story of an old, blind, wise, African American woman. She is confronted by a group of "young people who seem to be bent on disproving her clairvoyance and showing her up for the fraud they believe she is." One of them steps forward and says to her, "Old woman, I hold in my hand a bird. Tell me whether it is living or dead." In her interpretation of this allegorical scenario, Morrison chooses to read "the bird as language and the woman as a practiced writer." She does not, however, identify who the group of young people are in this story. Indeed, their role seems to be somewhat purposely undecided. They are at times a generation of young African Americans who desperately want to be taken seriously by their elders, who crave their wisdom, who want to be touched in significant ways by their experience. But they also represent a generation of young scholars, post-structuralist theorists, and purveyors of cultural studies, who have all participated in the discrediting of the very idea of the "author" and who have been – according to some – consumed with language and its paralyzing effects. Their work has in no small part advanced the policing duties of critical language in the academy – language invested in "maintaining the free range of its own narcotic narcissism, its own exclusivity and dominance" (Morrison, *Nobel Lecture*, 268).

No one is let off the hook in this scenario. All necks are on the line. The old woman, who represents the practiced writer, is upbraided for her undue investment in her good "name in the street," and her unwillingness to take seriously the young people's critique of her and her generation. The young people are called out for their ruse, their power play of flaunting the old woman's disability (her blindness) as a way of getting her attention. In all cases, however, what is most significant about this speech is its unflinching commitment to critiquing the "systematic looting of language" and the death of language. Her response to both, the "systematic looting of language" and the death of language, represents once again Morrison's commitment to linguistic freedom. The former, Morrison says, "can be recognized by the tendency of its users to forgo its nuanced, complex, mid-wifery properties for menace and subjugation" (Morrison, *Nobel Lecture*, 269). In the case of the latter, she says, "A dead language is not only one no longer spoken or written, it is unyielding language content to admire its own paralysis . . . Unreceptive to interrogation, it cannot form or tolerate new ideas, shape other thoughts, tell another story, fill baffling silences." In both cases, whether dealing with the looting of language or a dead language, one is always involved in a struggle for freedom. It is only through the dialogic, the interaction, the taking of the time to address one another that the story of the exchange between the old woman and the young people represents our hope of discovering some space of possibility, of freedom from these limits. This is what the old woman means at the end of the speech when she says to the young people:

> "Finally," she says, "I trust you now. I trust you with the bird that is not in your hands because you have truly caught it. Look. How lovely it is, this thing we have done – together." (Morrison, *Nobel Lecture*, 273)

Each time I have read Morrison's meditations on the limits of language in her Nobel acceptance speech, and especially her meditation on dead language, I have always been drawn to the figure of Beloved in the novel of the same name. One often imagines death as a space beyond retribution, a kind of ultimate limit. But when we consider the case of Beloved, we know that her suffering exceeds the limits of her life. Indeed, the fictional world is replete with moments in which death does not protect the dead – or at least "that which lives after us" – from the retribution sought by the living. Recall the dead Pericles of Sophocles' *Antigone* for whom Creon's edict forbids burial since he was a "traitor" to the state. One thinks of Dickens's dead Jacob Marley whose ghost is doomed to walk the earth for eternity in the chains of his sin as punishment for his miserly and unkind life. Or remember the biblical figure Jezebel whose body was never buried but was consumed by dogs for her wrongdoings according to the prophecy of Elijah. And there is, of course, the extra-literary example, which movie-goers may recognize, from *Ghosts* – a film which reinscribes the conventional ideas of heaven and hell at work in what is ultimately a moral universe, which consigns the transcendent soul, spirit, or essence either to eternal light and goodness or to eternal darkness and suffering. Whatever their particulars, each of these instances remind us that the dead, in the realm of art and representation, are not always free from retribution for their activities in this world or in the next; and if anything, death functions as a marker of a transition along a continuum which extends beyond that which we most commonly understand as "life."[5]

Documentation

But why this interest in death? It seems to me that Morrison recognizes the relationship between death and history. She recognizes that whether we are dealing with corporeality or with spirit, all of the spectacles staged to punish the dead (as in the examples mentioned) or to represent the past are really about, and staged for the benefit of, the living. These spectacles help us to make sense of our cultural existence in this postmodern world. Death in Morrison is rarely ever final. And it rarely represents the limitations we most readily associate with it. Whether in *Beloved*, *Sula*, *Jazz*, or *Paradise*, *Song of Solomon*, or *Love* – death seems ever to be an occasion for something more, the opening up of a larger domain for our consideration, a kind of invitation to free our calcified ways of thinking and knowing. Morrison recognizes what Foucault articulates about history and its "documents." In Foucault's account of history, its project is

> the reconstitution on the basis of what the documents say, and sometimes merely hint at, of the past from which they emanate and which has now disappeared far behind them; the document was always treated as the language of a voice since reduced to silence, its fragile, but possibly decipherable trace.[5]

That is, the document is the trace of the dead, the witness for the dead. It is quite literally "that which lives after us." However, when dealing with racialized subjects operating in cultural contexts somewhat different from those Foucault might have envisioned,[6] we must imagine the notion of the "document" in slightly broader terms. Let me suggest that in the telling of her personal and communal histories, Morrison uses memory as document. Morrison specifically makes use of the notion of "rememory" to envision and articulate the individual collective past of slavery. She uses the reincarnate spirit of the dead to authenticate hers. These observations represent only a few of the techniques used by Morrison to fiction a history. The ability to do so is but one example of a variety of discursive freedoms for the writer.

We may or may not be surprised to find that what Foucault imagines as the new role of "discontinuities" in historical analysis has always been on the agendas of the historian of labor, the historian of African Americans, and so on. I am not trying to suggest a kind of one-upmanship of Foucault by writers of color; but it is interesting, just as in this case, that often much of what Western theory imagines as the "new" can only be understood as such when the object of critique is delimited so as not to include the cultural production of, or the experiences of, marginalized subjects. The history of black thought is riddled with examples that demonstrate that the recognition and use of discontinuity has been around for some time. One thinks of the slave narratives and how many of them begin with discontinuous birth narratives. That is, the narrator does not know precisely when he/she was born or his/her exact age because the institution of slavery and trafficking of slaves often rendered it impossible to locate a precise date of birth. Still one wrote and told one's story in an attempt to "make sense" of one's life. One thinks of Du Bois's articulation of his famous notion of double-consciousness, the feeling of one's two-ness as a recognition of what could quite easily be seen as discontinuous parts in the struggle to understand one's place in the world, one's identity. One thinks also of James Baldwin's assertion that "if trouble don't last always, neither does power." Baldwin's assertion, though simply put perhaps, presses for continuity where there might at first appear to be none. This kind of recognition of the complex relationship between trouble in black life and the workings of power exposes what hegemonic ideologies work very diligently to conceal.

Legitimacy

Morrison's work takes this to new heights. As fiction-writer-become-historian, she inhabits the discontinuities of her history and locates, or indeed discovers, her creative historical projects in those discontinuities. The language of "rememory" itself might provide an interesting entrée into an examination of Morrison in this way. Morrison tells us, for example, that she did not do any more research for *Beloved* beyond the article that provided her with the facts of the Margaret Garner story: "I did a lot of research about everything else in the book – Cincinnati, and abolitionists, and the underground railroad – but I refused to find out anything else about Margaret Garner. I really wanted to invent her life."[7]

In addition to the intentionally disconcerting impact of the opening section of the novel, what is equally interesting about this beginning is that once we have read *Beloved*, we know that the narrator knew the story from the very beginning. This omniscient narrator possesses all the knowledge of the story and ably kindles a desire in us to know what she/he does. One of the by-products of this kind of circular narration is that the narrator is always in control of revealing what the reader knows, and when the reader knows it, in order to produce certain aesthetic, political, emotional, and psychological effects. In *Beloved* this voice is invested with even more significance as it will help us to sort out the terrain into which we have been thrust. Morrison's narrator is all we as readers have in this new narrative world, at first unrecognizable and unfamiliar, which is precisely one of the ways in which she/he is legitimized and authorized to tell the story. We believe the narrator, in part, precisely because we do not learn with the narrator; the narrator is always in the position of teaching and revealing things to us as readers, even up to the secret of infanticide, which rests at the very heart of the narrative. The political significance of investing the narrator with this kind of authority and legitimacy is that in histories such as those I have been describing, in which the voice and not necessarily the documents are primary, the believability and reliability of the storyteller is of the utmost concern.

In light of Sethe's having a history of scarification (in which the body itself quite literally becomes rather like a document of history to be read by others), the uses of the ghost in this text, and the representation of the "strong woman" (Baby Suggs) with almost mythic functions, it seems most important to speak briefly about the role of forgetting in Morrison. For in the history that Morrison creates, what one forgets is as important as what one remembers. Forgetting is not accidental in the process of "rememory" but is willful.

Beloved and the collective/communal voice

The idea of the collective experience of history and the telling of history is important for Morrison and bears further thought. How the collective body functions in the literature of slavery and the revisionist literature of slavery, as in *Beloved*, is interesting. While this is literally Sethe's story of slavery, we also know that it is not just a story about slavery. Morrison herself is quoted as saying that the novel is not about slavery: "It is a story about individuals and their experiences of slavery."[8] Sethe's story implies the impossibility of telling an individual tale. The slave body is both singular and collective. That is why so many moments in slave narratives describe the treatment of slaves other than the narrator. The other slaves are not the slave that is witnessing in the narrative, yet they are a part of a collective slave body constructed by the conditions of ownership which were legitimated by racial difference.[9] It becomes impossible to talk about the self singularly. The slave self is a self that is always engaged in a kind of collective corporeal condition that makes it impossible to speak of the self solely as an individual. And this has profound implications for the writing of history, some of which I have tried to explore here. Individual experiences of horror, torture, and scarred bodies are not in themselves meaningful. I do not mean by that statement to deny their personal significance, but only to say that these instances are individualized articulations that can be best understood within a larger cultural and communal logic or language, which sustains them and gives meaning to them. Slave experience literally "makes sense" and has meaning because it is located in the collective – which includes the experiences of a variety of slaves – that legitimizes the story of the slave doing the telling. Similarly, in the conclusion of *Beloved* the experience of the ghost Beloved in 124 "makes sense" (i.e., becomes legible) only in the context of the collective community. Only in the communal context can the black women and former slaves understand her for what she is and collectively exorcize her. After the exorcism, the narrator reports: "They forgot her like a bad dream . . . Remembering seemed unwise . . . So they forgot her. Like an unpleasant dream during a troubling sleep."[10] When the community collectively decides to forget her, Beloved ceases to be. The ability to read Beloved here depends upon a communal recognition of the linguistic codes that would be necessary to name the figure, now "disremembered and unaccounted for." Furthermore, there is the recognition in this passage that the forgetting is willful and deliberate. The "something that moves there" which one can touch if one likes is the presence of the supernatural. But to touch it is to acknowledge its ontology and to give it a phenomenal existence. Part of the contract of forgetting is the not touching. Remembering some things is obviously unwise. But Morrison also shows us, through the figure of Sethe, the price that forgetting can exact.

Jazz and the individual/liberating voice

If the narrator and narrative style in *Beloved* represent one approach toward narrative freedom, the narrator in *Jazz* takes that freedom to an entirely new level. The self-referentially disembodied narrator of *Jazz* is fascinating for a number of reasons. Some of these reasons have been discussed by a not inconsiderable number of critics including John N. Duvall, Henry Louis Gates, Jr., Philip Page, and Dorothea Drummond Mbalia, among others. Nowhere is the force and implication of that disembodied (and, once again, we might think at face value thoroughly liberated) narrative voice more keenly interesting than in the novel's final four paragraphs:

> It's nice when grown people whisper to each other under the covers. Their ecstasy is more leaf-sigh than bray and the body is the vehicle, not the point . . . They are inward toward the other, bound and joined by carnival dolls and the steamers that sailed from ports they never say. That is what is beneath their undercover whispers.

But there is another part, not so secret. The part that touches fingers when one passes the cup and saucer to the other. The part that closes her neckline snap while waiting for the trolly; and brushes lint from his blue serge suit when they come out of the movie house into the sunlight.

I envy them their public love. I myself have only known it is secret, shared it in secret and longed, aw longed to show it – to be able to say out loud what they have no need to say at all . . .

But . . . I can't tell anyone that I have been waiting for this all my life and that being chosen to wait is the reason I can. If I were able I'd say it. Say make me, remake me. You are free to do it and I am free to let you because look, look. Look where your hands are. Now.[11]

The only critic who comes close to appreciating the liberating and erotic possibilities enabled by this closing passage and the representation of the disembodied narrator is Duvall. He comments that this sexualized moment at the novel's end comes from an "odd and paradoxical admission on the narrator's part."[12] According to Duvall, "What is striking in this description is the narrator's assertion of a difference between her passion, which has always remained secret, and Joe and Violet's open heterosexuality. The narrator's closeted passion has remained unnamed, yet paradoxically, in the moment of enunciation, it becomes the unspeakable thing spoken."[13]

But what are we to make of this reading of the disembodied narrator? Again Duvall invites us to return to Henry Louis Gates's "sense of the indeterminacy of the narrator's sexual identity. If we read the narrator as both female and male," Duvall continues,

then the embrace between narrator and reader is large indeed, for it recognizes a wider variety of sexual–textual pleasures. The narrator's Whitmanesque acknowledgement of the reader's touch admits that there are a multitude of religions of the body, so that the touch represented in the final sentence may be imagined as occurring between man and woman, man and man, woman and woman; the embrace, in fact, may even be intergenerational or interracial.[14]

Still, it is very curious to me that when the disembodied narrator looks upon the reunion of Joe and Violet, what the narrator recognizes and longs for is not only the "public love" of Joe and Violet's heterosexual existence, but also the bodies that make that public love possible. The fact that this final representation of the disembodied narrator renders the narrator queer is intriguing, if by "queer" we mean outside the norm, the mainstream, what is allowable in public.

It is, then, the queer, disembodied narrator that envies them "their public love." The narrator's queerness is the price the narrator pays for the narrator's freedom. It is most often – and history will bear this out – those on the margins, outside the mainstream, who are in the best position to see our world most clearly. Abolitionists were ahead of their time in this way, as were women's suffragists and later civil rights leaders. We often look back upon such heroes and heroines with great appreciation for their contributions to our histories. We are not, however, always as aware of the price exacted (personal or otherwise) for those who choose – or who are chosen – to be a voice for freedom. *Jazz*'s narrator gives us a glimpse of what, by necessity, gets lost. The envy, the lack of public affection, the desire for another and the desire to have another desire you are not only laid bare for us as readers to look upon, but the "narrator-become-talking-book" offers itself to us when the narrator says, "You are free to do it and I am free to let you because look, look. Look where your hands are. Now." The book ends with the word that signifies the impossible in the realm of narrative – that is, the ability to narrate the present, the "now." As much as anything else, the disembodied narrator recognizes that for all its power language cannot sum up the now – which is the purview of the erotic. Both may just be the domain of the body.

Conclusion

The *lieux de mémoire*, places of memory, which are often located in the very discontinuities Foucault spoke of, are the very places that Morrison seizes, inhabits and uses to imagine, revision, and give voice to a history that has been long neglected or silenced by the very formality of the discipline of history and historiography. If legends and myths, as I think Morrison would agree, are the stories through or by which we authenticate cultures, then perhaps history is myth or legend with the weight and force of disciplinary authority. In any case, the *lieux de mémoire*, as Morrison suggests, may just be the places that offer the most liberating possibilities for telling, retelling, revising, and reimagining our collective cultural narratives.

NOTES

1. Rpt. in *Toni Morrison: Critical and Theoretical Approaches*, ed. Nancy J. Peterson (Baltimore: Johns Hopkins University Press, 1997). All other citations from this lecture will refer to this edition and be included in the text.

2. Much of the following section of this chapter is taken from an argument I made in an earlier published essay titled, "Speaking the Unspeakable: on Toni Morrison, African American Intellectuals and the Uses of Essentialist Rhetoric," Dwight A. McBride, *Why I Hate Abercrombie and Fitch: Essays on Race and Sexuality* (New York University Press, 2005).

3. "Unspeakable Things Unspoken: the Afro-American Presence in American Literature," *Michigan Quarterly Review* 28.1 (Winter 1989): 5. All subsequent references will be included in the text.

4. See Diana Fuss's "Introduction," *Essentially Speaking: Feminism, Nature and Difference* (New York: Routledge, 1989).

5. Michel Foucault, *The Archeology of Knowledge* (New York: Pantheon, 1972), p. 6.

6. I am thinking especially of those contexts in which people may not have written or officially recognized and documented histories, where history itself is a contested site that is created and recreated with each telling.

7. Quoted in Mervyn Rothstein, "Toni Morrison, in Her New Novel, Defends Women," *New York Times* (August 26, 1987): C17.

8. *Ibid.*

9. This is similar to an argument made by Howard McGary and Bill E. Lawson in *Between Slavery and Freedom* (Bloomington: Indiana University Press, 1992), pp. 1, 9–12.

10. Toni Morrison, *Beloved* (New York: Knopf, 1987), pp. 274–275.

11. Toni Morrison, *Jazz* (New York: Plume Books, 1993), pp. 228–229.

12. See John N. Duvall, "The Authorized Morrison: Reflexivity and the Historiographic," *The Identifying Fictions of Toni Morrison: Modernist Authenticity and Postmodern Blackness* (New York: Palgrave, 2000), p. 136.

13. *Ibid.*

14. *Ibid.*, p. 137.

13

DEIRDRE J. RAYNOR AND JOHNNELLA E. BUTLER

Morrison and the critical community

As Toni Morrison established her place within the American literary canon, her writing has been for the most part well received both by critics writing for popular culture and those writing for academe. The numerous accolades and awards honoring Morrison for her literature testify to her importance as one of the most prolific and talented writers of the twentieth and twenty-first centuries. Critical responses to Morrison's work focus on her audience, stylistic technique, and major themes, and explore the role she plays as a precursor to new voices in American literature, especially African American women's literature, given her instrumental influence in the Black Women Writers' Renaissance in the last decades of the twentieth century and as a book editor. The critical response is also informed by the critics' need to categorize Morrison as a black woman writer, African American writer, American writer, woman writer, and critic.

Whether in fiction or non-fiction, Morrison focuses her writing on a variety of topics including the intersections of race, class, and gender, questions of home and place, the connection between the individual and the community, self-definition, and the importance of cultural, familial, and individual history or rememory, and connections between, and nurturing roles of, African American folk culture and black cultural beliefs across the diaspora. Throughout her work, the author examines a number of themes including justice, love, power, death, and betrayal.

Morrison's commentary on her own work, in essays such as "Home" (1997) and "Rootedness: the Ancestor as Foundation" (1984) and numerous interviews with the popular press and academics, informs much critical response. In "Home," Morrison describes her overall writing project by stating that her novels explore "impenetrable, race inflected, race-clotted topics."[1]

In addition to foregrounding race and racism, she emphasizes the construction of identity and how identity is not only racialized but gendered as well. In "Rootedness: the Ancestor as Foundation,"[2] Morrison lays the groundwork for critics examining her writing by noting that her work is always political, always explores the conflict between the public and private aspects of one's life, and is always rooted in African American culture. To say her work is rooted in African American culture does not mean that individuals outside of the culture cannot relate to the themes addressed in her work. As evidence of her universal appeal, scholars such as Karla Holloway and Stephanie Demetrakopoulos provide a bicultural reading of Morrison's novels in *New Dimensions of Spirituality: A Biracial and Bicultural Reading on the Novels of Toni Morrison* (1987). This work incorporates Holloway's knowledge of West African epistemology and African American culture with Demetrakopoulos's expertise in women's studies.

Morrison's writing comes from a very personal/private space designed for the reading public both within and outside the academy. Her novels are required reading at both high-school and college levels, and her appeal can be seen in the numerous literature, African American studies, ethnic studies, and women's studies courses on college campuses that include her novels, essays, and edited works. Evidence of her widespread appeal can be seen in the response to her books by the popular press and the popularity of her novels, measured in terms of sales, and the selection of *The Bluest Eye*, *Song of Solomon*, and *Paradise* for the Oprah Book Club.

Whether critics come from the academy or outside, one major point of focus in their examination of Morrison's writing is her use of language, either as a way to attest to the author's skill as a writer or to emphasize the complexity of her writing. In these critiques there lies a danger of ignoring the stories and truths Morrison shares about American culture, the larger society, and the experience of African Americans. Many critics attribute the difficulty some readers have in interpreting her writing to what they perceive to be the complex language she uses. Yet, while Morrison definitely writes lyrical sentences, the lyricism must not be confused with complex syntax. Her narratives invite readers to construct meaning from what they read. In fact, Morrison's novels read as if the narrator is speaking directly to the reader, evoking response.

Trudier Harris in *Fiction and Folklore: The Novels of Toni Morrison* (1991) argues that Morrison illustrates the inextricable link between oral and written language. At the same time, as Harris and others interested in Morrison's use of orality point out, she provides a critique of written language forms in so far as the reader accepts the written forms as truth. The emphasis Morrison places on oral narrative links her contemporary written narratives to African and African American history as that history has been passed down through oral narratives. In "Unspeakable Things Unspoken"

(1990) Morrison writes: "The most valuable point of entry into the question of cultural (or racial) distinction, the one most fraught, is its language – its unpoliced, seditious, confrontational, manipulative, inventive, disruptive, masked and unmasking language."[3]

P. Gabrielle Foreman connects Morrison's use of language with magical realism and her mining of African and African American cosmology. The oral narratives that frame her novels do not "explore another or second reality, but rather [amplify] the parameters of our present reality."[4] Foreman places Morrison in the tradition of Alejo Carpentier, and discusses her use of the oral narrative "The People Could Fly" as exemplary of magical realism, distinguished by Marguerite C. Suarez-Murias from the fantastic or surreal by "the validity of interior worlds of faith which blossom in everyday realities and coexist with other available realities."[5] Although some critics attribute the flying myth in *Song of Solomon* to Greek mythology, Morrison acknowledges the African American folk roots of the flying African myth within her novel and questions why she has to explain when she is [recovering] history for her people, using her language on her own terms.[6]

In *Toni Morrison: Playing with Difference* (2003), Lucille Fultz argues that in addition to interpreting Morrison's writing, readers must also engage in analyzing her narrative strategy; both these aspects challenge readers much more than her actual use of syntax. At the same time, according to Fultz, readers must acknowledge shifts in meaning within and between texts by Morrison. In 2005, Fultz won the Toni Morrison Society Book Award for her comprehensive study of Morrison's writing.

In "The Contemporary Fables of Toni Morrison" (1993), Barbara Christian describes the importance of Morrison's novels in examining the historical conditions that shape race relations and black consciousness. She also argues that Morrison uses the motif of inversion in works like *Sula* and *The Bluest Eye*. According to Christian, this writer uses fables to interrogate the quest for womanhood among black females and, as Christian notes, the black cultural values that shape the quest.[7]

Morrison's narratives, whether about the pain of physical and psychological abuse on a little African American girl in *The Bluest Eye* or the evils of slavery in *Beloved*, give voice to the voiceless and record a history of a people, especially those she refers to as "ordinary people," who have been ignored or purposely forgotten. Morrison, modeling her fiction on the African American tradition of call and response, develops a connection between the speaker and the listener, the narrator and the reader. In the filmed interview, *Profile of a Writer: Toni Morrison* (1987), the author counters the interviewer's claim that she uses difficult language by responding that she does not use ornate or poetic words. Instead she notes that the "elaborateness or ornate quality" of the language she uses in her writing comes from "simple sentences where the reader is invited in with his or her own emotion."[8]

Barbara Hill Rigney also examines Morrison's use of language in *The Voices of Toni Morrison* (1991) in order to illustrate what she defines as the black feminine/feminist aesthetic in Morrison's writing. Other critics echo this theme: Marni Gauthier in "The Other Side of Paradise: Toni Morrison's Unmaking of Mythic History" (2005), Lisa Williams in *The Artist as Outsider in the Novels of Toni Morrison and Virginia Woolf* (2000), and Jan Furman in *Toni Morrison's Fiction* (1996). They more often than not explore how Morrison illustrates the destructive nature of patriarchy both within the mainstream American society and African American communities. Morrison's novels serve as "historical" narratives by showing the inextricable links between gender, race, and class. As Gauthier notes in describing *Paradise*, each chapter is named after the women in the novel and serves as "female authored counterhistories that correct the patriarchs' mythic history."[9] *Beloved, Jazz,* and *Paradise* raise questions about the power of language, the construction of history, and who has the authority to tell/write the history.

However, Charles Johnson questions what constitutes a black aesthetic and the social function of African American literature insomuch as the literature reveals oppression and chronicles African American history. From this perspective Johnson sees some of Morrison's work as lacking in intellectual profundity. In a 1993 interview with Jonathan Little, Johnson acknowledges Morrison's skill as a prose stylist, and he goes so far as to describe *Beloved* as the "penultimate" text of the Black Arts Movement primarily because of its poetic nature. But at the same time, Johnson raises the question of whether or not *Beloved* is truly an intellectual achievement because of what he perceives to be a lack of cerebral probing in the novel, and he wonders how realistic Morrison's depiction of slavery in *Beloved* is in terms of the question of infanticide,[10] given that she used the actual case of infanticide committed by Margaret Garner as inspiration for *Beloved*. In a discussion with Stephanie Stokes Oliver, recounted in the February 2006 issue of *Essence* magazine in an article titled "The Search for my Beloved Margaret Garner," Morrison notes that she wanted to examine the interior life of a slave through fiction, and this emphasis on informed imagining of the interior life provides readers with the intellectual challenge that Johnson believes is missing in this novel. In fact, scholars interested in the study of African Americans during the slave period and even African American autobiographical slave narratives will find *Beloved* insightful. Those individuals who wrote autobiographical slave narratives were often unable to provide readers a detailed account of the interior life of slaves, because these narratives were frequently financed by white abolitionists and were written to persuade those individuals with power in American society to challenge and dismantle the institution of slavery.

Beloved is not the only novel by Morrison in which actual historical events are incorporated in a fictional narrative. In analyzing mourning in African American culture in *Passed On: African American Mourning Stories* (2002), Karla Holloway explains that in *Jazz* Morrison's interpretation of black protests over the St. Louis race riot in 1917, namely the Silent Protest Parade in New York, resembles the work of social historians and shows the "cooperative venture of black fiction and black life."[11] Holloway also discusses representations of death and mourning in *The Bluest Eye, Song of Solomon,* and *Beloved.*

Critics like Marianne Hirsch in "Maternal Narratives: 'Cruel Enough to Stop the Blood,'" Trudier Harris in "Escaping Slavery but Not Its Images," Valerie Smith in "'Circling the Subject': History and Narrative in *Beloved,*" and Marilyn Sanders Mobley in "A Different Remembering: Memory, History, and Meaning in *Beloved,*"[12] offer a perspective in their criticism that challenges claims about the usefulness of Morrison's work and its intellectual achievement. Hirsch explores the connection between feminism and motherhood or the rejection of the maternal as illustrated by Morrison in *Sula, Tar Baby,* and *Beloved.* Harris examines how images of slavery in *Beloved* illustrate the difference between ownership and possession, whether one focuses on the slave-holder's claim to the black slave as property, the slave's attempts to claim ownership of his or her own body, or the slave woman claiming her children as her own. Smith illustrates how Morrison explores the relationship between literature and history and raises questions about the representation of the experiences and history of African Americans. Mobley argues that Morrison revises the slave narrative through her use of memory as a trope, and as a result the slave experience becomes "more accessible to contemporary readers."[13]

Many critics explore how Morrison challenges prevailing stereotypes of African American women, especially in the women-centered novels like *The Bluest Eye, Sula, Beloved, Paradise,* and *Love.* Morrison has indicated that she is interested in the evolution of a black female self. Part of this evolution depends on deconstructing the stereotypes of African American women found in the media and some literature by white authors. In the July 1988 issue of *Ebony* magazine, Morrison states she is interested in the evolution of self in black women. She goes on to discuss what she views as the compliment behind the stereotypes of the black mammy, the promiscuous Jezebel, and the emasculating/"henpecking" Sapphire. According to Morrison, if one breaks down these stereotypes one finds that black women are nurturing, comfortable with their bodies and sexuality, and "competent and strong."[14] In fact, she intentionally tries to project these qualities in her depiction of black female characters in an attempt to deconstruct the stereotypes.

A number of critics write about Morrison's depiction of the black mother in her novels. Andrea O'Reilly's *Toni Morrison and Motherhood: A Politics of the Heart* (2004) centers on the empowerment and disempowerment of the black mother within the context of the author's first seven novels. O'Reilly explains how Morrison develops themes of power, resistance, and healing through her depiction of both mothers and those whose ability to become a mother or act as a mother is compromised.

Critics also examine how Morrison resists polarizing gender in her narratives. Although she believes women often displace themselves and their own desires for those of others, the author acknowledges that something similar happens to some men. In addition to writing female-centered texts, Morrison also writes male-centered texts and fictional works that foreground the circumstances of African American men. For instance, she examines the plight of the black male slave through her depiction of Paul D, Sixo, Stamp Paid, and the conspicuous absence of Sethe's husband Halle in *Beloved*. In *Song of Solomon* she foregrounds the male quest theme through the depiction of Milkman, and she examines the development of black masculinity through the depiction of both Milkman and Guitar. In addition, Morrison examines relationships among black men and explores the effects of violence on black men in novels such as *Song of Solomon*, *Beloved*, and *Jazz* to name a few.

Rigney, similar to other critics, also examines music symbolism in Morrison's writing and sees connections between music and the narrative voice/orality of Morrison's novels. This critic points to examples ranging from women who literally sing the blues in Morrison's novels such as Claudia's mother in *The Bluest Eye*, Pilate and her mother Sing Byrd in *Song of Solomon*, to Sethe, Sixo, the chain gang, and Baby Suggs in *Beloved*.

Ashraf H. A. Rushdy, in "Daughters Signifyin(g) History: the Examples of Toni Morrison's *Beloved*,"[15] argues that *Beloved* is a "speakerly" text with Denver as both listener and storyteller. Just like an individual reading or listening to a Morrison narrative, Denver must create meaning from what she hears in order to retell the narrative.

Kathleen Marks argues, in *Toni Morrison's "Beloved" and the Apotropaic Imagination* (2002), that the apotropaic can be seen in many of Morrison's novels and may serve as a way of reading them. As Marks notes, the apotropaic "are those gestures aimed at warding off, or resisting, a danger, threat, or imperative. More exactly, apotropaic gestures anticipate, mirror, and put into effect that which they seek to avoid; one does what one finds horrible so as to mitigate its horror."[16] Marks illustrates how Sethe's act of infanticide is one of many apotropaic gestures in *Beloved*. Sethe commits the horrible act of killing her child in order to save her from a certain emotional and possibly physical death at the hands of slave-holders. Other apotropaic gestures in *Beloved*, according to Marks, include Sethe's use of "rememory" to keep "the past at bay," and the communal exorcism of Beloved from 124 illustrates both the "limits and ritual qualities" associated with the apotropaic.

As do a number of Morrison scholars, Herbert William Rice picks up where critics like Cynthia Davis and Susan Willis leave off in their early criticism of Morrison's work. According to Rice, the work of Davis and Willis serves as a precursor not only to his own writing on this author, but also to that of other Morrison critics. In "Self, Society, and Myth in Toni Morrison's Fiction,"[17] Davis analyzes Morrison's use of myth and folklore, the importance of naming for the author, her characters, and black culture, and the existential questions posed by Morrison's novels. Susan Willis,[18] as Rice notes, illustrates how Morrison rebels against "the male dominated bourgeois social model."[19] Rice uses the work of Willis and Davis as a framework for examining how Morrison's work is both a part of and separate from Western tradition. Like certain other critics, he uses the work of Bakhtin to describe Morrison's work. His criticism points to the universal appeal of her writing, concluding that the author does not use predictable patterns in her work, "because such patterns presuppose a 'last word,' a resolution. Rather she reinvents her alienation in each novel, making us aware of an unfinished world, both inside of us and outside of us, much bigger than any of us might have imagined."[20]

Morrison's numerous awards attest to the success and positive critical response to her writing. She received the National Book Critics Circle Award in 1977 for *Song of Solomon*. Morrison also received the National Book Foundation Medal for Distinguished Contribution to American Letters in 1996, the Condorcet Medal and Pearl Buck Award in 1994, the Modern Language Association of America Common Wealth Award in Literature in 1989, the Robert F. Kennedy Book Award for *Beloved* in 1988, and the National Humanities Medal in 2000.

Prior to receiving the Pulitzer Prize and Nobel Prize for literature, Morrison received two nominations for the National Book Award for *Sula* in 1975 and *Beloved* in 1987 and controversy erupted among literary scholars and critics over the national and international importance of her work. In 1987 the *New York Times Book Review* published an open letter with the signatures of 48 influential black writers and critics protesting her having been passed over for the Pulitzer Prize or the National Book Award. Morrison finally received recognition for her writing by earning the Pulitzer Prize in

1988, for *Beloved*, and in 1993, she became the first African American to receive the Nobel Prize for Literature.

Morrison's international appeal increased dramatically following the award of the Pulitzer Prize and the Nobel Prize. Her books have now been translated into twenty-eight languages or more. She belongs to prestigious international organizations as, for example, the Universal Academy of Cultures, an organization of artists, Nobel Prize winners, and intellectuals who have undertaken one major project: writing an international manual on racism and its destructiveness. The author is also a member of the International Parliament of Writers and the Africa and Helsinki Watch Committees on Human Rights. Toni Morrison's work within anti-racist and human rights organizations seems to be a natural extension of her project as a writer, and to complement her "speakerly" texts rooted in history and experience, inviting reflection on the present.

NOTES

1. Toni Morrison, "Home," *The House that Race Built*, ed. Wahneema Lubiano (New York: Pantheon Books, 1997), p. 9.
2. Toni Morrison, "Rootedness: the Ancestor as Foundation," *Black Women Writers (1950–1980): A Critical Evaluation*, ed. Mari Evans (New York: Anchor Books, 1984).
3. *Ibid.*, pp. 344–345.
4. P. Gabrielle Foreman, "Past-On Storied: History and the Magically Real, Morrison and Allende on Call," *Magical Realism: Theory, History, Community*, ed. Lois Parkinson Zamora and Wendy B. Faris (Durham, NC: Duke University Press, 2000), p. 298.
5. *Ibid.*, p. 300.
6. *Ibid.*
7. Barbara Christian, "The Contemporary Fables of Toni Morrison," *Toni Morrison: Critical Perspectives Past and Present*, ed. Henry Louis Gates, Jr., and K. A. Appiah (New York: Amistad Press, 1993), p. 74.
8. *Toni Morrison: Profile of a Writer*, dir. Alan Benson, LWT 1987.
9. Marni Gauthier, "The Other Side of Paradise: Toni Morrison's (Un)Making of Mythic History," *African American Review* 39.3 (2005): 407.
10. Jonathan Little, "An Interview with Charles Johnson (1993)," *Passing the Three Gates: Interviews with Charles Johnson*, ed. Jim McWilliams (Seattle: University of Washington Press, 2004), p. 107.
11. Karla F. C. Holloway, *Passed On: African American Mourning Stories* (Durham, NC: Duke University Press, 2002), p. 71.
12. Marianne Hirsch, "Maternal Narratives: Cruel Enough to Stop the Blood"; Trudier Harris, "Escaping Slavery but Not Its Images"; Valerie Smith, "'Circling the Subject': History and Narrative in *Beloved*"; and Marilyn Sanders Mobley, "A Different Remembering: Memory, History, and Meaning in *Beloved*," all found in *Toni Morrison: Critical Perspectives*, ed. Gates and Appiah.

13. Mobley, "A Different Remembering," p. 357.
14. Laura B. Randolph, "The Magic of Toni Morrison," *Ebony* 43.9 (July 1988): 106.
15. Ashraf Rushdy, "Daughters Signifyin(g) History: the Example of Toni Morrison's *Beloved*," *Toni Morrison's "Beloved": A Casebook*, ed. William L. Andrews and Nellie Y. McKay (Oxford University Press, 1999), pp. 140–153.
16. Kathleen Marks, *Toni Morrison's "Beloved" and the Apotropaic Imagination* (Columbia: University of Missouri Press, 2002).
17. Cynthia A. Davis, "Self, Society, and Myth in Toni Morrison's Fiction," *Contemporary Literature* 23.3 (1982): 323–342.
18. Susan Willis, *Black Women Writing the American Experience* (University of Wisconsin Press, 1987).
19. Herbert William Rice, *Toni Morrison and the American Tradition: A Rhetorical Reading* (Peter Lang Publishing, 1996), p. 11.
20. *Ibid.*, p. 142.

PART FOUR

Further Reading

WORKS BY TONI MORRISON

Novels

The Bluest Eye 1970
Sula 1973
Song of Solomon 1977
Tar Baby 1981
Beloved 1987
Jazz 1992
Paradise 1998
Love 2003

Short story

"Recitatif," a short story published in 1983 in *Confirmation: An Anthology of African American Women*. Ed. Amiri and Amina Baraka.

Drama

Dreaming Emmett, written for and produced by the Albany Repertory Theater in celebration of Dr. Martin Luther King's birthday in January 1986; unpublished.

Literary and social criticism

Playing in the Dark: Whiteness and the Literary Imagination. Cambridge, MA: Harvard University Press, 1992.
The Nobel Lecture in Literature, 1993. London: Chatto & Windus, 1994.
The Dancing Mind: Speech upon Acceptance of the National Book Foundation Medal for Distinguished Contribution to American Letters. New York: Alfred A. Knopf, 1996.

Editing

Race-ing Justice, En-Gendering Power: Essays on Anita Hill, Clarence Thomas, and the Construction of Social Reality. New York: Pantheon Books, 1992.

Birth of a Nation'hood: Gaze, Script, and Spectacle in the O. J. Simpson Case. With Claudia Brodsky Lacour. New York: Pantheon Books, 1997.

Children's books

The Big Box, 1999; The *Book of Mean People,* 2002; *The Lion or the Mouse,* 2003; *The Ant or the Grasshopper,* 2003; and *The Poppy or the Snake,* 2004. (Written with son Slade Morrison.)
Remember: The Journey to School Integration, 2004.

Lyrics/libretto

André Previn's *Honey and Rue,* 1992, and *Four Songs,* 1995.
Richard Danielpour's *Sweet Talk: Four Songs,* 1996, and *Spirits in the Well,* 1998.
District Storyville, 1982. Songs and story, unpublished. (Directed and choreographed by Donald McKayle.)
Margaret Garner, music by Richard Danielpour, commissioned and produced by the Detroit, Cincinnati, and Philadelphia Opera Houses which premiered at the Detroit Opera in May 2005 (available on the website of the North Carolina Opera House).

SELECTED CRITICAL READING

Andrews, William and Nellie McKay, eds. *Toni Morrison's "Beloved": A Casebook.* New York: Oxford University Press, 1999.

Bloom, Harold, ed. *Toni Morrison: Modern Critical Views.* New York: Chelsea House, 1990.

Bouson, Brooks. *Quiet as It's Kept: Shame, Trauma, and Race in the Novels of Toni Morrison.* Albany, NY: State University of New York Press, 2000.

Butler-Evans, Elliott. *Race, Gender, and Desire: Narrative Strategies in the Fiction of Toni Cade Bambara, Toni Morrison, and Alice Walker.* Philadelphia: Temple University Press, 1989.

Diedrich, Maria; Henry Louis Gates, Jr., and Carl Petersen, eds. *Black Imagination and the Middle Passage.* New York: Oxford University Press, 1996.

Dussere, Erik. *Balancing the Books: Faulkner, Morrison and the Economics of Slavery.* London: Routledge, 2003.

Duvall, John N. *The Identifying Fictions of Toni Morrison: Modernist Authenticity and Postmodern Blackness.* New York: Palgrave, 2000.

Evans, Mari, ed. *Black Women Writers (1950–1980): A Critical Evaluation.* New York: Anchor Books, 1984.

Fabre, Geneviève and Robert O-Meally. *History and Memory in African-American Culture.* New York: Oxford University Press, 1994.

Fabre, Geneviève and Claudine Raynaud, eds. *Beloved. She is Mine. Essais sur "Beloved" de Toni Morrison.* Paris: Université de la Sorbonne Nouvelle, 1993.

Fultz, Lucille P. *Toni Morrison: Playing With Difference.* Urbana: University of Illinois Press, 2003.

Furman, Jan. *Song of Solomon: A Casebook.* New York: Oxford University Press, 2003.

Toni Morrison's Fiction. Columbia, SC: University of South Carolina, 1996.

Fuss, Diana. *Essentially Speaking: Feminism, Nature and Difference.* New York: Routledge, 1989.

Gates, Henry Louis, Jr., and K. A. Appiah, eds. *Toni Morrison: Critical Perspectives Past and Present.* New York: Amistad Press, 1993.

Harris, Middleton; Roger Furman, and Ernest Smith, eds. *The Black Book*. New York: Random House, 1974.

Harris, Trudier. *Fiction and Folklore: The Novels of Toni Morrison*. Knoxville: University of Tennessee Press, 1991.

Heinze, Denise. *The Dilemma of "Double Consciousness": Toni Morrison's Novels*. Athens: University of Georgia Press, 1993.

Holloway, Karla F. C. *Passed On: African American Mourning Stories*. Durham, NC: Duke University Press, 2002.

and Stephanie Demetrakopoulos. *New Dimensions of Spirituality: A Biracial and Bicultural Reading on the Novels of Toni Morrison*. Westport, CT: Greenwood Press, 1987.

Keizer, Arlene. R. *Black Subjects: Identity Formation and the Contemporary Narrative of Slavery*. Ithaca, NY: Cornell University Press, 2004.

Kolmerten, Carol A., *et al.*, eds. *Unflinching Gaze: Morrison and Faulkner Re-Envisioned*. Jackson: University Press of Mississippi, 1997.

Kubitschek, Missy Dehn. *Toni Morrison: A Critical Companion*. Westport, CT: Greenwood Press, 1995.

Marks, Kathleen. *Toni Morrison's "Beloved" and the Apotropaic Imagination*. Columbia, MO: University of Missouri Press, 2002.

Mbalia, Doreatha Drummond. *Toni Morrison's Developing Class Consciousness*. Selinsgrove, PA: Susquehanna University Press, 1991:

Moreland, Richard C. *Learning from Difference: Teaching Morrison, Twain, Ellison, and Eliot*. Columbus: Ohio State University Press, 1999.

O'Reilly, Andrea. *Toni Morrison and Motherhood: A Politics of the Heart*. Albany: State University of New York Press, 2004.

Otten, Terry. *The Crime of Innocence in the Fiction of Toni Morrison*. Columbia, MO: University of Missouri Press, 1989.

Page, Philip. *Dangerous Freedom: Fusion and Fragmentaion in Toni Morrison's Novels*. Jackson: University Press of Mississippi, 1995.

Peach, Linden, ed. *Toni Morrison: Contemporary Critical Essays*. New York: St. Martin's Press, 1998.

Peterson, Nancy J., ed. *Toni Morrison: Critical and Theoretical Approaches*. Baltimore: Johns Hopkins University Press, 1997.

Rice, Herbert William. *Toni Morrison and the American Tradition: A Rhetorical Reading*. Peter Lang Publishing, 1996.

Rigney, Barbara Hill. *The Voices of Toni Morrison*. Columbus: Ohio State University Press, 1991.

Samuels, Wilfred D. and Clenora Hudson-Weems. *Toni Morrison: Twayne's United States Authors Series*. New York: Twayne, 1990.

Solomon, Barbara H. *Critical Essays on Toni Morrison's "Beloved"*. New York: G. K. Hall, 1998.

Stave, Shirley A., ed. *Toni Morrison and The Bible: Contested Intertextualities*. New York: Peter Lang Publishing, 2006.

Tally, Justine. *Paradise Reconsidered: Toni Morrison's (Hi)stories and Truths*. FORECAAST 3. Hamburg: Lit, 1999.

The Story of "Jazz": Toni Morrison's Dialogic Imagination. FORECAAST 7. Hamburg: Lit, 2001.

Taylor-Guthrie, Danille, ed. *Conversations with Toni Morrison*. Jackson: University Press of Mississippi, 1994.

Wall, Cheryl. A. *Changing Our Own Words*. London: Routledge, 1990.

Williams, Lisa. *The Artist as Outsider in the Novels of Toni Morrison and Virginia Woolf*. Westport, CT: Greenwood Press, 2000.

INDEX

Cambridge Companions to...

AUTHORS

TOPICS